North Sea Water in my Veins

The Pre-Christian Spirituality
of The Low Countries

North Sea Water in my Veins

The Pre-Christian Spirituality of The Low Countries

Imelda Almqvist

MOON BOOKS

Winchester, UK
Washington, USA

JOHN HUNT PUBLISHING

First published by Moon Books, 2022
Moon Books is an imprint of John Hunt Publishing Ltd., No. 3 East Street, Alresford
Hampshire SO24 9EE, UK
office@jhpbooks.net
www.johnhuntpublishing.com
www.moon-books.net

For distributor details and how to order please visit the 'Ordering' section on our website.

ISBN: 978 1 78904 906 0
978 1 78904 907 7 (ebook)
Library of Congress Control Number: 2021932912

A CIP catalogue record for this book is available from the British Library.

Design: Stuart Davies

UK: Printed and bound by CPI Group (UK) Ltd, Croydon, CR0 4YY
Printed in North America by CPI GPS partners

We operate a distinctive and ethical publishing philosophy in
all areas of our business, from our global network of authors to
production and worldwide distribution.

Contents

A brief note about spelling, translations and local customs

In linguistics, Old Dutch or Old Low Franconian is the set of Franconian dialects (i.e. dialects that evolved from Frankish) spoken in the Low Countries during the Early Middle Ages, from around the 5th to the 12th century.[1]

In this book I have used the local spelling of foreign language words, unless a common Anglicisation exists, therefore: Odin, not Óðinn (Old Norse) and the Dutch variant is Wodan.

One convention used by linguists, also followed by me, is that an asterisks indicates a missing letter or character, e.g. *bhat (proposed root stem for goddess Baduhenna).

Where Dutch source material is scarce I have provided comparative material from the same larger geographical region in an attempt to cast light on certain customs or beliefs, and have clearly indicated this.

I have provided a glossary of Dutch words (including modern, Old Dutch and Frisian words) for easy reference.

I frequently give suggestions for further reading. Where books appear in the endnotes without page numbers, I refer to the book in its entirety.

I have used the words he/she randomly. Some witches were male etc.

All translations from other languages (Dutch, Frisian, German, Swedish, Norwegian, Latin etc.) into English are my own, unless stated otherwise.

I am indebted to the people who have helped me with reading texts and translating quotes from Frisian. My own childhood dialect was West Frisian.[2] It is influenced by – but not identical to – Frisian. I have done background reading in about ten modern European languages to bring you this material – any errors are my own!

Last but not least: the Frisian Runes make a guest appearance in this book in an appendix. There is an introduction to working with the Anglo-Frisian rune row. To hear them pronounced and chanted please watch my video on YouTube. [3]

Typically Dutch

This is a list of sources and links for readers wishing to taste some Dutch culture (or even hear how spoken Dutch sounds). You will find the links in the footnotes. You can also find maps on-line showing what parts of the Netherlands were reclaimed from the sea.[4]

Song about Tanfana de Toverwitch [5]
- Sinterklaas article[6]

Videos
- Jan Klaasen is trumpeter[7]
- De Efteling[8]
- Traditional Dutch food with recipes[9]
- Tourist attractions in the Netherlands[10]
- Netherlands Tourist Information[11]

The Twelve Dutch provinces[12]

Drenthe	Flevoland	Friesland	Gelderland
Groningen	Limburg	Noord-Brabant	Noord Holland
Overijssel	Utrecht	Zeeland	Zuid Holland

Introduction

Why a book in English about the Pre-Christian (and Non-Christian) spirituality of the Low Countries?

The term Low Countries, also known as the Low Lands (Dutch: de Lage Landen, French: les Pays-Bas) and historically called the Netherlands, Flanders, or Belgica, refers to a coastal lowland region in northwestern Europe forming the lower basin of the Rhine–Meuse–Scheldt delta and consisting of Belgium, the Netherlands, and Luxembourg. [1]

This book is a love letter to my country of birth! I will start by naming my ancestors:

My name is Imelda Almqvist-Berendsen. I am the daughter of Herman Berendsen (deceased) and Cornelia (Nel) Berendsen-Oud. I am the granddaughter of Nico Oud and Martina Oud-van der Elst (maternal grandparents), and Arnold Berendsen and Elisabeth Berendsen-Vriezen.

If the Netherlands have one dedicated rune – it is LAGU: water! The water of the North Sea runs through my veins (and paintings) as the ink of my soul. The Netherlands are also known as *De Lage Landen bij de Zee* – The Low Countries by the Sea.

I moved to Stockholm in 1991 and have lived abroad ever since. At the time of writing, I have lived away from my country of birth for thirty years. My husband is Swedish and many people know me as an international teacher of both Sacred Art and Seidr /Old Norse Traditions. The latter field of focus is sometimes referred to as Norse Shamanism but there are major issues with that phrase (more about that later when we discuss *counter-cultural appropriation*).[2]

I have diagnosed myself with *geographical dysphoria*: A profound yearning for Scandinavia has haunted me since childhood. As a child I would look at the flat lands and straight dikes surrounding me and ask myself where the fjords and mountains had gone. I believe that this homesickness relates to previous lives set in the Far North, but not everyone will be open to that mindset.[3]

I am passionate about teaching courses in pre-Christian Northern European spirituality. Dutch people attend my courses in various locations. These students are *properly* Dutch in a way that I am not: they live in the Netherlands and Dutch has always been their primary language. They ask the obvious question: "When will you teach courses on the 'early' (meaning pre-Christian) spirituality of your country of birth? Your Dutch remains fluent, you read in almost all North European languages as part of research for your courses and books, why the gap?"

One immense benefit of having students is always being asked things that (on occasion) make me *question everything*. My initial responses were vague and reluctant: "Mm... yes I see what you mean.... One day perhaps.... Who knows..." The same question was asked again by other people, with greater urgency. By then I had started collecting tantalising snippets about indigenous goddesses and Frisian runes.

I asked my Dutch connections questions in return: what *is* happening in the Netherlands? In truth I had not kept up with things. Has there been a revival and inspired reconstruction of old indigenous (pre-Christian) spirituality, as is currently happening in all Nordic countries and (former) Celtic lands? I was told that *"sjamanisme" or "neosjamanisme"* (shamanism or neo-shamanism) in the Netherlands is generally either core shamanism or Native American 'inspired' (read appropriated): sweat lodges and medicine wheels abound. When I run searches, I find references to many practices imported from other cultures. There is no need for this!

I took the plunge and committed to one year of doing research. It was a joy to read in Dutch again (after years of mostly reading source material in Scandinavian languages).

One Dutch colleague tells me that he never even uses the

word *shamanism* (either on his website or in conversation) to distance himself from what passes for 'shamanism' in the Netherlands.

This book is *not* about medicine wheels, sweat lodges or dolphin healing (powerful as those modalities are). This book aims to unveil and present in a structured way what remains of the spirituality of the Low Countries, from a time before Christianity (the Church) worked hard to stamp out all heathen material. Thankfully they did not succeed, an incredible amount of material remains, often only thinly veiled! There is a case to be made for the word non-Christian spirituality (as opposed to pre-Christian), not everyone resonates with the word heathen or pagan.

I will declare upfront that I combine scholarship (reading source material and academic research papers in their original language wherever possible) with using my intuition and gnosis (personal revelation). In this book I will make a clear distinction between these two different *modi operandi*. The heart of my life is spirit-led work, in a wide range of manifestations (painting, writing, teaching, healing work).

Nothing is ever truly lost. The gods and spirits inhabit the Timeless Realm. They will present themselves to you in a very different way from the way they appear to me. They will actively enjoy doing so! Information from ancient times is stored in water (wells, rivers, oceans), our own blood (our inner ocean), our collective memory and in our ancestral field.

I chose to write this book in English (which surprised many Dutch people) so people with Dutch (or North-western European) ancestry who have another mother tongue, can access the material.

Every chapter of this book ends with an activity, encouraging you to actively work with the information offered and these principles. I hope that all readers will take from this book what they need from it – and feel inspired to make their own journeys of discovery. (Even during pandemics, we make soul journeys!)

For me writing this book brought many moments of feeling tearful, when the world as I previously knew it, turned upside down. I had not realised how deeply older beliefs and customs are still wired into Dutch culture (but often misinterpreted and even demonised). I grieve over the loss of ancestor worship, over forgotten goddesses and gods. I am glad that St Nicholas keeps making his annual pilgrimage to children in the Netherlands – but I was surprised to discover his true identity as a psychopomp!

The word dismemberment means taking apart, deconstructing. I hope that this book makes a small contribution to the process of re-membering and reconstruction of the spiritual heritage of the Low Countries. *To remember literally means to put all limbs back together again.*

Chapter 1

A very brief history of the Netherlands

God heeft de wereld geschapen, maar de Nederlanders hebben
Nederland gemaakt
God created the world but Dutch people made the Netherlands!

Jong geleerd, oud gedaan!
Learned young, (still) done in old age!
-Two popular Dutch sayings

In the Netherlands everything has been created or shaped by human beings. Nothing is truly *wild* or *untouched*. A considerable portion of land has been reclaimed from water and is situated below sea level today. This has an impact on the collective psyche of a nation.

Today we often speak of living in a 21st century global village or multi-cultural melting pot. From questions my students ask, I know that we often think of earlier cultures and tribes as being more clearly delineated and homogenous. In art we would speak of having *strong contour lines*. This is an illusion! People have always travelled, interacted with neighbouring tribes and looked for new lands beyond their immediate horizon. Using an example from the Netherlands, *a Frisian person could wear Scandinavian jewellery, possess a Frankish weapon and use Saxon urns for cremation ashes.*[1]

From this it follows that perception of identity was also more fluid than we commonly think. Geographical and political markers often decide ethnicity and, until today, ethnicity does not equal identity. (My own three children have dual nationality: Dutch-Swedish, but think of themselves as British because they have grown up in London!) Ethnicity is often perceived and defined only by outsiders; other groups referred to The Frisians inhabiting a treacherous watery borderland but they may not have called themselves Frisians.[1]

The Frisian Kingdom (West Frisian: Fryske Keninkryk), also known as Magna Frisia, is a modern name for the Frisian realm in the period when it was at its largest (650-734).[2]

The people we call the Frisians once occupied a large territory, stretching from the Rhine all the way up to the coast of Jutland in Denmark. There is another issue: due to severe flooding there was an exodus from the coastline of the Low Countries in the fourth century but a few centuries later new people moved into occupy those same lands (the North Sea having receded somewhat). Therefore the ancient Frisians (proudly claimed as ancestors by today's Frisians) were not the same people, or indeed (necessarily) the ancestors, of the people of the Northern Dutch province of Frisia today. What we can say with certainty is that they played a key role in the cradle of what became the Netherlands as we know it.[3]

Netherlands, Low Lands, Low Countries, Holland

The name Holland is derived from *houtland* (Holtland or Holdland), meaning a place where wood grows (woodland or forest). The name Holland is first mentioned in the year 1064.[4]

In the year 1076 the Count of Friesland (Frisia) had the name of his county changed to Holland because floods had separated off Friesland from the place called West-Friesland (West Frisia, situated in the province of Noord Holland today). My elderly mother lives here and, in old age, she often lapses into the West Frisian dialect I spoke as a toddler! Those floods ultimately created an inland sea now called *Het IJsselmeer*.

The provinces of Noord (Northern) Holland and Zuid (Southern) Holland do not overlap fully with the area formerly called Holland, as this also includes Noord Brabant and a chunk of the province of Utrecht. During the Eighty Years' War of Independence the region of Holland played a key role. It was seen as the most important of 'the seven provinces'. This may be why Nederland is often called Holland and many people use the names interchangeably. However, this usage is not correct: the country in its entirety is called the Netherlands.[5] Today my country has twelve provinces.

The Eighty Years' War of Independence (Tachtigjarige Oorlog in Dutch, 1568 -1648), was a revolt of the Seventeen Provinces, of what today comprises the Netherlands, Belgium and Luxembourg against Philip II of Spain, the sovereign of the Habsburg Netherlands. Eventually the Habsburg armies were ousted and the Republic of the Seven United Netherlands was established.

I will provide a very brief summary of the older history of the Netherlands.

The prehistoric forest under the North Sea and Doggerland

In the year 2015 a diver called Dawn Watson discovered a 10,000 year old prehistoric forest under the North Sea, just off the coast of Norfolk in England. Experts believe this forest may have stretched as far as Europe. She found complete oak trees (Rune AC) measuring eight meters long. This area was part of a much large zone known as Doggerland before it was flooded by the North Sea.[6]

I have become a little obsessed with Doggerland. We often mention Atlantis but we rarely mention this sunken land between the Netherlands and England.

Ice Age

The Saale Glaciation was the penultimate Ice Age (28,000 – 128,000 years ago). When the ice receded, it left large deposits of moraines, which in turn created mounds in the landscape. This process shaped the Waddenzee and the Dutch Islands in the north (*De Waddeneilanden*). Once upon a time the island of Texel used to be a peninsula and people could walk there. Archaeological finds there date from about 8,000 years BCE, including evidence of a wood henge.[7]

Polders and kwelders: land wrestled from the sea

For over 2000 years the Dutch people and their ancestors have worked daily to hold back the North Sea and even reclaim land from the sea. Around 400 BCE, the Frisians were the first people to settle in the Netherlands. They built their *terpen* (old Frisian for *villages*) as dwelling mounds for houses and entire communities. They also built the first dikes.

About 27% of the Netherlands is below sea level today. The areas reclaimed from the sea are called *polders.* Floods and the risk of dikes bursting will always be a serious national concern in the Netherlands. Average population density in the Netherlands in 2020 is 508 people per square kilometre (and rising).[8] The sea and tides also create *kwelders* or salt marshes: land created by sea water carrying mud which ultimately creates a landmass which does not flood during high water.

By the fourth century the Dutch coastal area appears to have become almost deserted again. In the sixth and seventh century BCE the kwelders of the Northern coastal strip were colonised by a new group of people, the (so called) Proto-Frisians, who made a very distinct type of earthenware. The Romans withdraw at the end of the third century. The Franks appear in the seventh century. (Until today Frank is a common Dutch boy's name).

On December 14th in the year 1287, the terpen and dikes holding back the North Sea failed and 50,000 people were killed. This is known as St. Lucia's Flood and it created a new bay, called De Zuiderzee (The Southern Sea) formed by flood water. Author Nigel Pennick points out that that countless previous floods must have destroyed a significant amount of both land

and culture already much earlier.[9] Dutch author Luit van der Tuuk gives a detailed account of this in his series of books about the history of the Netherlands.[10]

> ... *the disastrous medieval floods that killed so many in the Netherlands must have disrupted or destroyed so much, way earlier. Examples are the Zuiderzee, disastrous floods in 1282, St. Lucia's flood in December 14 1287 killed up to 80,000 and on November 18-19 1421, the St Elizabeth's Day Flood destroyed 72 villages killing c.10,000.*[11]

Pre-Christian times

Before Christianization, my country of birth was inhabited by Germanic and Celtic tribes. The area south of the river Rhine was part of the Roman Empire. The earliest inhabitants of the Low Countries lived mainly on the ridge of hills near present-day Utrecht. They subsisted on hunting and fishing. Archaeologists have found stone tools which indicate that Neanderthal people were roaming these lands during the last glacial period, which began about 110,000 years ago and ended about 15,000 years ago.[12]

Farming and animal husbandry arrived on the scene around 5300 BCE, but hunting and fishing continued. The imposing chamber tombs, called *Hunebedden,* date from this period. They are built from huge boulders delivered by the glaciers and can still be visited today. (Please note that not all Western European countries adhere to the same terms or conventions for naming these structures, which can cause confusion. The word *hunebed* is most commonly translated as passage grave – but archaeology shows many of them were not actually graves!)

Only the southern part of the Low Countries became part of the Roman Empire in 57 BCE, when the troops of Julius Caesar conquered modern day Belgium, as well as this area. The tribes living there were subjected to Roman rule and this marks the end of the Prehistoric period in the Netherlands.

Military forts were built at the location of present-day Valkenburg, Utrecht and Nijmegen. The Frisians, who lived in the northern provinces of Friesland and Groningen, were not under Roman rule but they engaged in trading with the Romans.

The Frisians were building their *terpen* (the word terp is derived from thorp or dorp, meaning village), while south of the Rhine the Romans built large villas where they lived in luxury, and following Roman custom, used slaves to farm the land.[13] The reign of emperor Trahan (98 -117) brought a long period of peace and relative prosperity, during which the Roman-occupied areas became part of the province of Germania Inferior. Roman power weakened during the third century. Germanic tribes, who had united and become collectively known as the Franks and Saxons, made frequent incursions into the occupied areas and in the year 406 a great invasion of Gaul put an end to Roman rule in the Low Countries.

During Roman rule and into the Early Middle Ages, the following tribes were resident in the Low Countries:

- North of the Rhine river: Germanic tribes (Low Franconians, Frisians, Tubanti, Canninefates and Batavians).
- South of the Rhine river: the more Celtic and Gallo-Roman Gaulish Belgae tribes of Gallia Belgica.

From the 8th century the Franks ruled Frisia. By then we are in the medieval period.[14] By that time we find farms and farmer's fields (called *geesten* – confusingly also the contemporary Dutch word for ghosts!)

In the more inaccessible coastal area, which flooded twice a day, human habitation was only possible in the strip of dunes by the North Sea. Here, two harbours and trade centers sprung up: Walacria (Domburg) en Scaltheim (Westenschouwen).[15]

Due to this rich cocktail of influences we need to realise

that the folklore and mythology of the Netherlands is rooted in pre-Christian Gaulish (Gallo-Roman) and Germanic cultures, predating the region's Christianization by the Franks in the Early Middle Ages.[15]

Another issue to be aware of is that Dutch mythology can refer to homegrown Dutch myths as well as myths (or stories and legends) from elsewhere (re)told in Dutch.

Timekeeping

The Germanic tribes used the solar year and lunar month for time-keeping. The numbers three, seven and nine were especially sacred to them.

Christianization brought a new form of perceiving time: the seven-day week. Most days of the week are named for Germanic gods in Dutch (but we also detect a lasting Roman influence):

- *Maandag*: Monday, is the Day of the Moon.
- *Dinsdag*: Tuesday, is the day of Tyr (the day of Mars Thingsus).
- *Woensdag*: Wednesday, is the day of Wodan/Odin.
- *Donderdag*: Thursday, is the day of Donar/Thor.
- *Vrijdag*: Friday, Frîja's day, the day of Frigg/Frya and Freyja.
- *Zaterdag*: Saturday, the Day of Roman god Saturn.
- *Zondag*: Sunday, is the Day of the Sun.

Some epic or legendary heroes, kings or leaders of the Low Countries[16] include:

- *Tuisto* or *Tuisco*, the mythical ancestor of all Germanic tribes.
- *Mannus*, son of Tuisto and founder of a number of Germanic tribes.
- *Ing* (Ingwaz, Yngve), founder of the Ingaevones Tribe.

- The Frisian king or hero *Redbad or Radbod* (more familiar to Dutch people using the modern spelling *Radboud*).
- *Folcwald* and *Finn*, heroes of the Frisian tribes.

We also find ancient deities of Druidic, Celtic and Gallo-Roman origin, especially in the south and throughout Flanders.

Activity #1 Pilgrimage or Sacred Journey

Write down a list of deities and divine beings mentioned during your childhood (from *any* tradition or spiritual orientation).

Think about your connection to the Netherlands (there must be a reason why you are reading this book!) Before reading further, please write some notes about what you know (think you know or don't know) about the pre-Christian era in The Low Countries and surrounding regions.

Write down any snippets of information your (grand) parents may have shared with you: did they observe traditions (however obscure)? Were they superstitious? Are there proverbs (or other sayings) you often heard in childhood (no matter in which language you heard them)?

If it all possible make or plan a trip to the Low Countries while reading this book (if you have already been there, relive memories, take out any photo album of photographs you may have) or talk to someone you know who lives there.

Chapter 2

Of Saint Boniface felling Donar's Oak (and about other sacred trees)

There were sacred woods long before there were temples
and altars
-Rudolph Simek [1]

[The Germanic peoples] consecrate woods and groves and they
apply the name of gods to that mysterious presence which
they see only with the eye of devotion
-Tacitus in his Germania [2]

Boniface and Donar's Oak

The oldest trees on Earth have, during their lifespan, lived
through incredible events:: the Trojan War, the Roman Empire,
the Medieval period. They span both heathen times and events
since Christianization.

Today we have Hollywood and we venerate movie stars
and celebrities (almost like gods). However, once upon a time
Europe was covered in dense sacred woods and the people of
Old Europe venerated trees. We may think of those people as
primitive heathens, but they would be horrified by the brutal 21st
century logging of the rain forest, the mass destruction of many
trees on which human life depends, *all for commercial gain.* No
trees means no oxygen, no firewood, no shelter, no habitats for
countless animal species and so forth.[3]

Saint Boniface (Latinised as Bonifatius) was born in the
Devon town of Crediton, in England, in the year CE 675. He
died near Dokkum in Frisia, circa 754. He was a leading figure
in the Anglo-Saxon mission to the Germanic parts of the
Frankish Empire, during the eighth century. He built significant

foundations for the Catholic Church in Germany and he was made archbishop of Mainz by Pope Gregory III. He died a martyr's death in Frisia, along with 52 other people. After his death he became the patron saint of Germania, known as The Apostle of the Germans.[4]

Boniface travelled to Utrecht in the Netherlands, where Willibrord, The Apostle of the Frisians, had already been working hard to spread 'the true faith' since the 690s. The two men spent a year working together.

Boniface's most 'famous' achievement was the felling of Donar's Oak (sometimes Latinized as Jupiter's Oak), near the present town of Fritzlar in Northern Hesse, in Germany. Local people used it as a focal point for worshipping the thunder god Donar (Thunor or Thor). Animal sacrifices were made and various rituals were practiced.[5]

According to his first biographer, Boniface started to chop the oak down, when suddenly a great wind, as if by a miracle, blew the ancient oak right over. When Donar did not strike Boniface down, the people present were overawed and, as the legend goes, instantly converted to Christianity. Boniface built a chapel dedicated to Saint Peter at the same site, from the wood of the tree. This chapel was the beginning of the Benedictine monastery in Fritzlar.

A church was indeed built there eventually, but only the Chatti Tribe, witnessing the event, converted to Christianity. Other nearby tribes were not impressed at all and Boniface met with a harsh reception.

We know this from so called *vitae* (life stories) that have been passed on to us. However, some authors have pointed out that the vitae (most likely) leave out the fact that this deed was well-prepared and widely publicized in advance for maximum effect and attendance. In contemporary language: *it was a set-up!* And Boniface had little reason to fear for his personal safety because the Frankish fortified settlement of Büraburg was nearby, so reinforcements were at hand in case things turned nasty.[6]

The *vitae* also inform us that Boniface cherished a special hope of converting the Frisians and in 754 CE he set out for Frisia, where he did indeed baptise a large number of people and then called a general meeting for the Roman Catholic rite of Confirmation at a place not far from Dokkum (between Franeker and Groningen). Instead of his converts, a group of armed robbers (or infuriated Frisians) appeared and hacked the elderly archbishop to death. They also killed his companions.[6] They ransacked the possessions of Boniface and his companions but found no riches, only chests full of manuscripts. They attempted to destroy these books, but they did not succeed entirely. Until today the *Ragyndrudis Codex* shows incisions that might have been made by a sword or axe (but some scholars doubt this). To this day Boniface's feast day is celebrated on June 5th in the Roman Catholic Church.

Soon legends sprung up. It was claimed that a visitor on horseback visited the site where a hoof of his horse got stuck in the mire. Where it was pulled out, a well sprang up. A church was built on site and the well became a "fountain of sweet water" to bless people.[7]

I was brought up in a Roman Catholic family. Roman Catholicism runs deep on both sides of my family tree. My maternal grandmother lived in a convent for a time, planning to be a nun. She later changed her mind, left the convent and got married instead, but she maintained close ties to the Church, the clergy and monastic people for the rest of her life. My childhood was punctuated by priests and nuns dropping in for coffee with Oma (Grandma).

Sacred Trees and Tree Sanctuaries

When Christianization started in the Early Medieval period many trees were cut down. The wood was then often used to build a chapel and to carve crosses or statues of Mother Mary.

On some occasions a sacred tree was preserved but a chapel was built nearby (or even in the tree!) At a later time, such statues and crosses were moved to a nearby church to draw people's attention away from the tree, but this usually failed.

A body of folk stories arose from this, about statues of Mary mysteriously returning to the tree, in the dead of the night. There are also stories about such trees beings struck by lightning but the dead tree recovering and sending out new shoots. The sites of some sacred trees *(boomheiligdommen)* remain popular until today.[8]

In Old Europe oak trees were commonly perceived as representing sacred masculine energy (Rune AC) while linden trees (called lime trees in Britain) embodied the sacred feminine.

Some well-known examples of sacred trees in the Netherlands and Belgium[8] are:

- The Holy Oak of Den Hout (Oosterhout).
- Fever tree at Overasselt.
- The *spijkerbomen* (nail trees), also *breukenbomen* (fracture trees) of Yde, Drenthe.
- Fever Tree in Breda (Liesbos).
- The Holy Oak of Heusen, in Belgium.
- *Achtzalighedenboom* (Named for the Eight Beatitudes spoken by Jesus in his Sermon on the Mount) in Lille. This tree originally had eight trunks and is called the most remarkable tree in Belgium.
- *Duizendjarige Eik* (Thousand-Year-Old Oak) near Lummen, Belgium.
- *Onze-Lieve-Vrouwe ter Eik* (Our Dear Lady In The Oak) in Meerveldhoven, Noord-Brabant. Here a chapel is built around the tree.
- *De Heksenboom* (Witches' Tree) in Sint Anthonis, Noord-Brabant.

Tree veneration in Old Europe

In Norse mythology, Odin and his two brothers, Vili and Vé, were walking on the beach one day. (The sources are not consistent, in some accounts Odin was accompanied by Hoenir and Lodur instead). Here they found two lifeless tree trunks (or possibly large pieces of driftwood), one from an ash tree and the other one from an elm tree. They used those pieces of wood to create the first pair of human beings: a man called Ask (Ash Tree) and a woman called Embla (Elm Tree). Odin, whose name means spirit or breath, gave them their indwelling spirit and the breath of life. Hoenir gave them comprehension or sense, and Lodur gave them the 'blooming hue' (or healthy colours) of a living and breathing human being. They were also given other qualities which define a human being (such as a heart, speech and hearing, intellect, the ability to move, and a sense of humour).

> Sense they possessed not, soul they had not,
> being nor bearing, nor blooming hue;
> soul [*önd*] gave Óthinn, sense [*oðr*] gave Hoenir,
> being, Lódhur, and blooming hue [*lá, læti, litr*].[9]

My Swedish surname is Almqvist and it means branch of an elm tree. My Dutch maiden name is Berendsen (and that means son – or child – of a person named for a bear).

Yew Tree

Yggdrasil is an immense tree that hosts all the realms of Norse cosmology. There is some confusion about what kind of tree it is: many sources describe it as an ash tree but others make a strong case for it being a yew tree. Some have suggested that it is a needle ash instead. Yggdrasil does not drop its leaves, which would make it an evergreen tree.[10]

The entire yew tree (*Taxus baccata*) is poisonous: its wood, bark, the needles and seeds. It is known as a death tree for good reason as it is a toxic and dangerous wood to handle. Shakespeare describes Macbeth as concocting a poisonous brew which includes 'slips of yew, silvered in the moon's eclipse'.

In Celtic culture the yew was the tree of death and resurrection and those themes continued into the Christian era. Yew shoots were buried with the deceased and ancient yew trees grow in many churchyards. (Yew trees have great longevity so some may predate the churches). Longbows were made from yew tree wood.[11]

In colloquial Dutch the Yew is called *de boom des doods* or *de venijnboom*, meaning the Tree of Death, or the Venom/Poison Tree. Taxus is derived from the Greek *taxon*, which means bow (as in the bow of an archer). Baccate means carrier of red berries. The resulting word *taxus* gave us the word *toxic*, meaning poisonous.[12]

In contemporary Dutch word *venijn* refers to the quality of a hidden sting or barely-veiled anger in a person's speech or manner, *venijnig* can even mean malicious or sarcastic, intentionally cutting or hurting another through one's words and tone. Even the weather can be described as *venijnig* in Dutch: a biting cold or icy wind that cuts right through clothing and knocks children off their bikes.

The English word yew might be derived from the Old-German syllable *ewe* (meaning eternal or relating to many aeons, it lives on in Dutch as the word *eeuwig* – eternal). It may also come to us from the Indo-European syllable *ei*, meaning red.[12]

The yew is a truly ancient tree species, known for its great longevity. It predates the Ice Age and is still around today. It has a unique way of growing new trunks from within its original root ball. This means that some yews today may be up to 4,000 years old, spanning a large segment of human (pre)history. Because of these qualities the Yew is associated with immortality, regeneration, rebirth, everlasting life and transformation. In esoteric terms it is often perceived as a portal for reaching both the Otherworld and our ancestors and this may be why it is a ubiquitous tree in so many graveyards.[13]

However, because yew trees grow extremely old, we can assume that many were in place *before churches were even built,* as they predate Christianity. Many churches and graveyards were deliberately positioned within a grove, or a circle of yew trees. Those circles and groves were a legacy of the Celtic druids. Celtic people spread over a large area, including the coastal regions of continental Europe.

In magical work, wood of the yew is used for protection, intentional dreaming and contacting ancestors. In hot weather yew gives off a resinous vapour which shamans may well have inhaled to induce visions. The wood was used for making lutes and carving objects but even the dust thrown up by sanding is poisonous.

The Pacific Yew is used today as an ingredient in medication for breast and ovarian cancer.[14] To my mind this information gives new meaning to the biblical story of the Tree of Life and Tree of Knowledge.

Norse God Ullr

Yew is a slow-growing tree, meaning that its wood is tough and resilient. In the mediaeval period it was used for making spears, hunting bows and even long bows. (Robin's Hoods long bows were made from yew wood).

Norse god Ullr has his own realm called Ydalir, Dale of Yew Trees and he is both an archer and hunter. He is attested in both ancient texts and archaeological records. Some people connect him to the Celtic deity Cernunnos (The Horned God as he appears on the Gundestrup Cauldron). Fertility god Freyr is sometimes depicted wearing antlers. It seems probable that Celtic, Gaulish and Germanic tribes all venerated a Divine Hunter or Male god of the Forest (such as the Finnish god Tapio), even if no name or records are preserved of this.

Yggdrasil

The Norse Aesir (the ruling sky gods who made a truce with their opposite number, the Vanir or land-and-fertility gods) attend a daily assembly by the tree. The branches of Yggdrasil stretch high up into the heavens and the world tree is said to have three large roots that reach different locations. One leads up to the sacred well called Urdarbrunnr (the Well of Urdr) in the heavens. The second one runs to a well called Hvergelmir. The third root leads to the third well: Mimisbrunnr (Mimir's Well).

The name Yggdrasil is most commonly translated as terrible horse or the horse of the Terrible One (i.e. Odin). Many different animals inhabit the tree: the squirrel Ratatoskr runs up and down the trunk to pass messages (and insults). At the top we find an eagle, while the dragon Níðhǫggr (Malice Striker) is forever gnawing both on the roots of the tree and on the corpses of the dead at Nástrǫnd (Corpse Shore). The Norns water Yggdrasil every morning. When the world as we know it ends, at Ragnarok, Yggdrasil is said to shelter another couple, called Lif and Lifthrasir, who will survive and populate the world following the current one. Yggdrasil therefore can be said to represent the principles of creation and destruction at the same time.

My personal impression of Yggdrasil is that of a world tree or cosmic tree and therefore an archetypal or ancestral tree. It is likely to have features of all tree species and not fit into one exact category. I also observe that Yggdrasil is situated in the other world, not our everyday world. The other world is non-material and known for being very shape-shifty. We access it using our imagination.[15] All conscious beings there (and Yggdrasil is one such being), will present itself in a way that holds the most profound teachings for us. Therefore, two different people could climb Yggdrasil (in a meditation or shamanic journey) on the same day and find themselves climbing trees that appeared very differently, perhaps recognisable as different tree species. It is equally likely that it may not even resemble a tree from everyday reality. In my own dreams and visions Yggdrasil sometimes appears as the Milky Way, the celestial spine (and highway) of our galaxy.[16]

Irminsul

There were two eminently sacred 'real' trees for the Germanic peoples: one was the Donar Oak and the other one was a sacred pillar called the Irminsul. The word Irminsul meant great pillar in Old Saxon. It was situated in the Teutoburg Forest, near the river Lippe at Eresburg (now Obermarsberg, Westphalia). It acted as the *axis mundi* or world axis in a very literal sense. To the Germanic heathen peoples, it was a sacred pillar connecting all words, from below the earth (the roots), to our everyday reality and the heavens or celestial realm. The oldest chronicle refers to it as a tree trunk erected in the open air. Some scholars think that it represented the old sky god Tiwaz (See Rune TIR).

The Irminsul was felled by Charlemagne, King of the Franks at that time, in 772 C.E. The temple area or sanctuary in which it was situated was destroyed too. The process of destruction took three days. The offerings of gold and silver left by Pagan visitors or 'pilgrims' were taken (read *stolen*) by the troops.[17]

The Nahanarvali tribe worshipped a pair of male deities, the Alci, within a sacred grove, where worship was overseen by a transvestite priest (Dowden, 2000). There is some disagreement about whether the Alci were gods, or instead wooden twin pillars, as certain researchers suggest that the word translates to wooden icon (Cusack, 2011). Regardless, trees were either the vehicle of worship, or provided the grounds in which worship would take place, or both. Other Germanic tribes paid respect to the mother goddess, Nerthus, in sacred groves (Dowden, 2000).[18]

Sacred Trees and Groves

In Germanic cosmology and myths trees play a key role. The Roman historian Tacitus wrote that Germanic cult practices took place in groves rather than temples. Some scholars link this to Yggdrasil as the cosmic tree and organizing principle of the universe. In his *Germania* Tacitus describes the groves of the Semnones and refers to a *castum nemus* (chaste grove) in which the image of the goddess Nerthus was venerated.[19]

Other examples of references to sacred trees in Germanic Europe from the Roman period:

- Rites held by continental Germanic peoples in groves.
- There was a *silva Herculi sacra* (wood sacred to Hercules) near the River Weser in Northwestern Germany.
- The Semnones held rituals in honor of the *regnator omnium deus* (god as the ruler of all).

Jan de Vries, a scholar of Germanic religion, noted that place names such as Frølund (Denmark), and Ullunda, Frösvi, and Mjärdevi (Sweden), in which the name of a deity is compounded with words meaning grove or wood, suggest a continuation of the same practice, but they are found almost exclusively in eastern Scandinavia; however, there is a *Coill Tomair* recorded near Dublin, an oak forest apparently sacred to Thor. This indicates how far the Norse gods travelled, just as the Celtic gods reached continental Europe.[20]

The reverence for individual trees among Germanic peoples is often commented on by medieval Christians, as an example of people slipping back into the heathen customs of their ancestors. The Church actively created associations and correspondences between trees and saints in order to stamp out this phenomenon and replace it with a more acceptable version. In our day we see a continuation of this 'merger' in the form of prayer trees.

After Christianization, trees continued to play a significant role in folk beliefs. References to trees, groves and woods also occur in many place names, even today.[20]

Toponymy

The science of place names is called toponymy. There are many Dutch place names containing references to trees or woods (or other geographical features), e.g. Hoogwoud (literally High Wood). The Germanic word *lauha(z)* means clearing in a forest and is found in many place names as *loo* or *le* (Almelo, Dinxperlo, Heiloo, Leuven, Baarle).[21]

A common ending is –*burg* (bourg in French), meaning fortress, and tells us where major fortresses were situated in Roman times: Oostburg, Luxembourg, Straatsburg, Middelburg, Tilburg etc. On occasion we find Old Saxon elements as well, for instance – run (Autun, Tungelroy) means enclosure. [21]

Modern Heiloo is said to have been named for the holy woods found there in Roman times. Some special events occurring in the 14th century made Heiloo a pilgrimage site dedicated to Mary Mother of God. The name Heiloo is derived from *Heyliche Loo*, holy woods. A farmer's son twice found a statue of Mary in a field while a rich merchant in Alkmaar, Johannes Mors, had dreams about a statue of Mary and was told to visit a local well, called Runxputte. He was so impressed that he funded a chapel here. Today the site called Onze Lieve Vrouwe ter Nood (Our Dear Lady – for those – In Need) in Heiloo remains a *bedevaartsoord*, a pilgrimage destination.[22]

The river IJ (dividing Amsterdam North from the rest of the city) started life as an arm of the Zuiderzee (now IJsselmeer). The more ancient name is Verremeer (far off lake) or Hellemeer (lake of the Goddess Hel or Holle). Dutch author Linda Wormhoudt connects this to Amsterdam North functioning as the Land of the Dead in the time of public executions.[23]

She also connects The IJ (Het IJ) to the souls of unborn children:

> *In Amsterdam aspiring parents rowed across Het IJ (a river*
> *separating the city of Amsterdam from the northern part of*
> *Amsterdam) at night, to a place called Volewijck, where bunches*
> *of babies were found hanging in the Kinderboom (Children Tree)*
> *at night. They called out to the searching parents and midwives:*
> *"Pick me! Pick me! I will be well-behaved every single day!" ("Pluk*
> *mijn, pluk mijn, ik zal alle dagen zoet zijn!")*[23]

In the western coastal area only a very small amount of Roman toponyms remain. They increase significantly further inland. This indicates a continuity in habitation by the indigenous population but not the colonizing culture[24]

Human sacrifice

The sacred grove of the Semnones, a Germanic tribe who belonged to the Suebi culture, is regarded by Tacitus as the most prominent of all sacred groves. In their groves they worshipped a *sky god who rules over all* (suspected to be Tiwaz, otherwise known as Tyr) through rituals including bloody human sacrifice. It is possibly that wood of the alder tree was used.[25] Here it is worth noting that:

> *In Finnish the word for alder [Alnus glutinosa] is derived from a*
> *word meaning "blood," which refers to the red sap the tree oozes*
> *when cut. Red pigment from the bark was once used as a dye and*
> *a face paint. There is an old superstition against cutting down the*
> *alder tree, ostensibly because it bleeds.*[26]

Those who entered the sacred grove were, at all times, bound by a chain, highlighting their inferiority in comparison with the highest god, and if individuals were to fall, they were required to roll out of the grove on the ground, as opposed to walking out (Dunn, 2013).[27]

Tolley (2013) also suggests, as does Gummere (1892) more broadly, that the tribe viewed the sacrifice of humans within the grove as representative of man's origins from the world tree, and therefore also recognised that trees also symbolised death.[26]

The Ogham

The Ogham tree alphabet is an early medieval alphabet used to write the early Irish language. It contains the encoded (or distilled) wisdom of the Celtic druids. Every letter is represented by a tree and written in the form of central line or stave with other strokes crossing or leading off this. These symbols can be found carved on the edges of some standing stones in Ireland and Wales (the Celtic heartland) but they were most likely used for magical purposes as well, carved on staves of yew. The Druids used it as a silent communication system. They also used specific gestures and hand symbols to make the signs. This is recorded in mediaeval manuscripts.[28]

The yew appears as *Idho* and the final letter, representing the last day of the Pagan year: the winter solstice (both death and resurrection). In the Frisian Rune Row, it is connected to the runes EOH and YR. Idho is said to guide the dead on their journey in the Otherworld just as it guides the living through the dangerous (sometimes deadly) winter season.[28]

Yew was sometimes called *the forbidden tree* as parts of it were used to bring on abortions. Tribal leaders were buried beneath yew trees perhaps believing that their knowledge and wisdom would merge with the spirit of the Yew Tree and that people could continue to access this by visiting yew trees.

Warden Trees

Scandinavia has a long tradition of families, farmers and homesteaders forming a special relationship with a so called Vårdträd or Warden tree. This is an old tree growing near the house. These guardian trees were said to have been taken from sacred groves as saplings (or cuttings) by pre-Christian Germanic peoples. As this tree grows it witnesses all events in family life and protects the homestead. It was believed that the *Vættir* (or wights) of the property lived under the roots of the warden tree or guardian tree. People made offerings and left out food and drink for the wights hoping for protection from diseases and back luck. In Norse cosmology a *vǫrðr* is a warden spirit, believed to follow from birth to death the soul (*hugr*) of every person.[29]

Harming that tree (often an elm tree), even breaking off a small twig or branch, was viewed as a great offense. The respect for this tree, and bond between tree and family, was often so great that people adopted a family name related to it. (Think of my Swedish surname: Almqvist means *branch of an elm tree!*) Cutting down or damaging such a tree would have an immediate effect on family fortunes.

Tree Spirits

In Old Europe there were many ancestor cults involving trees. There was a belief that after death the souls of the ancestors took up residence in trees.[30] This is why many forests and groves were so sacred and there were severe penalties and punishments for harming trees.[31]

Where we do not have detailed records of local practices it is often instructive to look at customs from the same larger region (in this case Northern Europe). In Slavic cultures we find the ancient belief in a tree spirit that enters buildings through the trunks of trees used in their construction:

Every structure is thus inhabited by its particular spirit: the domovoi in the house, the ovinnik in the drying-house, the gumenik in the storehouse, and so on. The belief that either harmful or beneficial spirits dwell in the posts and beams of houses is still alive in the historic regions of Bosnia and Slovenia and the Poznań *area of west central Poland. Old trees with fences around them are objects of veneration in Serbia and Russia and among the Slavs on the Elbe River. In 19th-century Russia a chicken was slaughtered in the drying house as a sacrifice to the ovinnik.*[32]

Slavic people also believed that a vegetation spirit is present in a sheaf of grain kept in the *sacred corner* of a home (meaning under the icon) and that the same thing goes for say, the branch of a birch tree or sprigs of thistle.

Boomheiligdommen – Sacred Trees and Tree Sanctuaries

In the Netherlands we still find many examples of trees that have a sacred purpose. People call those *'boomheiligdommen'* (tree sanctuaries) in Dutch.

- *Kinderbomen* (Children Trees).
- *Spijkerbomen* or *Breukenbomen* (Nail Trees or Fracture Trees).
- *Koortsbomen* or *Lapjesbomen* (Fever Trees or Rag Trees).
- *Kroezebomen* (Kroesebomen) are trees marking crossroads and property. boundaries (between farmers' fields and between districts).
- *Wensbomen* are Wishing Trees.

Kinderbomen or Children Trees

Trees are said to give newborn children their soul. In the past, people believed that the souls of children wishing to be born on earth lived in certain holy trees.[33] This may be related to the Old European belief that the souls of ancestors took up residence in trees. If one is open to the concept of reincarnation then such trees become portals where death meets rebirth.

In Amsterdam aspiring parents visited a Kinderboom situated north of the river IJ, near a burial pit for corpses displayed after public executions.[34]

Other than coming from the Children Tree, babies were also said to be found in cabbages, Pollard Willows, under *Kinderstenen* (Children's Rocks) or they were delivered by swarms of bees, or storks.

Spijkerbomen or Breukenbomen: Nail Trees of Fracture Trees

These were trees in which people hammered a nail to request the healing of fractures or hernias. The fractures were said to be fully healed once the bark of the tree had grown across the nail.

Koortsbomen of Lapjesbomen (Fever Trees or Rag Trees)

The general idea is that one can stop a fever or illness by tying a rag around a tree (often an oak or linden). Those rags were torn from clothing worn by the sick person. There needed to be direct contact between the tree and their body. The rag transmitted the fever to the tree, so the person afflicted was free of it.[35]

Certain rules had to be followed: the person tying the rag could not be observed, so the deed was often done at night. This person could not look back over their shoulder, while leaving the tree. If another person were to remove the rag (or another object such as a nail) from the tree, the illness would be transferred to them instead.

Fever trees were often associated with sacred mounds or hills. Here coins or jewellery were buried with the same purpose: an illness was cured by transferring the disease onto or into an object. There were often seven trenches or paths around such a mound.

The following Dutch nursery rhyme[36] still shows faint echoes of this:

Zakdoekje leggen

[Zakdoekje leggen, niemand zeggen,
`Kukeleku´, zo kraait de haan...]

Laying a hankie, telling no one
Kukelu, so crows the cockerel
I am wearing only two pairs of shoes
One made of cloth and one from leather
Here I'm laying my hankie
Look in front of you, look behind you
Whoever finds it may catch me!

Kroezebomen or Crossroads Trees

Kroezebomen[37] are trees (often oaks) marking crossroads and property boundaries (between farmers' fields and even districts). Such places where often used as a holy place for law-speaking and as an outdoor courthouse or assembly place. They became destinations for pilgrimages. Some kroezebomen acquired their own chapels. Some act as gathering places for communities and groups today (for instance as the starting point for a peace march).

Wensbomen or Wishing Trees

Wensbomen make wishes come true, according to folk belief. People will visit such trees and leave offerings. We find them all over the world, often decked with ribbons and rags. We also find wishing trees where messages on pieces of paper are hung in the tree. Wishing trees are a phenomenon found all over the world, from Korea to Turkey.

Once upon a time wishing trees were created during the Yule period by hanging ribbons in trees. (Today some people still put ribbons, as well as sweets, apples and candles in their Christmas tree). I have a Prayer Tree in my London garden, where my students and I hang prayer ribbons during sacred art workshops.

Because of the growing awareness of the climate crisis, I found specific sites and organisations that have harnessed this phenomenon in aid of this cause. This can take the form of a tree dedicated to wishes and prayers for the environment and mankind finding ecologically sound solutions. I also found a Dutch site[38] encouraging people to plant trees. It claims that people in the city of Rotterdam are planning to plant 100,000 trees –an addition of 3300 trees a year in just one big city! The site also makes a case for replacing every tree that needs to be felled by planting a tree elsewhere and it provides public information about accessing plans for tree felling in advance.

De Kerstboom – the Christmas Tree

The story of Boniface felling the Donar Oak continues and claims that a fir tree grew out of the fallen oak and became a symbol of Christ. Fir trees are triangular (in shape) and that was interpreted as a symbol for the Holy Trinity. This gave us the idea of the tree as a symbol of Christ and resurrection.[39]

The modern concept of the Christmas tree emerged in western Germany during the sixteenth century. Christian people brought trees into their home and decorated them with gingerbread, nuts and apples. In the seventeenth century the decoration became more elaborate. Big royal courts developed the habit of erecting trees with gold leaf on them and with paper decorationsand candles. The custom spread to royal courts all over Europe in the early nineteenth century. Germans emigrated all over the world and the custom spread with them.

In England Queen Victoria and Prince Albert popularised the custom (in the 1840s and 1850s). Victoria had a German mother and she grew up with the tradition of a decorated Christmas tree. A drawing of the royal family celebrating Christmas around a festive tree at Windsor Castle was published in 1848. The image 'went viral', as we would say today, and soon every British home had its own tree.

However, in some places such as the United States, having a Christmas tree was viewed as a foreign and new-fangled pagan custom until the mid-19th century. American settlers did not take to the custom initially.[39]

Tree Hermit

Gerlachus van Houtem was a man of noble birth who became a holy hermit after his wife died, in the 12th century. After a pilgrimage to Rome and Jerusalem he gave away all his possessions and moved into a hollow oak tree. He mixed his bread with ashes and made daily pilgrimages on foot to nearby religious sites. Local people had great respect for him but the monks in a nearby monastery became envious enough of his 'fame' to persuade the Bisshop of Liege to cut down the tree (to expose the gold and riches supposedly hidden there by the hermit). No treasure was found. Hildegard of Bingen, the famous Abdess, once sent him a gift of a wreath. When Gerlachus died, the water of the nearby well turned into wine on three seperate occasions. Today a church marks this place where his bones rest in a shrine.[40]

Activity #2 What is in a name?

- *Ancestral Discovery Activity – reflect on the meaning of your name (both first name, surname, nickname, married name and any middle (or other) names you may have*
- My own example:
- My maiden name is Berendsen. Son or child of a bear.
- Grandparents: (maternal) *Oud* and *van der Elst* (Old and a reference to Alder Trees), (paternal) Van der Vriezen, a reference to 'Freezing'.
- For those of you who have Dutch ancestry, reflect on both their family name (even if you don't use it yourself) and their first names: what do they mean?
- Do you know where your ancestors are from (region, province, town or village)? What does the name of that place mean?
- Connect with Dutch people and invite them to tell you

how they interpret those names and any associations they have.

- Meditation to seek audience with the Donar Tree and Honouring Ask and Embla.
- Do this activity outside! Visit an oak tree near you. Bear in mind that all the trees we see today are the children of both The World Tree (or Tree of Life) and ancestral trees that no longer stand. Trees have ancestors, just as human beings do. Some Germanic/Norse peoples go one step further: they say that *trees are the ancestors of human beings.*
- Go to a place where will be undisturbed for about half an hour.
- Honour our ancestral trees, Ash and Embla, in some way or form.
- Meditation or journey to visit your ancestral tree and discover where its roots reach.

Journey or meditate your way to the trees on the bottom of the North Sea and ask them to tell you about the Lost Atlantis of the North: Doggerland!

Chapter 3

Dutch Folklore and Folk Medicine

Kaaskop *(noun, literally Cheesehead)*
Idiot, stupid person
Mold for pressing Edam Cheese
Dutch person (term used in Belgium, derogatory)[1]
Person from Holland (term used affably in Holland)

Iemand was gierig, dan had ie z'n ziel an de duivel verkocht.
Someone stingy, it means that he had sold his soul to
the Devil.[2]

The focus of this book is the pre-Christian spirituality of
the Netherlands but I have also chosen to weave in some
contemporary material, to give people a sense of what it
means to be Dutch, what the Dutch mindset or spirit is. As
the three decades of my life away from the Netherlands have
been dedicated to practicing and teaching healing modalities, I
wanted this book to offer (some) information about traditional
cures and folk medicine as well. Please remember that what we
call 'alternative or holistic medicine' today was, for centuries,
the only form of health care most people had access to. These
were the remedies used by our ancestors.

Typically Dutch

We have an expression, often used with amused pride: 'typically
Dutch!' (*typisch Nederlands*). What *is* typically Dutch? Do we
have national characteristics?

Having lived abroad for most of my life I can list the things
that foreigners describe as quintessentially Dutch: windmills,
tulips, cheese markets, people living below sea level, dikes

(*dijken*), canals (*grachten*). The tourist attractions! We also find human qualities that people from other backgrounds define as Dutch: *thrifty* or *stingy*, *straight-speaking* or *blunt* (some say *rude* – Dutch people take freedom of speech to another level!), *progressive* (Dutch society takes a stand on drugs, prostitution and euthanasia that people from other countries consider immoral or risky – a sliding slope, undermining community values). Dutch people are said to wear their heart on their sleeve. They are *friendly* and *hospitable*, they welcome strangers with open arms – but if they are not pleased, they will tell you this to your face. The British qualities of *the stiff upper lip* (great self-restraint, no displays of emotion, stoicism even), dropping hints and *beating around the bush*, are not interpreted correctly by Dutch people (unless they have lived in Britain for decades). The one national trait mentioned by nearly every person who discovers my nationality, and who has visited the Netherlands, is that Dutch people will readily *switch languages* and speak fluent English, decent German and often basic French to foreign visitors.

How do Dutch people acquire fluency in foreign languages? Should other countries adopt the Dutch system for teaching foreign languages in school? The truth is simpler: the Netherlands are a very small country. We have a deep-seated collective awareness that only very few people in the world speak Dutch (including our Flemish-speaking neighbours across in Flanders and Afrikaans spoken in South Africa). Children grow up singing along to English pop songs. They play electronic games and make connections all over the world. Their focus on gaming forces them to become fluent in English at an ever earlier age. Due to a large volume of German tourists spending their summer in the Netherlands, children grow up hearing German spoken (many shops in the coastal areas have notices in German on their windows). It has been claimed that English is no longer a foreign language but that in reality it is the second language of the Netherlands. The truth in this statement will depend on how you define *bilingual*.

Folklore

Folklore[3] refers to the body of traditional beliefs, customs, memories, songs, poetry and stories of a community, originally passed from one generation to another orally (by word of mouth). It can also refer to a collection of myths or beliefs connected to a specific place or community. This can include local traditions, recipes and children's rhymes or games. Folklore is in a constant state of flux, always changing and developing, giving rise to new expressions, art forms and interpretations. Think of heavy metal bands singing about ancient gods and goddesses, or graphic designers taking inspiration from graffiti.[4]

Folk belief and superstition

There is a continuum between folklore or folk belief and superstition. In Dutch, superstition is called *bijgeloof*. [5] It refers to common beliefs in things that challenge the scientific worldview. This word is often used to refer to non-dominant religious beliefs and practices. Things work the same way as in English, one person's religion is superstitious nonsense by another person's reckoning. It reflects perspective and depends on who the speaker is (and how open-minded the speaker is regarding view-points and cosmologies different from their own).

Today some people will refer to astrology as superstition while others regard it as one of the most ancient sciences known to human beings. Until the 17th century there was no split between astronomy and astrology[6], between maths and sacred geometry, between chemistry and alchemy. This divide is relatively recent.

Traditional folk belief often concerns itself with the way that supernatural powers influence events on earth. By performing certain actions those forces can be called on, redirected or even cancelled. Knowledge about this allows people to increase their luck or ward off ill fortune.

One definition of magic is the ability to gain a larger influence over the shaping forces that define one's own life through greater consciousness and active relationship with such 'invisible' factors. When attempting to define the boundary between belief and superstition one soon finds oneself in muddy waters. In Dutch the word *bijgeloof*, literally a belief that there is more (between Heaven and Earth) is today often amended to *volksgeloof* (folk belief), a more neutral and respectful term. Note that the famous Roman author Tacitus referred to Christianity (the early Christian cults of his time, not Christianity in the well-organised form we know today) as *harmful superstition*.[7]

In our day Richard Dawkins, a caustic opponent of Christianity, describes students in Christian schools as being 'taught superstitions drawn from ancient scriptures'.[8] Some people believe that all religions are collections of superstitious beliefs. Some Christians condemn and carefully avoid any form of magic. The fear seems to be that practicing magic (even in a light-hearted or open-minded way) can open the door on demonic possession (meaning that the person can end up in the cast-iron grip of the Devil or Satanic forces).[9]

Christian Witches

Today I came across a reference to Christian witches as some branches of Christianity actively engage in magical practices. There is a book written by a Christian Witch who escaped the cult of Jehovah's witnesses and decided to walk her own unique path.[10]

The Dutch theologer Erik Borgman postes that superstition [bijgeloof] has a strong social component. In a culture where everyone believes something, that alone is enough reason for people to believe something. This is comparable to the reason why in western culture people do not eat dogs meat but are happy eating cows. On a rational level it does not make sense, but people do not do it because one does it. When everyone believes something it "just is", for the same reason.[11]

Most Dutch people are only mildly superstitious in the way many northern Europeans are. They are weary of the number 13 and they touch wood to ward off bad luck while a horse shoe or four-leafed clover brings good luck.[12]

Volksgeneeskunde and volksgeneeskunst (Folk Medicine)

The Dutch language uses two extremely similar words to refer to two different things:

Volksgeneeskunst refers to the full range of folk beliefs about illness and wellness and any remedies used to bring a cure. You could say that the defining characteristic is ordinary people 'acting as their own doctor'.

Volksgeneeskunde refers to professionals practising traditional forms of natural or herbal medicine and having spent years training in these disciplines, also known as holistic medicine. *Volksgeneeskunde* is also practised in South Africa and called *boererate*. An older generation believed that you should at least try to cure yourself, before you consult a medical doctor![13]

Here is a short passage about boererate, so the readers can see what written Afrikaans looks like:

Die gedagte aan boererate het onmiddellik by my opgekom, miskien omdat ek as kind die soort middele heel dikwels moes inneem ... of met 'n blikkie agter die bokke moes aanloop om die waardevolle kruie-uitskeidinkies huis toe te bring sodat die maselspasiënte daarmee verpleeg kon word![14]

Quality information about *volksgeneeskunst* is scarce. I was thrilled to obtain a copy of an out-of-print book from 1981 by Paul van Dijk.[15]

Before modern medicine the Netherlands had a wide range of healers: *piskijkers* (urine diviners), *beenzetters* (fracture fixers), *steensnijders* (stone carvers), *belezers* ("readers"/diviners), *koortsafnemers* (fever reducers), horoscope readers and many others specialists.[16]

The Ancient Celts, who also reached the Low Lands, had druids. Their successors were the Germans who had *de lacheners* (wizards, the contemporary word *lachen* means laughing in both Dutch and German). Their job was driving out sickness demons (*ziektedemonen*).

All over Europe, indeed, all over the world, indigenous healing methods involve ingredients we consider dubious and unethical today: the penis of a wolf, the heart of a raven, the brains of cats and lizards, the bone of a frog boiled alive....[17]

Het Galgenveld in Amsterdam Noord was the public site of executions by hanging. Perhaps surprisingly the executioner became an expert and healer in his own right, as his profession made him familiar with fractures and wounds. He was a liminal figure, operating in the danger zone between Life and Death.[18]

The successors of witches were *hellevegen*: women who specialised cupping, childbirth, reading horoscopes etc. By the 7th century the Netherlands had *monnikkengeneeskunde*: Roman Catholic clergy (even bishops) who practiced healing and curing, using ancient techniques with a Christian overlay. This contributed to the Christianization of plant names[19]:

- Valerian – duivelsklauw (Devil's claw).
- Hondsdraf (Ground Ivy, Glechoma hederacea) – duivelskandelaar (Devil's candelabra).
- De smeerwortel (Comfrey) – duivelsboon (Devil's bean).
- St Jans Kruid duivelsdruif (Devil's grape).

In the Medieval period we find *barbiers* (barbers), later called *chirurgijns* (the forerunner of *chirurgen* – surgeons). In addition to cutting hair and shaving, they offered bloodletting and treatment of wounds and fractures.[20] We need to remember that the profession of modern medicine, as we know it today, only developed after the Industrial Revolution in the 18th century.[21] Before that, disease theory followed very different guiding principles[22]:

- Law of Sympathy.
- The Doctrine of Signatures developed by Paracelsus.[23]
- Theory of the Four Humors (*Humoraalpathologie* in Dutch).[24]

The Law of Sympathy is based on the belief that all expressions in the physical world reflect a primordial unity 'behind the scenes'. This is the key principle behind phenomena such as synchronicity (meaningful coincidence) and omens or portents (hints and foreshadowing of things to come). Modern science dismissed this but the idea has come back into vogue courtesy of quantum mechanics and the concept of quantum entanglement.[25]

The Doctrine of Signatures dates from the era of Galen and Dioscorides. It states that plants resembling various body parts can be used by herbalists to treat ailments of those body parts. Botanist William Coles (1626–1662) offered a Christian justification: God had made 'Herbes for the use of men, and hath given them particular Signatures, whereby a man may read ... the use of them'.[26]

Fatal outcomes have occurred (e.g. birthwort was once used widely for pregnancies but it is carcinogenic and damages the kidneys). Today this same principle is still followed in homeopathy, as *like cures like,* but the dose is negligible: the active ingredient is watered down so heavily that only an energetic effect remains.

> *By similar things a disease is produced and through the application of the like is cured.*[27]
> -Hippocrates (460-377 BCE), Father of Medicine

The Theory of the Four Humors views the processes occurring in the human body as an interaction between four fluids: blood, phlegm, black bile and yellow bile, associated with, respectively, air, water, earth and fire. They were also connected to the seasons (e.g. blood represented spring). Maintaining the right balance was crucial to physical and mental health so treatments involved a process of re-balancing. Bloodletting, for example, was a cure for diseases caused by 'the human body containing an excess of blood', which is medically impossible.[28]

Volksgeneeskunst makes use of six different categories and healing methods (and many practitioners combine several)[29]:

Magical means

Driving out demons or in Church idiom 'exorcism'.

sprinkling with Holy Water (before Christianity: using the healing power of water from natural springs and wells).

Amulets and talismans.

Strijken or Magnetiseren (healing massage).
- *Aanblazen* (blowing off pain, even today Dutch mothers will blow on a child's sore knee to blow the pain away).

Sympathetic medicine
- Medical astrology.
- Precious stones.

Healing substances and objects, even animals
- Herbs and plants.

- Bodily fluids (even corpses!).
- Leeches.
- Snow, sticks, stones.
- Purging.

Animal-assisted therapy (in the past sick people were wrapped in gory fresh animal skins, today we see e.g. dogs and horses used in work with autistic children)[30]. *To cure gout, take a dog to bed with you.* Advice from the Achterhoek, province Gelderland, but nearer Amsterdam in De Zaanstreek we find *rheumatiek-hondjes*, dogs helping people to manage the symptoms of arthritis.

"Christian magic"
- Speaking prayers or reading out healing formulas (*'gezondbidden'* – praying someone back to health, requires a very pious person, but today even Heathen/Pagan communities operate prayer lists and prayer trees etc.)
- Votives and statues.
- Holy water, holy bread, holy wine etc.
- Pilgrimage (the non-Christian version is now commonly called a *sacred journey.*

Secret medicine
Miracle substances with undisclosed ingredients (often the domain of quacksalvers), i.e. powdered horn of unicorn. Germanic people perceived disease agents and intrusions as small worms.

- Heartworm causes heart disease.
- Toothworm causes tooth decay.
- Fingerworm (*fijt*) causes a skin infection at the bottom of a finger, (often following a puncture wound).

The *bezweringsformule*: spell or magical incantation

The simplest form of such a formula is also found in children's rhymes:

> *"Koorts, koorts, ik ben niet thuis, ga maar naar een ander huis!"*
> "Fever, fever, I am not at home, please go visit another house"
> (Comparable to the nursery rhyme: rain, rain, go away, please come back another day!)

One interesting fact is that in Belgium healing formulas often start off with an example of a cure. This reminds us of indigenous healing sessions starting with a litany of Creation, to call something back to its state of original perfection. Healing needs to have a community dimension. Perhaps a human life is one long healing?[31]

Sacred Numbers

The numbers three and seven, as well as multiples of those numbers, are considered sacred in healing. In formulas the words are often repeated three times. After childbirth, days number three and day nine are considered risky. Nine is, arguably, the most special number in Norse and Germanic cosmology.

Some means to treat fever[32]

- Make an infusion of nine plantain leaves in brandy and drink.
- Carry nine plantain leaves in a pouch around your neck.
- Hang nine plantain leaves on your door...

Sevens

It has been claimed or observed that:

- The seventh son has healing powers (not easily tested in

the modern era of 2.4 children!)

- A pregnancy was viable only after seven months of gestation (today's figure is 22 – 24 weeks).
- In acute illnesses day seven and day fourteen are (reportedly) critical (in pneumonia the fever drops after seven days).
- The human body renews itself completely every seven years (due to cell regeneration).
- Babies grow seven milk teeth on both sides during the first seven months of their life.
- Girls used to start menstruation at age fourteen (but this happens earlier today, at 12 – 13 years).
- Multiples of seven are key years in a human life, where major changes occur because one 'epoch' ends and another starts, people die most often during a year that is a multiple of seven, compared to their birth date. (Globally speaking the average age at death is about 70 but that rises to 80 in Western society – and is still rising).

'Corpse Therapy'

In the past mummified human corpses, especially the bodies of young men dying a violent death, virgins and unborn babies were viewed as powerful medicine (ground up and generally applied in powder form). In the sixteenth century Egyptian mummies were all the rage but a more manageable supply of bodies came from public executions. (Another profitable side-line for executioners!)[32]

In the Low Countries there is a case on file of an epileptic boy being made to drink fresh blood taken from a decapitated criminal. In the past criminals were executed by hanging on the Amersfoortse Berg (a place called the Mountain of Amersfoort) for dishonesty. One tailor (called a *Laakman*, someone who makes or sells bedsheets and table cloths), who was unfairly sentenced and killed, is said to be still walking around the area, carrying his head under his arm. He is singing:

> *"Little Laakman Laak (Literally: Little Sheetman Sheet)//The sheet*
> *I cut too short//My poor soul I forgot"*

Our cleaner reported that she saw him. It is possibly but perhaps she was hysterical (Dutch for 'in a state').[33]

Professional prayer services

We have already looked at prayer trees and fever trees. Belgium had so called *bidzaligers* (literally: those who bless through prayer) who would make a pilgrimage on behalf of a sick person (in return for a gift or charitable donation). People would also make pilgrimages to churches and leave offerings there in form of food and animals (pig's heads, fruit, butter).[34]

Unicorns

This mythical animal had a tremendous reputation as a panacea. Even some animals were treated with this ingredient and got better. This would suggest that we cannot speak of the power of suggestion alone! However, as more people travelled long distances and the world 'grew smaller', it was discovered that the horns of unicorns resembled rhinoceros and oryx antelope horns but actually were narwhal horns.

A well-known doctor called Cardanus (1501 – 1546) claimed that the night sky held all the answers, even to all diseases! This refers to the sacred art of the medical horoscope, still practiced today.[35]

Some treasures from the National Story Archives (De Verhalenbank)

To tap into the mindset of The Low Countries, I trawled the archives of De Verhalenbank[36], a treasure trove coordinated by the Meertens Institute. It offers a vast collection of stories from present and past and from all provinces, in their local dialects.

The material ranges from fairy tales and legends to jokes, riddles and eye witness accounts of memorable events.

Many of these stories are written down in the local dialect of the narrator (or near the border, in German):

Tsjin pine yn 'e holle mat men in hier út 'e holle lûke, dan kriget de holle lucht.
When you have a headache, pull out one hair to 'air' the head.

'Broodjeaapverhaal' or Monkey Sandwich Stories

Reading many of these stories some observations can be made. Contemporary developments and life in the (so called) global village spawn new stories (and new superstitions) all the time. I found one story sparked by the Ebola virus: *No worries about contracting the Ebola virus because after death you will resurrect as a zombie. Nothing to get stressed about at all!*

This is classified as a 'Broodjeaapverhaal' (literally a monkey sandwich story), meaning a made-up story that is told to others as real and factual. It usually plays on latent fears and prejudices in the listener. At the time of writing (May 2020) the culprit would have been the Coronavirus.[37]

This is what Frisian looks like:

Ik lei op bêd op 'e rêch mei de hannen ûnder 'e holle. Doe kom der in âld frommeske oan mei in blauwe tipdoek op 'e holle, in âlde, grize kadoffert.
Ik wie oan 't stjerren ta, doe't se kom. Doe't ik op 'e side komme koe, wie 'k forlost. It wie in nachtmerje.
-Translated from Frisian by Ytje and Annie de Meer
I was lying on my bed with my hands under my head. Then an old woman came, wearing a blue headscarf. I was close to death when she came with a great offer of a gift. When I rolled over on my side I was released from a nightmare.

Babies

Storks brings babies but babies can also grow in the hollow of a knotty willow tree or even in a large cabbage.[38]

My wife was pregnant and while lighting the stove a flame burned her head. My baby daughter was born with the same red mark on her head.[39]

Ghost ('t Spook)

The soul of a person who had moved boundary markers on the land did not find peace after death and was often spotted in the evenings, floating above the fields and calling out: "Where shall I leave it?" The village priest advised the farmers to reply: "Exactly where you found it!" A burly and brave farmer's son dared call out this reply and the rock dropped down in exactly the right place.[40]

Encounters with the (local) Devil

De Langesleattemer man op gyk of roer

Three old skippers from Leeuwarden (in Frisia) tell stories where they make a distinction between the *'Langsleatter man'* and the *'devil'* of *Eernewoude*. They conclude that the latter is probably a prankster called Freark Prûk (Helffrich). The man who often lies down on the boom of the mast of a boat is probably the devil of Eernewoude.[41]

So here we find a local devil or demon (as opposed to the Christian figure of The Devil).

Don't come and torment me tonight...

V. D. Berg offers a method for checking if there is a nightmare in the house: bake a pancake or ketelkoek (a cake made in boiling water). If there is a nightmare in the house, the (pan) cake won't be done and leave the pan wonky. He also says that when a farmer's wife bakes cake and the cake fails in some way (turns out lopsided or half-baked) people would say: "There are witches present in the house!" (Dated c. 1874)[42]

Note about the Frisian language

Frisian is a West-Germanic language. In the early Middle Ages, Frisia stretched much further south and Frisian was spoken between the delta between the rivers Schelde and Weser. The Frisians were in touch with Scandinavia using sea routes.[43] Because of this connection and exchange the Scandinavian languages acquired some Frisian words! (Just as the English language acquired Old Norse words. Did you know that the following common English words are Scandinavian in origin: husband, horse, knife, knot, land...?)[44]

Today Frisian is spoken only in the province of Friesland and in the extreme western part of the province Groningen. A different kind of Frisian is spoken in Germany. A distinction is made between the following types of Frisian:

- Westlauwersfries (the Netherlands)
- Stadfries (Spoken in the towns and cities of Friesland)
- Saterfries (Germany)
- Eiland-Noord-Fries en Vastelands-Noord-Fries (on the coast and on the islands)

Frisian became a formal language of the Netherlands in the twentieth century. From 1955 children have been taught in Frisian in the lower year groups of primary (elementary) school.

Moving with the times

Theo Meder, a researcher of folklore and folk stories based at the Meertens Instituut, explains that some superstitions fade over time but they are replaced by new superstitions related to 21st century events and technology.[45] The example he uses is that in the past people feared the Devil but we now live in fear of the radiation of micro-wave ovens, chem trails or inoculations for children causing autism. (Please note that I am not commenting on the veracity of these beliefs). And did you know that of all cats, black cats stand the highest chance of ending up in an animal shelter? Nothing to do with witches at all but black cats are not very photogenic (compared to fellow felines with different colouring), in photographs they appear as furry black holes or blobs. People are social-media-conscious today. We actively curate our public image.[46] Our pets (and even children) often suffer for the cause of our public image.

Merkeldagen or *lotdagen*: 'fate days' used to predict the weather in months to come[47]

2 February, Merkelday of the Holy Virgin, after the Purification of the Virgin feast, the snow falls on hot stones.

14 February, Valentine's Day, if the Earth is blanketed in white this day, the fields are filled with joy.

20 July, Saint Margaret (Sint Margriet), if it rains this day, we face six weeks of rain.

1 November, All Saints, is a water day or a winter day.

2 November, All Souls, going without fire this day does not save on firewood from the woodshed.

11 November, St Martin's Day (St Maarten), mist in the night makes winter short and gentle.

25 November, St Catherine's Day, frost on this day means frost for six weeks to come.

30 November, St Andrew (Sint Andries), if the saint buckles under snow the corn harvest will fail next year.

The fourteen Emergency Helpers or Holy Helpers (Noodhelpers)

My students of Seidr and Northern Tradition work often yearn for 'pure material', unpolluted by centuries of Christianity and other influences. This is an illusion. The realistic choice is reconstruction work with material from the 8th century (never knowing for sure whether our efforts resemble what people did then) or accepting Christian magic as part of the bargain.

In Roman-Catholic regions the veneration of saints and patron saints played a major role in folk medicine. This phenomenon includes relics, votive gifts and pilgrimages. In the Roman Catholic church there are fourteen Holy Helpers people can call on for assistance with specific matters or ailments. This group makes its first appearance in the German Rhineland area in the fourteenth century. Their emergency may be related to bubonic plague epidemics.

There is a long-standing folk tradition of calling on saints for intercession and healing

The fourteen saints or Holy Helpers are:

- Achatius, martyr, called on for relief from headaches.
- Barbara, virgin and martyr, fever.
- Basius, bishop and martyr, sore throat.
- Catharina, virgin and martyr, pestilence and bubonic plague.
- Christoffel, martyr, pestilence.
- Cyriacus, deacon and martyr, deathbed temptations.
- Dionysius, bishop and martyr, headaches.
- Erasmus van Formiae, bishop and martyr, stomach and gut complaints, is also knowns as Saint Elmo.
- Eustachius, martyr, arguments and differences of opinion in families.
- Joris, soldier, martyr and abbot, sick pets.
- Margaretha, virgin and martyr, pregnancy.
- Pantaleon, bishop and martyr, patron saint of medical doctors.
- Vitus, martyr, epilepsy.

I was brought up Roman Catholic but translating this list into

English hit home to me how the Church preaches about one omnipresent and omniscient male god instead of the heathen pantheons of an earlier time and yet they have created.... *an alternative pantheon!*

The key concept here is intercession: saints set an example of living a life as true to God and close to God as humanly possible and nearly always dying a martyr's death, dying for their faith (think back to St Boniface and the Donar's Oak). Because they are so close to God, living human beings can pray to them for intervention, to plead their case to God. Another key idea is that the way these saints lived and died gave them expert experience of the suffering you experience now. This means that they are uniquely placed to speak to God on your behalf.

The Roman Catholic Church has come under criticism for this. She has been called a 'whore' for 'sleeping with the enemy'. A more sober way of saying the same thing is that the Roman Catholic Church was founded as a compromise between Roman Pagan traditions and the then emerging Christian faith.

Early Catholicism strongly disagreed with actual Bible teachings and the church barred followers from actually reading and studying the Bible. Protestants (non-Catholic believers in Christ) did not want the compromise. It is something that has been talked about for a while now.[48]

In order to survive, the Church felt compelled to accommodate earlier pagan beliefs, deities and customs in Christianised form. Some would say that these Saints really are Christian images imposed on much older heathen deities.

Due to reforms that swept the Roman Catholic Church many saints have been *reviewed* and some have been demoted, lost their saint-status. I believe some saints are still *under review*.

Reading about this reminds me of the secular process where Pluto was a planet until an astronomer found a larger object than Pluto far out in space, now called Eris. Scientists reevaluated what constitutes a planet and demoted Pluto to dwarf planet status in 2006. Many people have voted for it being reinstated as a planet![49]

The Catholic Church removed 93 saints from the universal calendar and revoked their feast days in 1969 when Pope Paul VI revised the canon of saints and determined that some of the names had only ever been alive as legends or not enough was known about them to determine their status.[50]

Today we make a distinction between canonized saints and inspirational figures ordinary people still call saints.

Many of the saints revered during the era of the Knights Templar (12th and 13th centuries) were removed from the liturgical calendar in the sweeping reforms of the Catholic Church in the 1960s. Up to 40 saints were no longer to have their own saints' days.[51]

Legend had that St Christopher carried a child who grew increasingly heavy across a river -- the child was supposed to be carrying the weight of God. But there wasn't enough historical evidence the man ever existed, so Pope Paul VI dropped him.[52]

My grandmother often talked about St Christopher (Sint Kristoffel). People would have St Christopher amulets in their cars as he was (possibly remains) the patron saint of travel. He was loved and prayed to by many, yet he got the chop.

The Church began honoring saints by the year 100 CE. The practice grew from the long standing Jewish practice of honoring prophets and holy people with shrines. ... Canonization has only been used since the 10th century. Prior to that saints were chosen by public acclaim. With that process, some saints' stories were distorted by legend and some never existed. In 1969 the Church reviewed all the saints on its calendar to see if there was historical evidence of each saint's existence. After discovering that there was little proof that many saints including some very popular one's ever lived, some were dropped from the calendar of feast days.[53]

Other saints who suffered a similar fate were Saint Ursula, Saint Nicholas (who gave us Santa Claus) and Saint George, usually depicted in art as slaying a dragon. According to legend Saint Ursula was the leader of a group of 1,000 virgins who were murdered in Cologne by the Huns. Saint Ursula is the patron of the Order of Saint Ursula, a congregation of nuns dedicated to educating girls.[54]

It is clear that some of these saints (leaving aside whether they ever existed as *real people* or not) replaced earlier local heathen deities in the popular imagination. From years of shamanic practice I know that once such a phenomenon, historically accurate or not, is created, it becomes inspirited and a relationship is established. From a spiritual point of view this means that praying to St Christopher or St Ursula for assistance or protection, will set an energetic trajectory in motion, only part-powered by our own focus and belief. The energy invested by the collective adds power and substance too. This group manifestation then becomes powered by the Other World in return, meaning that on a magical level (because this is a form of magic!) one can get results working with these saints. The fact that they have been demoted by the Vatican does not change this – a long history of intercession and miracles for ordinary people continues to power this belief, this phenomenon. It is not unlike charging a cosmic battery.

Down-to-earth

One quality Dutch people are said to possess in abundance is being *nuchter*. It means down to earth, not easily swayed, not prone to exaggerations or flights of fancy.

One typically Dutch invention is *The Monday Morning Monster*: a name for a machine (supposedly) assembled on a Monday, that never works properly... The 'nuchter' Dutch have a quirky sense of humour!

Activity #3

Make a serious attempt to learn an ancestral language which currently is a foreign language for you. What can you learn from the process, without pressure to achieve fluency?

If that is a too tall order, listen to songs in this language, or listen to friends/family members speaking it and observe how this feels.

If you are not language-minded, commit to learning just five words or phrases in an ancestral language. Using those will give you 'goodwill credits' with native speakers!

In Dutch

Hallo! – hello!

Tot ziens! – See you!

Dankjewel (familiar form) or Dankuwel (polite form) – Thank you!

Ik heet (or: mijn naam is).... – My name is ...

Chapter 4

Ancient indigenous gods and goddesses venerated in the Low Countries

Germanic Heathen deities

Ask any Dutch person to name some Germanic heathen gods and you will probably hear two names: Wodan (Odin) and Donar (Thor). People may be able to specify that Odin is the main god (or Allfather) and Donar is the Thunder god. Ask people about female deities, ancient indigenous goddesses, and you will receive a blank look. Only people who self-identify as pagan or heathen and who have researched the topic, will be able to tell you more. They are likely to mention Vrouw Holle and Nehalennia.

The names of most (but not all) ancient gods and goddesses in The Low Countries have Germanic origins but we also find Norse, Celtic, Gaul (and other) influences. Heathen religion was never static or monolithic[1], it was always evolving and changing.

Here are some local Dutch names of Germanic deities:

- **Arcanua**, archaeologists found an enamel rooster with her name stamped on it (in Burchten, Limburg, in 1976).[2]
- **Arduina** or **Arduinna**, location-specific goddess of the forest and Ardennes region, Belgium.
- **Donar**, Thor, called *Stavo* in Frisia/Friesland.
- **Fosite,** Fosta or Fosite might be the female half of a deity pair Foste-Fosta.[3]
- **Fostera,** goddess of agriculture describe as pale-skinned with blue eyes, might have been venerated by Frisians. According to sources a sanctuary or deity domain called *Fositesland* used to exist.[3]

- **Nehalennia** (goddess from the province Zeeland with a strong connection to the sea).
- **Tanfana** (also *Tamfana*, a goddess from an area called Twente in the east of the Netherlands, whose name was recorded in the first century).
- **The Witte Wijven** or **Witte Wieven** (literally translated meaning white women but actually meaning *witty or wise* women, are figures similar to the Norse Völva who became supernatural women after death).
- **Vagdavercustis** (ancient goddess of the Batavians mentioned on an altar near Cologne).
- **Wodan** *(Odin, Woden, Wotan)* as the leader of De Wilde Jacht or The Wild Hunt (appearing in different guises such as Gait, Derk or Henske).

In the time of the Roman Empire there were sanctuaries and temples dedicated to a very large number of *matres* or *matronae* in the Netherlands (see Chapter 6). They were ancestral mothers, deities people made offerings to for protection, healing and guidance.

Dutch author Ineke Bergman wrote a book dedicated to reviving ancient and indigenous goddesses of the Netherlands titled: *Godinnen van Eigen Bodem* (Goddesses from Our own Soil). Her take is that in pre-historic times, when people still lived in harmony with nature, an overarching Great Goddess was venerated. Different tribes had their own local version of this archetypal deity. Their image of her was shaped by the land they lived on. When a new religion preaching about one male god arrived on the scene, these female deities started vanishing (or as Bergman puts it: *they moved to the realm of the human unconscious instead*). Certain key values faded out of our collective awareness along with them: unity, coherence, balance between giving and taking, respect for all life forms, the awareness that we all have our place in a larger Web of Life.[4]

Bergman provides exercises for people to connect with some of these goddesses. She runs a (Dutch-language) Facebook group by the same name[5], dedicated to unearthing information about female deities of the Low Countries. In 2012 Bergman created a list she calls *The Alphabet of Goddesses, Wise Women and Saints in our regions*. This list is not complete. It continues to grow and change as more information becomes available, courtesy of the internet and more people actively working on research and reconstruction. If we include the Matrones, there were many goddesses indeed. About 1,100 different stones with description to the matronae have so far been found.

A balancing viewpoint is required here: there is no academic consensus at all that such a peaceful overarching Mother Goddess once existed. The work of pioneering Lithuanian-American archaeologist and anthropologist Marija Gimbutas, known for her research into the Neolithic and Bronze Age cultures of Old Europe remains controversial. Some praise her theories highly, others challenge many of her conclusions.[6]

Some male deities

To balance the female preponderance of this chapter. I first provide examples of some *male* gods venerated in The Low Countries. I highly recommend the Hearthfire Handworks website (for its comprehensive listing of old deities in many locations).[7]

(The) Alci

According to Tacitus[8] the eastern Germanic tribe of the Naharvalians worshipped two young brothers at an ancient grove.[9] Tacitus associated these two brothers with the Roman Castor and Pollux, who were inseparable and even followed each other in death, when they became two stars in the night sky (in star constellation Gemini, The Twins). The priest at the grove dressed as a woman and the sanctuary contained no idols of the two brothers. It is possible that some Germanic tribes had their own version of the Castor and Pollux myth, which can point to a common Indo-European origin, Mediterranean influences, or a coincidental similarity.[10]

In terms of the runes, they are associated with Rune EH (or EHWAZ), said to represent both twins and horses. They are often linked to the Sun goddess (Sowilo/Sunna – see Rune SIGEL) and appear in Bronze Age petroglyphs all over Scandinavia (dated 1,800 BCE to 500 BCE).

Foste or Fostare

On the Dutch island of Ameland a god named Foste was worshipped. In 866 CE his temple on the island was destroyed by fanatical Christians, and from the wood a church was built. Nothing is known about this god but it is likely that he was a local variant of *Forseti* (or Forsite), who was the Germanic god of Justice. There is some confusion about location, some historians connect him to Helgoland in Denmark instead. Ineke Bergman wonders about a possible deity-couple: Foste (or Fosite) and Fosta (or Fostare).[4]

Lugus

Lugus, god of light or the sun, was one of the most popular deities of the Celts. Several cities were named after him, Lugdunum (Lyon) in southern France, Lugdunum Batavorum (Leiden) in the Netherlands, and Luguvalium (Carlisle) in northern England. Lugus was also worshipped in several sites on the Spanish province of Tarraconensis, including the tribes of Gallaeci, Astures, Cantabri and Celtiberians.[11]

Pater Rhenus

Is Latin for Father Rhine, said to resemble Neptune and have two horns, possibly representing the fork in the river, where De Waal splits from De Rijn. This river marked the boundary of the

Roman Empire and acted as a main artery for trade. Riverbanks were popular places for offering ceremonies and locating shrines and temples.[12]

Rekwaz

Some Roman sources mention a god named Requalivahanus. Requaliva is probably a Latin interpretation of Germanic *Rekwaz* or *Rekwaliwa*; rekwaz is an old Germanic word for darkness (Gothic: *riqis* and Old Norse: *rokkr*) while *liwa* is old Germanic for water, so Rekwaz may mean The Dark One and Rekwaliwa interpreted as Dark Water.

Rekwaz may have been a god of Darkness or Death but other sources portray him as the god of forests or trees. An alternative theory is that Rekwaz is one of the names of Wodan. Many Germanic gods had multiple names in various languages and dialects; besides that, they were also referred to with poetic metaphors (*kennings*) and nicknames *(heiti)* which described some of their characteristics.[10]

Saxnot, Saxnōt, Saxnote or Seaxneat

Was a Germanic god of the Saxon tribe, often compared with Tiwaz/Tyr, the brave warrior god. (See RUNE TIR). He was venerated in England as well as in North-Western Europe. He is the third god named in the Old Saxon Baptism Vow,[13] also known as The Baptism Vow from Utrecht, discovered in Mainz, Germany. The Nordic word *sax* means scissors and *neat* (see RUNE NYD) means need/necessity.

Sucellus

Sucellus was possibly the god of feast and providence and consort of Nantosuelta, the goddess of nature and water. He is depicted as carrying a long-handed hammer and a cauldron. May have been asked for protection or food supplies; may be linked to the Irish Dagda (who already had a magic cauldron and club on wheels). Sucellus was accompanied by a raven and a three-headed dog, linking him to death and soul conductors. Worshipped predominantly in Italy and Britain.[14]

Thunar/Donar/Thor

Some altars and Roman texts mention gods such as Magusanus Hercules, Mars Halamardus, Jupiter tonans, Hercules, etc. These are believed to be Romanized names for the Germanic god Thunar, who was also known as Donar or Thor, the Romans had a habit of relating native gods to their own. So, although Thunar is a well-known god, I have decided to list his Roman names, to avoid confusion. He was one of the most important gods of the Batavians and an altar dedicated to him was found near the Dutch village of Ruimel.

Tiwaz

Some Roman sources mention the god Mars Thingsus, this was another name for Tiwaz, *thingsus* may refer to the Germanic folk assembly (þing) in which Tiwaz (also known as Tyr/Tiu) played an important role. (RUNE TIR)[15]

Vosegus

A personification of the Vosges, a region with mountains and forests in eastern France. Vosegus was a god of nature or the animals in that region, depicted carrying a pig under his arm.[16]

Warns

Believed to have been worshipped by the Saxon tribe of the Warnians, probably identical to Wodan. The modern Dutch village of Warnsveld is believed to have been named after him as well as the Frisian village of Warns. In Austria there is a city called Warnsdorf and in the Czechian Sudetenland there is also a Varnsdorf, though whether these cities have been named after the god Warns is unknown.[10]

Scholarly Reconstruction

A few pointers before we proceed with the goddesses; it is important to note that some Proto-Germanic deities have been reconstructed[17] and pertinent at this point to refer the reader to the appendix 'Further Scholarly Discourse' at the end of this book, which considers both the reconstruction of Proto-Germanic deities and the 'Goddess Alphabet' of the renowned scholar, Ineke Bergman. Also, before we continue, please note that the following linguistic acronyms apply:

- OHG = Old High German
- OHS = Old High Saxon
- OE = Old English
- OF = Old Frisian

Directory of Goddesses

Abnoba

Abnoba was a goddess of the forest and river. Abnoba is a Romano-Celtic goddess who was popular in the Black Forest (in Germany).[18]

(The) Alaisiagae: Friagabis and Fimilena

These goddesses are associated with The Alaisiagae, two Celtic and Germanic deities worshipped in Roman Britain (at a Roman fort on Hadrian's Wall) as well as in the town of Biltburg, near the German-Belgian border. They were known by two sets of names, one Celtic *(Beda and Boudihillia)* and one Germanic *(Friagabis and Fimmilena)*. Beda is Friagabis and Fimmilena is Boudihillia. They were likely goddesses of war and battle, worshipped at a military site. The Alaisiagae had Mars Thingsus (Mars of the Thing – Public Assembly) as their consort. This name refers to the Germanic god Tyr or Tiwaz. Tyr was the Norse god associated with oath-taking and the Thing. (See Rune TIR)[19]

Simek suggests, given that the goddesses are accompanied by the god of the Thing (Mars Thingsus) that Boudihillia and Friagabis could be related, respectively, to the Frisian *bodthing* (summons) and *Fimelthing* (sentence). The modern German city of Bitburg was once known as *Beda Vicus* or Beda's village.[20]

Some digging produced one intriguing further reference: The Alaisiagae are believed to have been two Valkyries, one of them was Bed, who could aid people in lawsuits, and the other one was Fimilo, who could divert danger. Their names are probably Latin and it may be possible that the Romans misinterpreted a local worship of Valkyries.[10]

Alateivia

Goddess, possibly associated with healing. (Known in Gaul, with a worship site at Xanten)[21]

Alfrodul (v. Alfrodil)

In Norse mythology it is prophesied that the Sun (perceived as a female giantess) will one day birth a daughter who is no less beautiful than she herself is. This daughter, Alfrodul, will be her successor and follow the path of her mother in the sky:

> *One daughter is born to Alfrodul [Sun] before Fenrir [the wolf] destroys her. When the Gods die this maid shall ride her mother's paths [The Prose Edda].*[22]

Ammaca/Gamaleda

During the restoration of a brewery in Maastricht (Limburg) in 1894, an altar stone was found and the inscription remained partially legible: *Ammacae sive Gamaledae (...) vndi.* The name Ammacae is derived from *ammait*, which means old woman and probably means venerated mother or honourable mother. The Sanskrit word amma means mother goddess.[23] The Hebrew word ammah means mother or origin.[24]

The Gothic word *aikei* means mother, as does the Old High German word *eidi*, which is related to the Old Norse word *edda*, usually translated as grandmother. Gamal (*gammal* in contemporary Swedish) means old, making gamaledae *old honoured wise mother*. They are sometimes perceived as two different goddesses while others perceive the titles as different appellations for one goddess.

Ancamna (v. Ancama)

In Gallo-Roman religion, Ancamna was a goddess worshipped particularly in the valley of the Moselle River. She was commemorated at Trier and Ripsdorf as the consort of Lenus Mars, and at Möhn as the consort of Mars Smertulitanus.[25]

Arcanua

Arcanua is mentioned in Roman writings, she was worshipped in the Netherlands and may be connected to the Geleenbeek region. Her name means 'the mysterious or mystical one' in Latin. Her name could also be a Romanized Germanic name because it is believed that she was venerated in the area before the Romans invaded. In 1976 amateur archaeologists found a bronze and enamel rooster in Burchten (Limburg), with Arcanua's name stamped on it. In 1982 a bronze leaf was found there. The rooster is hollow and may have been used for burning candles, incense or oil.[26]

Arduinna (v. Ardbinna)

Arduinna is the Goddess of the Ardennes Forest and of hunting.[27] She was worshipped in the region called Belgium and Luxembourg today (plus small segments of France and Germany). Some call her *De Dame van de Bossen* (The Lady of the Forests) or *De Berengodin* (The Bear Goddess). Near Villers-devant-Orval in Luxemburg at Margut there was hilltop sanctuary dedicated to Arduinna. The root of her name comes from the Gaulish word *arduo*, meaning height, making Arduinna the Goddess of Heights.

She protected both flora and fauna and received animal sacrifices on her feast day. She extracted fines from hunters who killed animals on her land. She protected its animals and she was propitiated with offerings so that the hunt would be successful. My sacred art students have worked with her. Her attributes are a wild boar and a spear. We have one statue of her riding a wild boar.

There is a minor planet called 394 Arduina, first spotted by astronomers in 1894.

In comparison the Norse goddess Freyja also rides a boar called Hildisvíni, in the poem Hyndluljóð. She meets the volva Hyndla and together they ride to Valhalla (Freyja on her boar and Hyndla rides a wolf) in search of discovering the ancestry of her protégé Óttar. (Actually the boar is Óttar in disguise!)[28]

It is an indisputable fact that there was an altar dedicated to Ardbinna at Gey in what is today Kreis Düren, in the German state of Nordrhein-Westfalen. Gregory of Tours informs us that a monk called Walfroy the Stylite found the people of Margut too devoted to Arduinna in the sixth century. They would drink and chant in her honour. Walfroy attempted to eradicate her cult by destroying the sanctuary and installing himself atop a large pillar he had erected nearby. He vowed that he would live on only bread and water and would not descend until Arduinna's followers abandoned her.[29]

Astrild

Appears as a Nordic name for the figure known as Amor or Cupid in Greco-Roman culture. She probably originated in the writings of 17th-century poet Georg Stiernhielm and does not appear in Norse mythology.[30]

Atesmerta

Known from one single inscription, discovered in France, in 1918. Her altar was found together with bones, fragments of pottery and coins from the third century CE. Her name means the same thing as Rosmerta: Great Purveyor or Good Provider. Her name appears to be the female version of the god Atesmertius (equated with Apollo).[31]

Atla

One of the nine daughters of Aegir and his wife Ran in Norse mythology. These gods of the sea have daughters, the Nine Wave Maidens, who together mysteriously gave birth to the god Heimdallr. Her name means fury and she was responsible for overseeing the grinding of the world mill. Atla and her sisters may have given us the archetype of and fairytales about mermaids. Sailors made sure to be on good terms with the Wave Maidens just to stay safe on their ocean crossings.[32]

Baduhenna

Baduhenna is a Frisian Goddess. She is solely attested by the Annals where Tacitus records that a grove in ancient Frisia was dedicated to her, and that near this grove 900 Roman soldiers were killed in 28 CE. The location may have been north of the modern city of Velsen, where Heiloo is situated today.[33]

We know little about her other than that she received offerings in her holy grove. Her name may have been derived from the Proto-Germanic *badwo: *battle*. It has been suggested that Baduhenna is etymologically linked to the Irish Celtic Badb whose name derives from the Proto-Celtic *bodwo or crow, both likely deriving from a common Proto-Indo-European root, perhaps *bhat (*to hit*).[34]

Tacitus describes an attack by the Frisians on the Romans, who had invaded their lands. Peace prevailed for a time until Ollenius became the Roman ruler and demanded taxes from the

Frisians (payable in aurochs and skins, which the Frisians did not have access to). Some Frisians sold all they could to make the payments and some even sold their wives and daughters into slavery but soon rebelled.[35]

In the year 28 CE the Frisians formed their own small army and attacked a Roman fortress called Castellum Flevum, where Ollenius was hiding. The Romans requested reinforcements from a fortress at the place called Nijmegen today. In response to this, the Frisians withdrew into the Forest of Baduhenna (The Baduhennawald), an inaccessible area they knew intimately. This, as well as the use of small weapons such as hand-axes (Rune YR), gave the Frisians the upper hand in the continued battle. The Frisians killed 900 Roman soldiers that day. Tacitus writes that the Romans had become so paranoid, and so afraid of betrayal that, in the confusion and battle frenzy they even killed 400 of their own soldiers.[36]

As a teacher of Seidr and Northern Tradition teachings, I think that 'madness' is a mistranslation. I believe that the correct word here is (battle) frenzy, and that would place Baduhenna in good company, such as the Celtic goddess called The Morrigan but also Norse goddess Freyja (as the Picker of the Slain) and her troop of Valkyries. The formidable Celtic goddess Badb, said to represent one face or facet of The Morrigan, reportedly flies over battlefields in the shape of a crow. This is how she brings panic, confusion and paranoia to the enemy forces. Today we refer to this event as The Battle of Baduhenna Wood. The location is believed to have been near Heiloo in the Netherlands, but this has not been proven. It took place between the Frisii (Latin for Frisians) and a Roman army led by the Roman general Apronius.

Barbet

The existence of a goddess called Barbet is heavily disputed. Christian (Roman Catholic) history speaks of three *Beten* (also written as *Bethen* and *Beden*). Their names varied in different regions:[37]

- Einbet(h), Ambet(h), Embet(h), Ainbeth
- Worbet(h), Borbet, Wolbeth, Barbeth
- Wilbet(h), Willebede, Vilbeth, Firpet

These names refer to three saints, also known as the Three Virgins.

Their cult exists since the late Middle Ages in smaller churches and chapels in Northern Italy (South Tyrol) and the western part of Germany up to the Rhineland. There are also spare traces in the southeast of the Netherlands. We know the oldest of these three saints from the 12th century, the other two, among them Barbeth, is known since the 14th century. Their cult became a little bit more substance after in the 15th and 17th century these three saints were declared as companions of the better known Saint Ursula.[38]

Church leaders later then changed Borbeth (Barbet) to 'Babette'. In the Romantic period a theory was floated that these three saints had originated from a Germanic triple goddess or pagan trinity, comparable to The Norns or possibly linked to a Gaulish-Germanic triple mother cult as part of the Matronae phenomenon. There is no evidence for this. In 1936 a German called Hans Christoph Schöll from Heidelberg came up with a new idea that the three saints were developed from a Germanic triple goddess (Indo-European in origin). His theories do not stand the test of etymology but in the closing decades of the 20th Century, some people adapted Schöll's theory and placed the so called 'Bethen' at the heart of a gynocentric oriented heathen religion. Archaeological finds were deliberately interpreted (manipulated) to support this.[38]

Berchta

Berchta (also see Chapter 12) means The Shining One and she was a protector of children and women. Grimm's writings provide glimpses of a Germanic area where Berchta was a psychopomp (a guide to the afterlife), with a special responsibility for babies and children's souls. In other tales Frau/Vrouw Holle has the role of soul conductor or goddess presiding over Death and Berchta (also *Perchta* or *Perchten*) is a brighter figure, linked to light. In one tale about Berchta, a grieving mother spots her recently-deceased little boy following a group of children along a hillside. The children are following a motherly figure, wearing a white gown. The boy breaks away to address his grieving mother. He holds a bucket of water saying these are his mother's tears. Then he tells her not to weep for him, for he is safe and sound with the White Lady.[39]

Berchta reportedly wears a belt with three golden keys attached. (This is a feature she is said to share with Norse goddess Frigg). These keys are said represent the three stages of a cosmic process: life-death-rebirth. She wears her long black hair in braids on the side of her head, and wears a white gown. Like all old goddesses she was demonized, so in later stories she appears as a hag or crone, a dishevelled elderly woman. This may indicate Berchta as embodying a triple goddess (traditionally maiden, mother, and crone) or reflect an overlay imposed by the Church, or possibly both.

She is connected to spinning and checks on distaffs and spinning tools during the Twelve Nights period. The southern German city of Berchtesgaden was possibly named after her.

In *Fjölsvinnsmál*, a maiden or goddesses named Biort (Bjort) is mentioned. This may be the Old Norse name of Berchta, or Berchta may be a kenning, a poetic metaphor for a powerful goddess worshipped over a large area in Northern Europe.[10]

Berkana

Berkana or Bjarka (Old Norse – Frisian rune row: BEORC) is a rune named for the birch tree and often perceived as the rune of the mother (goddess). Some authors make the leap to speaking of a Birch Goddess, but here we are on slippery ground in terms of source material.

> *You will notice that rune books and sites about birch folklore tend to be vague about exactly who the "birch goddess" might be. That might be because only one the three rune poems mentions a deity, and that deity is [trickster god] Loki:*
>   *Birch has the greenest leaves of any shrub;*
>   *Loki was fortunate in his deceit. (Norwegian Rune Poem)*
>   *The Old Icelandic Rune Poem emphasizes the greenness of birch as well, no doubt a reference to its quickness in leafing out. The Anglo-Saxon rune poem, however, calls it 'poplar', probably because birch is uncommon in England. (That it means poplar, and not birch, is clear from its description of a tree that grows tall, and spreads by suckers, not seed.)*[40]

Birch will grow on land that has been burned or devastated by floods. It grows fast and loves sunlight. It is also one of the first trees to grow foliage in spring (I love observing this at our house in Sweden). Birch brooms and twigs are used for purification, said to drive out evil and as an anti-septic. The names for birch go back to an Indo-European root, *beryoza*: 'to shine'.[41]

Slavic folklore is more forthcoming about Birch: there is an Eastern Slavic holiday of birch trees called *Berezozol*, on April 11th. Birch twigs are used in making brooms. The spirit of the Birch tree was perceived as a young girl and associated with feminine power. It is used in health rituals and healing ceremonies and often used alongside oak (to represent masculine power). There is a dark side as well: a Belarusian song speaks of a birch tree growing on the bride's grave after the groom's mother poisoned her. (The Facebook group called Magpie's Corner offers information about Slavic traditions).[41]

Brigantia

Brigantia or Briganti was a tutelary goddess of the Brigantes, protector of the eponymous Brigantes, the largest British tribe in Yorkshire and northern Britain in late antiquity. Her name may translate as high or noble, and Brigantes would then mean noble ones or highlanders. She was a goddess of springs, streams, river and water cults, and corresponds to the Irish goddess Brigit in Ireland.[42]

Burorina or Burovina

May have been associated with abundance. She was known in Gaul and Germania. Her name was found on an altar near Domburg in Zeeland.[43]

Cantismerta

Derived from Gaulish *cant* – 'with' and smert – 'purveyor, carer', this name was probably understood in the sense of 'all-purveyor'.[44]

Catharina

Saint Catherine of Alexandria is also known as Saint Catherine of the Wheel, a Christian saint and virgin, martyred in the 4th century. More than 1,100 years after her death Joan of Arc identified her as one of the saints who appeared to her and gave her guidance. Her feast day is on 24 or 25 November, depending on the region. Some modern scholars believe that the legend of Catherine was based on the life and gruesome murder of Greek philosopher Hypatia (where the roles of Christians and pagans are reversed: she was killed by Nitrian monks belonging to a fanatical sect of Christians).[45]

Cobba
Goddess. Associations uncertain. (Known in Gaul, worship site near Utrecht in the Netherlands.)[43]

Cunera
Cunera was the daughter of English king Aurelius, on the Orkney Islands. She joined St. Ursula, when she set out from Britain on a pilgrimage to Rome with her 11,000 virgins, but her party was massacred by the Huns at Cologne. Redbad (Radboud), King of Frisia was so struck by the beauty of Cunera that he saved her from this event by hiding her under his mantle and he carried her off to Rhenen, his capital on the Rhine. (Historians hotly debate the historical accuracy of this account).

Radbod, the King of Rhenen, is said to have brought her into his palace, when she had been rescued from that death which overtook the eleven thousand virgins. While there, she kept herself constantly in the presence of God, serving him day and night, by vigils, abstinence, and other good works. While strictly observing his commandments, she despised the pomps of this life, advancing steadily from virtue to virtue. The poor were constant objects of her care.[46]

Damona
A goddess worshipped in Gaul, connected to thermal springs. Her name is sometimes translated as Divine Cow, connecting her to ancient goddesses such as Egyptian Hathor and to motherhood.[47]

Domnu, the Goddess of the Deep
Domnu and Dānu are Goddesses of the Abyss, Chaos and Old Night. Here we find a Celtic-Hindu Connection.

I am Domnu the spirit that moves in the abyss beyond time,

My face is desire, my eyes sees all, my pain is loneliness, and my womb gives birth to all,

And my breast will feed the voided,

For I am Domnu mother and bringer of life and bringer of death renewed,

I am the eye that sees, I am the heart that thinks, and the tongue that speaks,

I am the three I am the one, I am the Mother of all.

And an eternal mist spread to the fire eternal, and the mist was cold that fire eternal.

-Unknown[48]

Dorothea

Virgin and martyr, Dorothea of Caesarea suffered during the persecution of Diocletian, 6 February, 311, at Caesarea in Cappadocia. She was brought before the prefect Sapricius, tried, tortured, and sentenced to death. On her way to the place of execution the pagan lawyer Theophilus said to her in mockery: 'Bride of Christ, send me some fruits from your bridegroom's garden.' Before she was executed, she sent him, by a six-year-old boy, her headdress which was found to be filled with a heavenly fragrance of roses and fruits. Theophilus at once confessed himself a Christian, was put on the rack, and died.[49]

Einbeth

The Norns were not only worshipped in Scandinavia but also in many other Germanic areas. In southern Germany they were worshipped as *Matres* or *Matrones*, names given to them by the Romans who tried hard to match all deities to their own pantheon. In other parts of Germany, the Norns were called *The Three Eternal Ones* and their names were Einbet (Urd), Barbet (Verdandi), and Wilbet (Skuld).

Epona

Epona was worshipped in the Netherlands, especially by the Roman and Celtic occupiers there. It is believed that they were the ones who brought this goddess to the Netherlands since she was not of Germanic origin; Epona (Great Horse) was the Celtic goddess of horses.[50]

Erecura (also Aerecura or Herecura)

Goddess, thought to be Celtic in origin, depicted with the same attributes as Proserpina or Persephone, on an altar from Sulzbach. She is associated with the underworld, goddess of the deep earth.[51]

Ertha

Nothing remarkable occurs in any of these tribes [of northern Germany], except that they unite in the worship of Hertha [Ertha], or Mother Earth. They believe that she interposes in the affairs of men, and visits the different nations in her chariot. On an island of the ocean stands a sacred and unviolated grove, in which is a consecrated chariot, covered with a veil, which the priest alone is permitted to touch. He becomes conscious of the entrance of the goddess into this secret recess; and with profound veneration attends the vehicle, which is drawn by yoked cows.

At this season all is joy; and every place which the goddess deigns to visit is a scene of festivity. No wars are undertaken; arms are untouched; and every hostile weapon is shut up. At this time, only peace abroad and at home are known.

At length the same priest conducts the goddess, now weary of mortal intercourse, back to her temple. The chariot, with its curtain, and, if we may believe it, the goddess herself, then undergo ablution in a secret lake. This ritual is performed by slaves, whom the same lake instantly swallows up. Hence arises a mysterious horror and a pious ignorance of these events, which are beheld only by those who are about to perish.[52]

Exomna

Exomna was worshipped by the Batavi[53] in the Netherlands. Her name means *without fear* in Latin, which may suggest a Roman origin or a Romanized version of a Germanic goddess.[10]

Eir

Eir (help, mercy) is a Goddess of healing and patron deity of healers. The ancient text Fjölsvinnsmál informs us that there is a Mountain of Healing or Medicine Mountain in Norse cosmology where a mysterious goddess resides, surrounded by Nine Maidens or Disir (deified female ancestral spirits). Climbing this mountain can bring healing miracles, no matter how ill or 'diseased' a person is, and return people to wholeness and holiness. Eir is one the nine maidens in Menglöð's company.[54]

Fanna (also known as Waldacha)

Frisian goddess of the hunt and protective deity of forests and woodland, depicted as holding a bow in her hand[43], (a female counterpart of the Norse god of archery called Ullr?)[55]

Ferda or Freda

Both local Dutch names for the goddess Freyja who was venerated, along with Meda in the sanctuary called Hymeleferda near Stavoren in a sacred woodland called Ferwolda, (the source is the controversial 19th-century Oera Linda book).[56]

Feruna

A fertility goddess from the Dutch province of Twente. The local organisation *Ferunagenootschap* provides the following information:

Feruna is a goddess associated with the origin or life, tender beginnings. The farmers in an area called Usseler Es (near the city of Enschede) honoured her while planting new crops, near an ancient elder tree. She was worshipped in Spring and viewed as protective deity of all young creatures.

The artist Judith Schepers learned about Feruna at the kitchen table of her late grandmother, who lived for almost a century. She knew the farmers in the area and was familiar with their stories. Younger generations in the same area have forgotten all about Feruna. She might be related to Tanfana (who has beaten oblivion by positioning a big boulder in the market area of Oldenzaal. We have no written sources for Feruna, only an oral tradition on the verge of extinction due the internet and social media.[57]

Fimmilena

Fimmilena is a goddess associated with the þing/Thing (Germanic legislative assembly). She is one of two *Alaisiagae* (most likely 'venerated ones'), who are named in three inscriptions near Hadrian's wall in Cumbria.

The name *Fimmilena* seems to be related to the Frisian legal term *Fimelþing*. The exact meaning of this term is uncertain, but it has been interpreted as 'moveable assembly'.[58]

Flora

In Roman culture flora was the goddess of the flowering of plants. Titus Tatius (the Sabine king who ruled at the time of Romulus) is said to have introduced her cult to Rome, where her temple stood near the Circus Maximus. Her festival, called the Floralia, was instituted in 238 BCE. A representation of Flora's head, distinguished only by a floral crown, appeared on coins of the republic. Her name survives in the botanical term for vegetation of a particular environment.[59]

Fostare/Fosta/Fostera/Phoseta

Was a goddess depicted with long hair, blue eyes, bareheaded, wearing a short-sleeved robe and slippers while holding three ears of corn in her left hand. She was a goddess of agriculture, central to the daily life of the Frisians.

Ineke Bergman reports that the goddess Fostare called her to a well named *De Willibrordusput* in Heiloo. Her search next took her to Friesland and the island of Ameland. From descriptions of Willibrord's life we know that a male god called Fosite or a goddess called Fosta were honoured in Friesland. The name Fostera occurs in the old, previous, name of Westergeest: Fosterahiem. Ameland used to be called Fostaland! She says that we will never know exactly what happened in Magna Frisia, the ancient Frisian Kingdom (c. 500 – 734 CE) but we can all tap into memories held in our Collective Unconscious.[60]

Fru Freke

A Dutch version of the Norse goddess Frigg, Old High German Frīja, Low German Frike or Freke ((Fru Freen, Fru Frien, Fru Freke, Fru Frick, Fuik, Frie), Lombardic Frea.

The name *Frijjō* (Old Norse *Frigg*, Old High German *Frīja*) ultimately derives from PIE *prih-y(a)h, cognate to Sanskrit *priya* (dear, beloved), which in Germanic split into two etymons, one covering the semantic field of 'love, courtship, friendship' (think of the English word *friend*), the other covers the field of 'freedom' (English word *free).

Our modern weekday Friday is named for Frigg. In Old English this was called frigedæg. Friday, in Old Norse, was called both *Freyjudagr* and *Frjádagr*, in Faröese *fríggjadagur*, and in Old High German it was never *Frouwûntac, but *Frîatac, Frîgetac*, now *Freitag*.

In contemporary Dutch her name is directly related to the contemporary word *vrijen*: making love. *Frigaholdam* or *Frouwa* are local variants of the same name.[61]

Frya

She may be a fictional Frisian goddess described in the

controversial 19th-century Oera Linda book[62] or her name may offer an alternative spelling for the historical goddess **Frijjō**.[61]

Frijjō as Frigg-Frija (an abbreviation of short for Old Norse *Frigg*, Old High German *Frīja*) is the reconstructed name offered for a hypothetical Germanic love goddess and spouse of Wodanaz (Wodan-Odin), who later splits into two distinct Norse deities: Frigg and Freyja. Her Anglo-Saxon name is *Frig*, Old High German is *Frija* and Low German is *Frike* or *Freke* (we encounter her as *Fru Freen, Fru Frien, Fru Freke, Fru Frick, Fuik, Frie*). There is evidence that the name Frya[63] or Frigg simply means Lady. In some parts of Sweden and Germany the three stars in the asterism known as Orion's Belt are known as Frigg's distaff or spindle. Our contemporary English words *freedom* and *friendship* are derived from the same Indo-European root stem. Their Dutch equivalents are *vrijheid* and *vriendschap*.[61]

Ganna

After the famous Germanic seeress Veleda was captured and relocated to Rome, the Germans drafted a virgin named Ganna to take on the role of Veleda and seeress of the Semnones. She too was politically active and acted as a diplomat for her tribe in negotiations with Roman Emperor Domitian (who ruled from the year 81-96 CE). She even made a 'pilgrimage' to Rome and returned safely. Her religious duties would have included divination, prophecy and magical incantations. Her name may well be connected to the Old Norse word gandr (magical wand).[64]

Garmangabi

The name of this goddess was found on a Roman altar stone in Great Britain, it was created by Suebians who served in the Roman army; 'gabis' means gift, and there are theories which link her to the northern Germanic Gefjon (Frigg). (See Rune GYFU).[65]

Gerdr, Gerda

In Norse mythology, Gerðr is a jötunn, goddess, and the wife of the god Freyr. Gerðr is attested in the Poetic Edda, compiled in the 13th century from earlier traditional sources; the Prose Edda and Heimskringla, written in the 13th century by Snorri Sturluson; and in the poetry of skalds. Gerðr is sometimes modernly anglicized as Gerd or Gerth. The Dutch version is Gerda.[66]

Góntia or Ghent (Belgium)

Góntia, also known as Guntia, was a Celtic goddess. Her name may be etymologically related to the Celtic word condate (confluence). She may have been the tutelary deity of the river Günz, which is near Günzburg in Germany. She also appears to be connected with the Belgian city of Ghent.[67]

Haeva or Hafna

The name of this Batavian goddess was found on an inscription found near the Dutch city of Wijk bij Duurstede. It is unknown who Haeva was but it is believed by some that she was the wife of the god Thunar, her name probably means 'Exalted One'. A goddess of water and the sea. (The contemporary Swedish word for the sea is *havet*).[43]

Hariasa

Hariasa was worshipped in Germany and she is thought to have been a war goddess, other names for her were Harimela or Harimella, 'hari' means battle or war in old western Germanic.[43]

Harke

Jacob Grimm wrote in Teutonic Mythology that 'Harke flies through the air in the shape of a dove, making the fields fruitful'.[68] Harke is a giantess of German folklore from the Brandenburg and Thuringia regions. Her name means *to rake* (harken in Dutch) related to the harvest and care of the earth. She is a dweller of wild mountain forests but she moves around on her holy days. Folklorist Benjamin Thorpe wrote that 'At Heteborn, when the flax was not housed at Bartholomew-tide [August 24], it was formerly the saying, 'Frau Harke will come'.

She – and other land spirits –are deeply tied to agricultural fertility, and there is a symbiotic relationship between spirits and living humans, an exchange of gifts and energy (Rune GYFU). Harke is also a mistress of wild animals, protecting and herding them on her mountain, as well as a mistress of the hunt. She decides whether hunters will catch game (or not) and woe betide those who hunt without giving her due respect![68]

Hertha

Hertha was an Earth goddess, probably a local variation of Nerthus, some scholars also link her to other fertility goddesses, such as Berchta or Holda. the name Hertha may have been derived from the Proto-Germanic words 'hertan' (heart) or 'erþaz' (earth).

> *Hertha's themes are rebirth, kinship, health, longevity and tradition. Her symbols are dormant trees and snow. In ancient times, on this day people venerated Hertha, the Teutonic Goddess of fertility, domesticated animals, magic and nature. In Germanic tradition, Hertha descended through the smoke of any fire today and brought gifts, much like an early Santa Claus figure (giving Her solar associations too). Her connection to nature has survived in the name for our planet: Earth.*[69]

In the dunes behind today's venue *Kraantje Lek* in Haarlem there once stood a wooden temple dedicated to Hertha, on the shore of the river Spaarne.

Hel

Hel, (Hela is a popular but incorrect Latinized form), the Goddess of the Underworld, is the eldest child of Angrboda and Loki. She is the Goddess of Death in the cosmology of the Nine Worlds, and the Guardian of the Underworld. She is often depicted in her half-rotted or half-skeletal form, divided down the middle vertically.[70]

Hludana

In the terp village of Beetgum, Friesland (the Netherlands) in 1888, a votive stone was found with the following inscription:

To the goddess Hludana, the tenants of the fishery, when Quintus Valerius Secundus was head tenant, paid their due, willing and according to what they have earned.[71]

The name of Hludana (slight variations in spelling occur, *Hludanaz = 'Loud One') also appears on several stones in the Netherlands and Germany. Indeed, the image of a woman seated on a stone and the inscription – the Latin name and language, the connection with water, boats and trade – recall the votive stones of Nehalennia.[72]

Scholars debate whether she may be linked to (or even identified as) the old Norse goddess *Hlóðynn*, mentioned in de Voluspa, Gylfaginning and Skáldskaparmál, mother of Þórr (Thor) and/or Víðarr. Others claim that she may be related to Holle. We have only five votive stones to go on.

Hludana was probably a goddess of fishing. Like Nehalennia she was connected to both the sea and rivers. The Dutch people were a sea-faring nation. They were also keen traders and 'natural born businessmen' (and remain so until today).

Hretha

Anglo-Saxon paganism venerated Rheda (Latinized from OE

as *Hrêðe* or *Hrêða*, possibly meaning "the famous" or "the victorious") as a goddess connected with the month 'Rhedmonth (from Old English *Hrēþmōnaþ*). Rheda is attested solely by Bede in his 8th century work *De temporum ratione*. While the name of the goddess appears in Bede's Latin manuscript as *Rheda*, it is reconstructed into Old English as *Hrēþe* and is sometimes modernly anglicized as Hretha (also Hrethe or Hrede). *Hrēþmōnaþ* is one of three events that refer to deities in the Anglo-Saxon calendar—the other two being *Ēostermōnaþ* and *Mōdraniht*.[73]

Hruoda

Hruoda is also known as Hrede in Anglo-Saxon, Grimm briefly mentions her as a Spring goddess and she may be related to Ostara, though in most sources they are named as separate goddesses. One interesting fact is that the Anglo-Saxon calendar has the month March named after her: Hrethmonath.[10]

Hurstrga, also (Deae) Hurstaergae
(The Hurstaerga Goddesses)

The name of the goddess Hurstrga was found on a 30 cm high altar stone near Tiel in the Betuwe area, the Netherlands, in the 1950s. This stone dates from ca. 200 CE, when the area was occupied by the Romans. This stones has a Latin inscription giving thanks to the goddess in the name of a particular person (Valerius Silvester). Since the altar stone was found in the area of Bergakker in the Betuwe, this is also where Hurstrga's sanctuary may have been. The name Bergakker suggests a place higher than its surroundings. Likewise, the part hurst in the name Hurstrga means something like 'bush', which may indicate a sacred place. The area of Bergakker has revealed several archaeological finds, including a scabbard with runic inscriptions (unique in this area) and a silver votive plate showing three Matronae, or mother goddesses. What we may have here is a sanctuary devoted to the cult of Hurstrga, the local goddess of the Bergakker area.[71]

Holle *(Chapter 12 is dedicated to her)*

Idunn

In Norse cosmology Idunn is the goddess of rejuvenation and wife of Bragi, the god of poetry. She was the keeper of the magic apples of immortality, which the gods eat to preserve their youth. When, through the cunning of trickster god Loki, she and her apples were seized by the giant Thiassi and taken to the realm of the giants, the gods quickly began to grow old. They forced Loki to rescue Idunn, which he did by taking the form of a falcon and shape shifting Idunn into a nut (or sparrow in variants of the myth). He flew home carrying her in his talons.[74]

Iseneucaega or Senucaega

Most likely a goddess of the hunt, worshipped by the Batavians in the Netherlands. We know about this goddess from a damaged altar with an inscription that is hard to decipher, dated 222 CE. Segments to text were hacked off because it contains a *'damnatio memoriae'*, cursing the memory of Emperor Severus Alexander. This allows a precise dating of the stone but it is impossible to fill in the missing text. No remains of the temple Severus Alexander built have been found. The stone shows a goddess holding an arrow accompanied by a dog. She is assumed to be a goddess of the hunt, not unlike Roman goddess Diana. This altar was found in 1930, near Zennewijnen and Tiel.[75]

Korenmoeder

De Korenmoeder is the Corn Mother (also Roggemoeder or Rye Mother, depending on the type of grain). According to folklore Dutch people would make a *graanpop*, a corn dolly made from grains, as part of a ritual to increase the fertility of the land and future harvests. These creations were sometimes called Great Mother, Old Woman, Old Man and even Virgin or Witch (depending on location and harvest time).[76]

Kunigunde (v. Cunegonde)

Kunigunde, Kunigunda, or Cunigunde is a European female name of German origin derived from 'kuni' (clan, family) and 'gund' (war).[77]

Kere or Ker

A Dutch form of Celtic goddess Cerridwen (?)

Lucia, St Lucy

Saint Lucy (Santa Lucia, 283–304) was a wealthy young Christian martyr who is venerated as a saint by Catholic, Lutheran and Orthodox Christians. Her feast day is 13 December, on the unreformed Julian calendar the longest night of the year. Her name is derived from the Latin word lux, lucis 'light'.

She is the patron saint of those who are blind. Saint Lucy is one of the very few saints celebrated by members of the Lutheran Church, in Scandinavia. On her special day a procession is headed by one girl wearing a crown of candles (or lights), while others in the procession hold only a single candle each.

In Bavaria we find the *Schiache Luz* (bad or ugly Lucy). She appears as the *Lutzelfrau*, bearing a distinct resemblance to Perchta! She is ugly, dressed in rags, carries a sickle, has an iron nose and inspects all spinning equipment. Scary things occur: obnoxious children are thrown in a river; she is said to cut the tongues of children with shards of broken glass and their intestines are wound up on distaffs...[78]

Dark Lucy also reminds us of the Slavic Baba Yaga. In Scandinavia her wicked counterpart, the *Lussi*, actually haunts *Lusinatta* (Lucy's Night), flying through darkness like Holle with her ghostly retinue of *Lussen, Lussiner* or *Lussegubber* ('Lucy's kids').

Lucy night was also associated with divination: at midnight young men would scan the night sky for any *Luzieschein*: a mysterious play of light, containing the shapes of things to come. Young women were to then find a willow tree, pull back the bark, cut a small cross in the green wood below, moisten the wood and press back the bark to heal. Peeling it away again on New Year's Eve would reveal new patterns for reading the future.[78]

Lutgardis van Tongeren *(saint)*

Lutgardis[79] was born in Tongeren, Belgium as a rather frivolous girl.[75] Due to a financial family setback she had no access to dowry and was forced to enter a convent at age twelve. She was a visionary and mystic with a gift for prophecy, perceived as a patron saint of blind and disabled people. She performed miracles. She became the Mother Superior of her convent.[80]

Margaretha

Saint Margaret died a martyr's death in AD. 306. She is the patron saint of women in childbirth.[81]

Meda

The town of Medemblik in Noord Holland was founded in her honour because a golden statue of her was found there. She was honoured by virgins as the Goddess of Love near Stavoren, in a sanctuary called *Hymeleferda*, as well as in the sacred wood *Ferwolda*. Married people instead venerated a goddess called Ferda or Freda (variants of Norse Freyja) as the Love Goddess in the same locations. The name Meda means virgin or girl. Her festival was in May, once known as 'The Month of Virgins'. She protected innocence and virginity.

In a document from the year 985 CE, Medemblik is called Medemelacha. Lacha refers to the small nearby river De Leek. Medemelacha would then mean 'Virgin on the River Leek'. The town is said to owe its name to a golden statue which dazzled and flashed in the sunshine, so guiding the fishermen home.[82]

Matronae (See Chapter 6)

Mona

A goddess of the sea. There was a sanctuary dedicated to her in Dokkum in Friesland. Mostly likely there was another sanctuary on the island of Ameland.[83]

(Matres) Mopates

Near Nijmegen in the Netherlands an altar of the goddess Mopates was found, it was dedicated to her by M. Liberius Victor, a corn trader and Nervian citizen. In the form of the *Matres Mopates* she is often depicted as a threesome. Dutch author Judith Schuyf demonstrated that the Church imposed Christian conventions, such as the holy trinity, on older culture and customs. This meant that in the Middle Ages several 'trinities' of three women, or three female saints, were venerated and depicted together. When the Romans left the region, at the end of the fourth century CE, the name Mopates became 'Moffet' and that name survived as the name of a local forest.[84]

Nantosuelta

A Celtic goddess worshipped primarily in Gaul. Sometimes depicted together with Sucellus ('Good Striker'), the Gaulish god of agriculture. Her name was reconstructed by linguists and approximations in proto-Celtic mean 'She of the Winding River' or 'She of the Sun-drenched Valley'. Her attributes were a raven (linking her to the dead and the underworld) and Gaul craftsmen depicted her as holding a pole with a dove-cote mounted on top.[85]

Nehalennia

Nehalennia was a goddess worshipped in and around the Netherlands, in the place where the Rhine river meets the North Sea, in the 2nd and 3rd century BCE. We have found votive descriptions and altars dedicated to her. We know that temples were built in her honour.[82]

In the year 1645 gale-force winds assaulted the coast of the southern Dutch province Zeeland and exposed an ancient temple on the island of Walcheren. Votive objects and 28 altar-stones, dedicated to Nehalennia, were found. Scholars believe that Nehalennia's original temple was destroyed by Christian missionaries in 694 CE. In the centuries that followed even more altar stones and objects washed ashore.[86]

Other historians believe that this temple and the land it stood on was reclaimed by the sea some time in (or after) the third century CE. Whatever the truth may be, imagine a temple from over a thousand years ago rising from the waves, it must have been a spectacular sight![86]

The altars, inscriptions and offerings have been studied very closely. Nehalennia also re-captured the imagination of local people: a new temple to her was built in the town called Colijnsplaat, in the year 2005.

Scholars and authors do not agree on their interpretations of the name Nehalennia. Some think that her name implies that she was a death goddess (based on the Latin word necare – to kill) while others think that her name reflects that she was a River Goddess (ne = new, hel = stream/river and ennia = goddess).

Nehalennia's attributes are a ship and rudder, a dog and apples (sometimes baskets holding other types of fruit as well). However, her most striking attribute is a horn, possibly a cornucopia or Horn of Plenty. She is generally perceived as a goddess of water: streams, river, the ocean, and seafaring.[87]

Her other attributes are a dog, often depicted as sitting at her feet, which makes Simek classify her as a Death Goddess. Dogs often act as psychopomps or soul conductors (as do other animals such as horses and ravens). She often has one foot positioned on the bow of a ship. This likely expresses a role as a guardian or protector of sea-faring people. She may have had power over water and oceans. Dutch people have always been sailors and traders.

Nehalennia also appears with loaves of bread and not just any type of bread. Hilda Ellis Davidson identified the bread concerned as a *duivekater*; a type of sweet bread baked in the shape of a bone to resemble an animal sacrifice to a deity. The recipe originates in Amsterdam and surroundings (and is especially popular in *De Zaanstreek area*). A *duivekater* even appears in a painting by Jan Steen from 1658. The general idea was that if the gods were pleased with the offering, the Devil would stay clear. (*Duive* is the genitive of *Duivel*-Devil and a *kater* is a tomcat!) Dutch people still eat them today but most are not aware of the history of this type of bread! It does make us wonder what exactly Nehalennia's connection to death was, but the sea as always claimed her share of the dead by means of drowning and ship wrecks. You can find the recipe online.[88]

Near Walcheren we also find the lost city of Ganuenta, believed to have been situated on the Colijnsplaat. Some authors claim that Ganuenta was the capital of the Frisiavones, but it is more likely that it was situated in Menapian territories, and that Frisiavones lived further north.[89]

Most of Nehalennia's altars were found in the Oosterschelde, one arm of river De Schelde, today a nature reserve. Typical inscription found on a votive stone:

DEAE NEHALENNIAE DACINVS LIFFIONIS FILIVS V(OTUM) S(OLVIT) L(IBENS) M(ERITO)

"To the goddess Nehalennia, Dacinus, son of Liffio, has payed his promise with pleasure and reason."[89]

Nemetona

'She of the Sacred Grove', is a Celtic goddess with roots in north-eastern Gaul. She is thought to have been the eponymous deity of the Germano-Celtic people known as the Nemetes; evidence of her veneration is found in their former territory along the Middle Rhine as well, in the Altbachtal sanctuary in present-day Trier, Germany.[90]

Nerthus

Roman historian Tacitus mentions an island where a ritual was held in honour of the goddess Nerthus and the island he is speaking about is probably one of the Frisian islands (also called *wadden*) forming a long chain along the Dutch, German, and Danish coast.[91]

> *"On an island of the sea stands an inviolate grove, in which, veiled with a cloth, is a chariot that none but the priest may touch. The priest can feel the presence of the goddess in this holy of holies, and attends her with deepest reverence as her chariot is drawn along by cows. Then follow days of rejoicing and merrymaking in every place that she condescends to visit and sojourn in. No one goes to war, no one takes up arms; every iron object is locked away. Then, and then only, are peace and quiet known and welcomed, until the goddess, when she has had enough of the society of men, is restored to her sacred precinct by the priest. After that, the chariot, the vestments, and (believe it if you will) the goddess herself, are cleansed in a secluded lake. This service is performed by slaves who are immediately afterwards drowned in the lake. Thus mystery begets terror and a pious reluctance to ask what that sight can be which is seen only by men doomed to die."*
>
> *- Description written by Tacitus, Germania 40, 9 (98 CE)[91]*

In the Netherlands, Germany, and Denmark mummified bodies have been found in peat bogs. Historians think that those bog bodies were either criminals or human sacrifices. Many had their throats cut and others had cords around their neck (strangulation). They may have been sacrificed to Nerthus.

Most scholars equate the western Germanic Nerthus with

the Norse Njord, making them a hermaphroditic or transgender deity. This dual aspect is common in ancient religions and probably has spiritual meaning.

In later periods Nerthus was also referred to as 'Nar' or 'Ner' in the Netherlands, the Gooi area in the Dutch province of Utrecht used to be a Germanic gau (province) called *Nardinckland*, it was named after Nardinck, which was the old name of the modern city of Naarden; Nar – is derived from Nerthus and – dinck is an old Dutch word for þing/Thing (the Germanic folk assembly); thus, Nardinckland means "Nerthus'-þing-land".

The tribes of the Reudignians, Avionians, Anglians, Varinians, Eudosians, Suarinians, and Nuitonians were all known for their worship of Nerthus.[91]

During the early Middle Ages there was a local custom in some parts of the Netherlands, Belgium, and Germany in which the people rode a ship on wheels through the country while dancing around it and celebrating, this procession sounds very similar to the Nerthus ritual that was described by Tacitus, it was later forbidden by the church.[91]

The Norns or Nornen *(See also: Schikgodinnen)*

The Norns were not only worshipped in Scandinavia but also in many of the other Germanic areas. In some areas of Germany, the Norns were called The Three Eternal Ones and their names were Einbet (Urd), Barbet (Verdandi), and Wilbet (Skuld).

In Southern Germany they are called *Heilrätinnen* (wellbeing councillors), in Northern Germany *Metten* (from 'messen' – to measure out), in Tyrol they are the *Gachschepfen*, (those who rapidly scoop water from the well). This name links them to the wells at which they were worshipped, including Leutstetten. Their role as councillors shows that the Norns were not only feared and appeased, but also asked for guidance.[92]

Odilia

Saint Odile of Alsace, also known as Odilia and Ottilia, born c. 662 – c. 720 at Mont Sainte-Odile), is a saint venerated in the Roman Catholic Church and the Orthodox Church. The current Roman Catholic liturgical calendar does not officially commemorate her feast day of 13 December (the same feast day as St Lucy), but she is commemorated on this day in the Orthodox Church.[93]

Ostara

Ostara (the festival) takes its name after the Germanic goddess, Eostre/Ostara, who was traditionally honoured in the month of April with festivals to celebrate fertility, renewal and re-birth. It was from Eostre that the Christian celebration of Easter evolved, and indeed the naming of the hormone oestrogen, essential to women's fertility. The Goddess Ostara has the shoulders and head of a hare.[94]

Quiteria

St. Quiteria was a fifth century virgin martyr and saint. Her name comes from the title that the Phoenicians gave to the goddess Astarte – Kythere, Kyteria, or Kuteria – which means *the red one*. St. Quiteria was the daughter of a Galician prince. Her father wanted her to marry and renounce Christianity, but Quiteria fled. Her father's men found her at Aire-sur-l'Adour, in Gascony, and she was beheaded on the spot.

The Church of Sainte-Quitterie in Aire-sur-l'Adour is dedicated to her. This church was on the pilgrimage route called the Way of St. James. St. Quiteria was especially venerated in the border region shared by France and Spain, which included Navarre. However, there are many churches dedicated to her in France, Spain, Portugal, and Brazil. Her relics were buried at Aire-sur-l'Adour, but were scattered by the Huguenots.[95]

Rana (local version of Norse goddess Rán?)

Rán (also Rån) is a Vanir (Dutch Wanen) goddess of the sea who rescues drowning people with her fishing net. She is married to Aegir. They live near the island Hlesey and have nine daughters together, the so called Wave Maidens (barenmeiden): *Bára, Blóðughadda, Bylgja, Dúfa, Hefring, Himinglæva, Hrönn, Kólga en Unnr* of *Blödughadda, Bygleya, Dröbna, Dusa, Hefrig, Himinglätfa, Kolga, Raun, Udor of Unn.*

A folk-belief quoted in one of the Icelandic sagas is that if drowned people appeared at their own funeral feasts, it was a sign that Rana had given them a good welcome into her hall.[96]

Roggemoer, Roggeannegien, *(see Korenmoeder)*

Rosmerta

Rosmerta is a Gaulish goddess. Her name is usually translated as Great Provider (but some translate it as Dew-of-the-Sea).[97] Her husband (or consort) was Esus (Lord or Master) who was identified with the god Mercury or Hermes. She was worshipped in South-western Britain, Gaul, and along the Rhone and the Rhine rivers. She was often depicted holding a patera or offering-dish and she sometimes carries a ladle or sceptre. Her unique attribute is a milk churn.[98] She was often linked to the Roman god Mercury and depicted with his caduceus (the rod with two entwined snakes) which makes her a goddess of healing.[99]

Rufia Materna

In Millingen a gravestone was found with an inscription dedicated to Rufia Materna, probably an indigenous priestess. Her mother had the stone raised, in the early centuries CE, and also dedicated a woodland to her. Millingen was a strategic location, close to the fork in the rivers Rhine and Waal, on the opposite riverbank from the Roman fortress Carvium.[100]

Rura

Altar stones, dating from the 3rd century CE, dedicated to this goddess were found near the Dutch city of Roermond. Her name suggests that she was the goddess of the river Roer (Dutch) or Ruhr (German).[101]

(The) Saligen or Saeligen

Some authors try to establish a link between the Bethen and the *Saligen* or *Wild Women*. The Saligen are nature spirits, living in the mountains of the Bavarian, Austrian and Swiss Alps, where the magical mountain called The Schlern is situated.

The Saligen sometimes help humans with their work, but if one calls them by name or offers them clothing, they disappear forever. In this, they behave in a very similar way to the dwarves and house spirits of the Germanic tradition.[102]

> *Mountain legends here are rich with stories of herb-women, 'wild folk', "wood and water spirits, giants and a magical garden of roses blasted to a naked crag by dwarf King Laurin. Also cursed by him were protective mountain spirits who tended his roses, the so called Saeligen, who were thereby transformed into witches, either flying off to their Sabbaths or left clinging to the mountain slopes in the form of wildflowers, the Aquilegia einseleana, commonly called Schlernhexen.[102]*

Schlern is the mountain where witches are said to hold their Sabbaths, congregating on stone benches called *Schlernhexen* (Schlern witches). Today these are depicted as cute 'tourist magnets' but this hides a darker reality.

Sandraudiga, Sunna

Sandraudiga is a Germanic goddess, attested to on an altar stone with a Latin inscription from Tiggelt, near Rijsbergen in North Brabant. The stone is in the National Museum of Antiquities in

Leiden, today. The meaning of her name is debated, but might mean *she who dyes the sand red* or *'Goddess of the Sandland'*. Some people consider her the protective deity of the cities Zundert and Zandrode, which may have been named for her. She is depicted with long hair, bareheaded, wearing a short-sleeved top and slippers, holding three sheafs of wheat in her left hand.[103]

Schikgodinnen *(see also Nornen)*

Often appearing as a threesome, these are the goddesses of Fate. The Norns are called *Nornen* in Dutch. Their names are Urdr, Skuld and Verdandi.

Sequana

A river goddess. Sequana was a tutelary goddess of the Sequanae tribe, who occupied territory between the Saône, Rhône and Rhine rivers. Sequana was also a goddess of healing, depicted wearing diadem, standing on a boat with her arms spread out.[104]

Sinthgunt (Old High German)

She appears in the Old High German Merseburg Incantations, where she is mentioned in a horse cure. She is referred to as the sister of *Sunna (Sol, Sigel, Sowilo)*. Together they are cited as producing charms to heal a horse. This pair is followed by a mention of *Friia and Uolla*, also sisters.[105]

The 19th century scholar Sophus Bugge proposed her name means 'the night-walking-one' (meaning the moon). This is problematic because the Moon, Mani, is male in Germanic mythology. Simek states that the historical record lacks evidence for any cult of personified celestial bodies among the ancient Germanic peoples. The abundance of petroglyphs in Scandinavia appears to tell a different tale.[106]

Many finds indicate a strong sun-worshipping cult in the Nordic Bronze Age and various animals have been associated with the sun's movement across the sky, including horses, birds, snakes and marine creatures.[107]

Sirona/Tsirona

Her cult centered on Gallia Belgica but reached across north-west Europe. An elaborate shrine and temple complex at Hochscheid in Germany was the main center of her cult. She was connected to thermal springs and healing waters. She had several husbands.[108]

Sowilo/Sol/Sunna (See Rune SIGEL)

Sol (ON) or Sunna (OHG) is the reconstructed name of the rune representing the Sun. The sun is perceived as female in Norse cosmology. The Merseburg Incantations call her Sinthgunt's sister.[106]

Tanfana

The goddess Tanfana (also Tamfana) hails from Twente. Once again, we find debates (and disagreements) about the origin of her name. Fana is a Latin word meaning 'temples' and Tan is the (contemporary) German word for pine tree (think of the Christmas song: O Tannenbaum). However, it has also been pointed out that Tan is an Old Germanic word for water while fana means sanctuary (which may connect her to goddesses with watery realms such as Holle, Hel, Nerthus and Frigg's Fensalir etc.)[109]

> The name 'Tan' may also be derived from Proto-Germanic 'tanhuz', which means 'tough', and another possibility is that it was connected to hills or mountains; the old Dutch word for 'sand ridge' is 'tange', a name element which is still present in some place names, the Icelandic word 'tangi' means mountaintop.[110]

In the area of the Tankenberg near Oldenzaal stood the *Groote Steen* (Big Stone). It may have represented Tanfana (see RUNE

PEORTH). According to local legend female spirits wearing white robes (Witte Wieven) gather here to drink beer once a year. The *Groote Steen* was moved, possibly to halt the veneration of Fan. There still is well on the Tankenberg (since rechristened as a 'fountain'). It is likely that this played a key role in ancient rituals.[109]

Tacitus mentioned that the Marsi Tribe had a temple dedicated to Tanfana. He provides a (gruesome) description of how forces led by Germanicus massacred the men, women, and children of the Marsi, during the night of a major festival, near the location of a temple dedicated to Tanfana. Bergman suggests that Tanfana lives on in the Dutch children's verse Anneke, Tanneke, Toverheks[111]:

Anneke Tanneke Toverheks//Waar ga jij wel naartoe?//Ik trek de hele wereld rond//En word dan toch niet moe
Maar ikke wel, riep toen de hond//En gooide Anneke op de grond
(Refrain 2x)
Anneke Tanneke Magical Witch
//Where are you off to?//I travel around the world//But it doesn't tire me.//
But it does me, then called the hound// And threw Anneke on the ground (Refrain 2x)

Anneke gauw weer opstond//Ging zonder hond de wereld rond//Vloeg toen op haar bezemsteel//Naar haar roze luchtkasteel
De hond toen Janneke daar zien staan
Die blaft naar haar de volle maan (2x)
Anneke got up quickly//Travelled the world without the dog//Then flew on her broomstick//To her pink castle in the clouds
The dog saw Janneke standing there//He barks at her, the full moon (2x)[112]

If this song is indeed about Tanfana, then Tanfana, who became demonized and dismissed a witch in Christian times, would have been a healer and quite possibly a death goddess too. We can still see her standing on the Moon; we can also catch a glimpse of her pink castle in the clouds, at sunset and sunrise!

Ursula

Abe de Verteller[113] links her to a hill just south of Amersfoort, called the Heiligenberg (Mount of Saints). Local legend states that it was created by Ursula and her 11,000 companions. This hill appears in many local stories. *Witte Wieven* (Chapter 7) and wandering lights have been spotted there. There is a ghost lifting people up and dropping them elsewhere. Witches' Sabbaths are said to occur here too and all indications are that this is a sacred heathen place, a place of power, as much as any mount(ain) of Saints. The pit created by collecting earth for mound building is a pond today, called Het Zwanenwater (The Swans' Water) .

The 11,000 maidens (or virgins) travelled by ship, on a pilgrimage to Rome, and decided to dance on the waters of the North Sea, where the pounding of their feet created the holy island of Helgoland. (We'd better not ask how a ship travelling from the Netherlands to Rome passes Helgoland, I guess!) On their way back home from Rome, Ursula and most of her handmaidens were murdered by Attila the Hun. The exception was Cunera who was rescued by Frisian king Redbad (Radboud).

Abe makes Ursula the Low Countries version of Celtic bear goddess Artio and links her to the asterism Ursa Major in the night sky. He suggests she may also be a Christianised version of Vrouw Holle and the Heiligenberg her Holy Mountain.

Vagdavercustis

This goddess was worshipped at the city of Cologne (Köln) in Germany, she is believed to have been a goddess of trees and wood and was also worshipped by the tribe of the Batavians in the Netherlands.[114]

Valcallinehis
Was the goddess of the river Waal.[115]

Veleda *and* Ganna

Bergman wonders whether they were goddesses of the Batavi but my own research unearthed the following information: Veleda was a priestess and prophet of the Germanic tribe of the Bructeri who achieved some prominence during the Batavian rebellion of CE 69–70, headed by the Romanized Batavian chieftain Gaius Julius Civilis, when she correctly predicted the initial successes of the rebels against Roman legions.[116]

She was an ancient oracle who addressed her audience from a tower (linking her to the Norse Vǫlva speaking her prophecies from a high or raised seat!) She had assistants who passed the questions and messages back and forth. Closer study of the text shows that this was probably a public office performed by a succession of women. These prophetesses-turned-goddesses on Earth were among the most important leaders of their tribal units, apparently holding both religious and secular powers.

The area then known as Germania caused the Roman Empire great trouble. On one hand, the Roman general Germanicus earned military glory on the Rhine. On the other hand, the Germans massacred more than 10 percent of the entire Roman army at the Battle of the Teutoburg Forest

Tacitus described Veleda as '*a maiden of the tribe of the Bructeri, who possessed extensive dominion*'. She took her role as the leader of a rebel government seriously, working as a negotiator. She was not only a political leader and channel for divine guidance, according to Tacitus she became a goddess in her own right!

Eventually she was captured and she may have become a priestess at a temple in Ardea, not far from Rome. However, the

Germans continued their ancestral tradition of selecting certain women for the role of priestess and prophetess on behalf of the community. Veleda's successor was *Ganna*.

Vercana

Vercana is an unknown goddess mentioned by the Romans, the Germanic name of this goddess may have been *Werkanaz (Worker) which points to a connection with labour.[117]

Vesunna

A Celtic goddess venerated in Roman Gaul. She probably gave prosperity, abundance and good fortune (as she carries the cornucopia). A temple dedicated to her stood in the French city of Périgueux. She is identified with the Roman guardian goddess Tutela.[118]

Viana

Was a forest goddess from Vianen, in the province of Utrecht, where she had her sanctuary.[119]

Viradecdis

The name of this goddess has been found on Roman altar stones in Belgium, she possibly was a Celtic goddess though the –dis ending points to a Germanic origin. One altar dedicated to her was found near Vechten, in the Netherlands (today). She was a goddess of the Tungri people, who lived in the area south-west of present day Liege. Her name probably indicates an association with honesty or truthfulness, or uttering truth.[120]

Walpurgis

Walpurgisnacht is a European festival celebrated on the night of April 30th (Beltane on the Celtic calendar), named for Saint Walburga (OHG Valpurga) whose feast day is on May first. It is a magical night for witches to attend their Sabbaths. On the

Brocken, the highest peak in the Harz mountains, it is believed that the witches banned and burned may return for just one night. Sweden has a tradition of building huge bonfires. This is festival where winter meets spring, death meets rebirth through fertility, and Christianity meets heathen customs.[121]

Wilbet

Probably refers to the Bavarian Bethen, a female triads of saints rooted in pre-Christian spirituality. In Bavaria, these three women are mostly known as Ainbeth, Borbeth and Wilbeth. Since their names all end with 'beth', they are usually called *'die drei Bethen'* (the three Bethen). The following variants occur

Aubet, Cubet and Quere
Ainbet, Gwerbet and Wilbet
Embede, Warbede and Wilbede
Ambede, Borbede and Wilbede
Ainpet, Gberpet and Firpet

In modern German *beten* means to pray (the Dutch word for prayer is *gebed*). Firpet or Firbet, the name of the third woman on the Leutstetten image, in modern German resembles 'Fürbitte' (intercession, Dutch: *voorspraak*).[122]

Bavaria has a tradition (almost extinct) of three women in disguise, known as *Berchten,* moving in procession through the village on January 6th (Epiphany) or the evening before.

This is also the day when 'C+M+B+2004' (CMB with crosses between them and the date of the new calendaric year) is signed with white chalk above every door of the house. In general understanding this means 'Christus Mansionem Benedicat' (May Christ bless the house), some authors point out that CMB are also the first letters of Catherine, Margaret and Barbara, the later Christian names of the three Bethen.[122]

This tradition marks a connection between the Winter Solstice and a goddess of the land, because the Venerable Bede calls Christmas Eve *Modranecht* (Mother's Night or Night of the Ancestral Mothers) in his *Historia Ecclesiastica*. This, and the appearance of the three 'Berchten' during the twelve holy nights, indicates that our ancestors did not only celebrate the return of the Sun but also various deeply feminine aspects of Mother Earth.

Witte Wieven *(See Chapter 7)*

Xulsigiae (Gallia Belgica)

Triple goddesses venerated at the healing spring in Augusta Treverorum, present-day Trier.[123]

Yrsa (*Yrse, Yrs* or *Urse*)

Based on my own research she was not a goddess but a tragic heroine in early Scandinavian stories or song cycles. Some references in Beowulf appear to have been taken from her tradition.[124]

Zizarim

The goddess Zizarim was worshipped in Germany, in later times she was also known as Zisa or Ciza and in Switzerland the people called her Cisara, in the German city of Augsburg she was worshipped as the protector of the city, her holy day was the 28th of September. A temple dedicated to her was located in a forest on the Zisenberg hill but it was later destroyed by Christians, she was associated with Tiwaz, who was the god of war, and she may have been his wife or consort; an interesting sidenote is that Tiwaz was called "Ziu" in some areas in Germany.[125]

Zisa

Zisa or Cisa (possibly another form of Zizarim) was a goddess worshipped in Augsburg, mentioned in an 11th century manuscript. The city of Augsburg was once known as Cisaris, named for this goddess who saved the city from a Roman invasion. Her feast is celebrated on 28 September and her name is preserved in the name of a hill, called Cisenberg. Jacob Grimm suggested she was the consort of Norse god Tyr (Ziu in Old High German). Scholars say that the source texts do not confirm any of this and that she was an innovation of the post-medieval period.[126]

Goddesses only known by name
(but no further information)[127]

Alateivia
Sunucsal
Vihansa

Personal encounters with The Old Ones

Baduhenna

At our house in Sweden, I started by creating an altar to Baduhenna at Dark Moon, intuitively choosing items that might please her. They included feathers and a raven mask. When Darkness cloaked the surrounding forest, I lit the candles and spoke my prayers. I danced by the altar to invoke her. It soon felt like I was dancing inside her. That she was a great corvid who had feasted on me. Strangely, this was not scary, instead it was deeply reassuring because it connected me to the great cycle of Life-Death-Rebirth.

For one week I kept part of my attention on Baduhenna all the time. As I went to bed one night, a bird kept me awake. It was busy rummaging under the roof. This brought the sensation of sleeping in the nest of a great Corvid, *a great Predator Mother who won't hesitate to kill in order to feed me.* The price for this tender care is knowing that one day I too, at least my corpse, will be eaten, will become food for hungry beings other than myself. This is the deal for all children of the Mother Goddess, who is by necessity also a Death Goddess.

I collected red rowan berries for her altar, to represent drops of blood. Two ravens accompanied me as I hiked to the nearby lake to watch the sun rise. When Sunna (the Sun, personified as a female giantess in Norse cosmology) rose over the lake, they shrieked loudly and flew off. Next, I started painting her. I felt a desire to carve her name into rock, using the runes of the Frisian Futhark, so she would not slide into oblivion (but I didn't do this). I don't think she would handle oblivion well – she might shape shift into an even more ferocious bird (perhaps a sea eagle?) and come for us, if she does not receive her portion, her allocated share of the dead.

Birds linked to the Winter Crone are consequently be birds of darkness and birds of prey – the owl and the eagle, raven, crow, seagull, heron, and cormorant. According to Marija Gimbutas' theories of death and regeneration, based on her archaeological excavation from Old-European sites, the birds of prey are a central part of the excarnation (de-fleshing) practice of that time, associated with ideas of transformation and regeneration. Equally wild animals associated to Her would be: wolves, boars, the sow etc. [128]

In another dream I saw the face of an old woman. She had raven feathers instead of hair. Half of her face was blue, half a moon, a 'Waning Blue Moon'. She had only one eye, but that eye was glistening with ferocious intelligence, the alert eye of a Raven. Looking into that eye I saw the night sky and the stars, just as they had appeared over the Forest the night before. In the dream I understood that the stars were the souls of the dead, shining brightly in a reversed world where humans have blue-black wings, and birds walk the earth as dinosaurs. I woke up and felt that Baduhenna had responded to my invitation. She was definitely keeping me company!

Connecting with ancient deities

This can be done in many different ways; the key ingredient is an open heart and genuine desire to connect.

- Do some research and make note of details that speak to you. Those will act as doorways or portals to the deity concerned.
- (If possible) read blogs and articles written by other people working with this same god or goddess (the internet has gifted us a proliferation of on-line shrines and altars, often with key words provided and attributes listed).
- Use any spiritual technique available to you (guided visualisation, meditation, sitting out, using a form of divination such as runes, Tarot cards or other) to tune in.
- Do not rush and think carefully about your level of commitment:
  - Are you just curious and making a one-off exploration?
  - Are you interested in a more long-term commitment of honouring this deity and forming a relationship?
- Treat deities the same way as humans you love: show respect and never make promises you know you are not going to be able to keep.
- Make or bring some offerings. Please note that offerings do not need to be physical (but can be: tobacco, alcohol, some sage or mugwort burned etc.) but they can also be a song, a poem, a promise to pick litter on a beach or reach out to a person in need (etc.)
- Find some time where you are going to be undisturbed. Bring a notepad and pen. Light a candle and request an audience with the god or goddess…
- Write notes while impressions are fresh in memory.

- Did things go well? Place some item symbolising this goddess on your altar (assuming you have one), examples are: keys, a precious stone, a photograph of ancestor or sacred place, some sea water, a shell etc.
- If you don't have an altar in your home, consider creating one. (If you have a tiny home or travel a lot: create a mobile travel altar. If you have cats or toddlers: make an altar in a shoebox with a lid and move it out of reach once you are done).
- Keep a wish list of follow-up meditations/journeys and other deities you'd like to seek an audience with.

Activity #4 Honouring Neglected or Forgotten Gods

You now have an extensive list of deities and divine beings!

- Select one whose name or location grabs your attention. Follow the suggestions above and connect with him/her. Make notes!
- Choose a 'deity of the week', create a dedicated altar, and for one week focus on him/her, make offerings, write unique prayers or poems, make drawings/paintings/ music etc. about what you perceive. Make notes. Did you gain an ally?
- Run a 'spiritual investigation' and choose one name, a being of which nothing else is known. Request an audience. Make notes. Perhaps write a blog about your findings so others can compare notes? (Examples are Alateivia, Sunucsal or Vihansa).

If you have an appetite for meeting even more deities, please consult the footnotes for links to helpful compendiums and listings.[129] Compile your own information and compare notes with others.

Last but not least: make a commitment to start celebrating

the ancient festival of *Modranecht* (The Night of the Ancestral Mothers) in way that feels right to you. Honour your personal mother, godmother, spiritual mother, aunts, grandmothers and all female relatives in the family line.

Chapter 5

The Wild Hunt (De Wilde Jacht)

The Wild Hunt and its leader have many different names in Dutch:

Helse Jacht, Rebelse Jacht, Jacht van Hänsken met de hond (with the dog), Tilkesjacht, Telmsjacht, de wilde jacht van Tütü, de Kefkesjacht, De wilde jacht van Tüpis, Knuppeljacht, Turkusjacht, Jacht van de eeuwige Jood (the Hunt of Eternal Death), Tieltjesjacht, Juulkesjacht, Jacht van Hakkelbeernd en Jacht van Jakko.
-Dutch terms for the Wild Hunt[1]

Wild Hunt, Woden's Hunt, The Raging (or Furious) Host (Germany), Herlathing (England), Mesnee d'Hellequin (Northern France), The family of Harlequin (France), Cŵn Annwn (Wales), Cain's Hunt, Ghost Riders (North America), Herod's Hunt, Gabriel's Hounds, Asgardreia (Asgard ride in Scandinavia), 'The Devil's dandy dogs' (Cornwall), De Wilde Heir, De Wilde Jacht (Netherlands)
-Names for the Wild Hunt from other regions in Europe[2]

Veneration and demonization of the Dead

One key feature that most tribal, indigenous and ancient cultures share, distinguishing them from contemporary Western Culture, is an active relationship with the ancestors and the dead.

Some authors have made a case for St. Nicholas (Chapter 11) being associated with the ancient phenomenon of The Wild Hunt, where a deity or another legendary figure leads a ghostly army travelling across the Northern European winter sky, especially the nights in the dead of winter, between December sixth (the birthday of St. Nicholas) and January sixth (Epiphany).

The general concept is that, at a certain time of year, the veil between worlds thins and the dead will visit the living, often in disguise. In Heathen times it was understood that not all the dead rest in peace forever after, some souls of the deal continue to roam the land and visit the living (in all seasons). Therefore, one of the purposes of The Wild Hunt is to sweep land and sky clean of old energy (energetic manifestations that serve no more) and the souls of the unquiet dead.

Deep winter once held real terror as Death preyed on the weak and vulnerable. Scandinavian people expressed age as *how many winters a person had lived.* This holy terror was felt deeply by our pre-Christian ancestors and lives on in many Yuletide traditions.

Let's make one crucial point upfront: Hell (note the double letter l) is a Christian invention. Pre-Christian people did not believe in Hel as a realm of eternal damnation of the human soul. However, there was a general cultural awareness that death can be compromised and that not all the dead automatically arrive in an idyllic location in The Afterlife. Christianity deliberately replaced this nuanced and realistic cosmology with the more dualistic and simplistic model of three destinations after death:

- Heaven (god-fearing 'good Christians' fly straight up to Heaven).
- Hell (the realm of damnation and eternal punishment).
- Purgatory (an intermediate state after physical death dedicated to purification – but some orientations within Christianity, such Protestantism deny that this realm exists).

Purgatory was invented in the 12th century. It was not included in the original teachings of Christ (as the Kingdom of Heaven was). What did exist long before the birth of Christ was the belief in a period of purification after death; and that saying prayers (which became the prayer cycle called The Office of the Dead in Church) supports this important process.[3]

Germanic tribes knew an underworld called Hel, domain of the goddess Hel (possibly Holle, scholars do not agree on this). Wells were seen as access points to this realm. Frigg's domain, for example, is called *Fensalir*: the hall in the marshes. The Church Fathers actively projected Christian overlays on the more ancient customs they could not stomp out. Onto Hel, as a watery realm of both death and (re)birth, domain of both the deceased and those waiting to be born, the Christian dogma of Hell as a fearsome realm of punishment was projected.

In the 14th century the old mystery and miracle plays transition from Latin to the vernacular[4] and morality plays appear on the scene. To state the obvious: literacy rates were low, few people had access to books before the invention of the printing press, even if they could read, there was no law requiring children to attend school, the internet would not be invented for many centuries to come. Morality plays acted as a form of education and entertainment at the same time.

Guising, costumes and masks

Traditionally children wear masks when they go trick-or-treating at Halloween. Masks allow us to inhabit another identity, to briefly become Another or The Other. In the medieval period the word mask became synonymous with 'devil's mask'[5], while before that, masks were associated with amusement and feasting. Even masks that did not actually depict the devil (think of animal masks) were understood to represent the different manifestations of the Devil.

This was one of the reasons why masquerades were, or became, risky. A masked person was said to be easy prey for the Devil, so masking up was *dangerous*. The church actively tried to abolish the habit of masking and masquerades.

It makes sense that the period of penitence and serious self-reflection, Lent, is preceded by abundant feasting or a carnival. It can be seen as one final explosion of excess before the mood changes.

The use of masks and role reversal were also key ingredients in earlier Heathen festivals such as *Saturnalia*, *Kalendae Januariae*, *Brumalia* and *Matronalia*. They involved games and parties, the exchange of gifts as well as behavioural excess and obscene songs. In that period masks became linked to travesty, an exaggerated or grotesque imitation.

Matronalia (Feriae)[6] was a Roman festival celebrating Juno Lucina, the goddess of children (literally 'Juno bringing children into the light') and also motherhood and women. It took place on the first day of the year, which was the first day of March, the month of warrior god Mars, also known as Feriae Martis.

Mothers and all women received gifts, wore their hair loose and were not allowed to wear belts. They also cooked a meal for the household slaves, who had the day off work.

Festivals involving role reversal have acted as a safety valve since ancient times: so called *travesty* obliterates any gender boundaries, the distinction between 'good' and 'bad' dissolves briefly making these festivals truly dangerous as well as exhilarating, authority figures were humiliated, children ruled families instead of their parents, the very boundary between the dead and the living became blurred too.

There is great wisdom behind such festivals: giving the less privileged or disempowered groups in society a lot of power for a few days a year actually contributed to the larger social order being preserved. After those 'wild' days things went back to normal and most people behaved once again as was expected of them. This prevented a seething of deep-buried resentments or festering of deep-seated desires boiling over so dramatically that society, sooner or later, itself became endangered. It was also good for the gene pool: unexpected sexual liaisons countered in-breeding and challenged community/cultural boundaries imposed on sexuality.

The same principle is embodied by the Trickster archetype[7] in all cultures. The sacred clown is one version of this. Tricksters challenge the established order and introduce new, exciting, even dangerous elements. They are change agents and prevent staleness and stagnation.

Al Ridenour speaks of 'excess and unconventional vitality' in a liminal space where rule-breaking occurs[8] in his book about Krampus:

> *While we are used to think of the Krampus in very contrary terms – i.e. as an enforcer of the social norms – from the side of the costumed participant, the experience is quite the opposite: a Krampuspass member embraces the role of Devil, allowed taboo acts that include disturbing the peace, intimidating, striking or otherwise manhandling his neighbor, as well as special freedoms with the opposite sex, thanks to the anonymity provided by his costume.[9]*

The Cult of the Dead

In many pre-Christian cultures a cult of the dead formed part of the end of year period, where the transition between years was marked. The Old Year was sent packing with a great deal of drama and noise, especially all things unwanted/old/expired/obsolete/worn-out/harmful/weak and so forth. This process involved a literal cleaning of homes and living spaces as well as ritual cleansing. The new cannot arrive when the old fills all the space.

One key feature was scapegoating: sometimes a literal scapegoat was created or other times certain people in the community had the sins of the collective projected onto them (in other words they were blamed and demonized) and they were then expelled or even executed. One could say, perhaps, that the witch trials or witch hunts were one gigantic manifestation of this principle, one group proclaiming themselves as pure/ innocent at the expense of a literal black sheep: evil/unwanted/ dehumanized.

What has struck me repeatedly while writing this book is the connection between the scapegoat and references from all over Europe to a connection between the Devil and goats. We have all seen pictures of Satan with hooves.

In Northern Europe the last sheaf of grain bundled in the harvest was perceived as containing the spirit of the harvest, and having magical properties. It was sometimes called the Yule Goat (Julbocken)[10] and until today such goats are made from straw and placed under the Christmas tree. Swedish people used to regard the Yule Goat as an invisible spirit calling to check on the Christmas preparations. People played pranks by placing a straw goat on the land of neighbours without them noticing.

In his book Veneficium, Daniel Schulke[11] speaks of an other-world location: The Goat-Fold of Azazel, the Heath of the Billygoat. It is a spirit meadow, both an actual place and a state of embodied power. He explains that when grain was planted, a portion of the seed is offered to the Devil to ensure a good crop:

Four seeds in a hole
One for the birds
One of the mice
And one for the Master

Next, he introduces the Devil-in-the-Grain, Mahazhael, or Sovereign Witch Father in deified form: The Corn God. He undergoes ritual slaughter for the sustenance of all but is resurrected in transmuted form.

The abundance of a good harvest is based on death: grain dies so humans and animals can eat. The Devil appears to be the Christianised (demonized) form of an earlier fertility god, a Master of the Animals, priapic and hoofed, who possesses a raw animal power and pure life force that is profoundly sexual and amoral. By this I mean that it does not concern itself with the rightness or wrongness of things, just a primal desire to procreate and bring new life. Life's desire for the continuation of Life, at all cost.

Ancient Slavic festivals honour a god (Dazbog) represented by a white goat. People still dress up as goats to bring forth his power. Sweden has the julbock (Christmas Goat) and Finland has the Joulupukki. Finding very similar figures near the Baltic and North Sea coasts of the Old German Empire suggests a southward spread from Scandinavia, a parallel of the first wave of migration that brought Germanic peoples south into the region between Germany's Oder & Elbe rivers around 1000 BCE.[12]

Author Theodore Storm had the Schimmelreiter, a phantom rider, appearing on the shorelines of Northern Frisia in Theodor Storm's 1888 novella.[13]

The male leaders of the Hunt were very specifically wild men, or wild spirits (selvaggi, salvatici or homines selvatici). Before the 'Christianising' of Europe these wild men were probably fertility spirits, which may explain their connection with animals, notably the stag. The myth of the Wild Hunt became a popular literary and artistic device, which may be why it is still so familiar to us. In particular, Herne the Hunter, a horse riding ghost with antlers upon his head, thought to torment cattle and rattle chains has been commonly linked to the Wild Hunt within English folklore.[14]

In some areas The Wild Hunt is connected to evidence of local fertility cults and the Hunter is the Fertility Deity. In other locations the Hunter is the leader or king of the fairies, such as Gwyn ap Nudd in Wales and West England. It is only towards the end of the Medieval period that the Wild Hunt becomes associated with witchcraft (Chapter 9). A conflation then occurs, where witches are said to participate in the Wild Hunt and their leader is Satan or a demon.[14]

This notion is also connected to the concept of Witches flying off to Sabbats on either broomsticks or the backs of animals, which became one of the main accusations made in witch trials and accusations.[14]

If only human beings would learn from such events, so history need not repeat itself! For me these are all teachings of the Rune THORN (Elder Futhark: Thurs). Here we meet The Other, we move from the undivided primal consciousness of UR (contemporary Dutch Oer) to fear of what is Not Us. The higher octave manifestation is setting healthy boundaries. The lower octave manifestation is demonization.

Demonization creates individuals or a group of people who are rejected and do not belong. Such people sometimes make the extreme choice to join a Satanist Church, to be with others who understand about being an outsider. Not just that, but a group focused on a being who rebelled and was made the Ultimate Outside and carrier of Evil by the one male Christian God: Satan, The Devil.

Around the year 1020 CE, Bishop Burchard of Worms cautions against *'what pagans did and still do on Jan 1st, in the guise of a stag or cal'*. He also rants against Holda and witchcraft, *a host of devils transformed into the likenesses of women, riding on certain beasts during special nights, 'members of the company of demons'*.[15]

Appeasing and venerating Ancestors

Historians inform us that most of the current European cultures and tribes had Indo-European warrior ancestors, who arrived from the Eurasian steppes and conquered most of Europe, along with a large part of Asia. Those collective *deep ancestors* all had a Cult of the Dead.

In India the term *Pitri/Fathers*[16] refers to the Hindu ancestors.

They are said to live on the dark side of the moon and they receive offerings at Full Moon. They participate in a sacramental meal set out for them. Dark Moon or Waning Moon is known as Pitri-Paksha, a time when ghosts and the dead need appeasing, or they will become active and dangerous. The sacred text known as the Rig Veda demonstrates how the dead received prayers already 3,000 years ago!

The general idea behind appeasing ancestors is that that they remain content and return to their abodes in the Afterlife or Other World (depending on cosmology) and therefore do not endanger either the living or the structures which make up the backbone of contemporary cultures and societies.

At the time of the Roman Empire, the Romans expected a visit from the dead between 15–21 February, the feast of the *parentalia*.[17] The (hearth and public) fires were extinguished, civil servants took off their robes and dropped their roles, the temples closed and people were not allowed to get married. In this period the dead were honoured with rites and domestic observances. On the final day people brought wreaths to the graveyard as well as salt, bread soaked in wine and pansies. This was all in aid of a reconciliation and truce with the dead.

Belarus is the place where the cult of the dead survived, intact, well into the 19th century, covered with only a thin Christian veneer. They hosted a supper for the Dziady or Holy Grandfathers[18]. No Church Feast is conceivable without the dead receiving their allocated share, meaning that the honouring of the dead occurs at regular intervals in the Church Year. Meals were served to the dead in graveyards. My US colleague Susan Rossi and I perform Dumb Supper Ceremonies with students, continuing this tradition.

The Church eventually created a Feast Day called All Saints (on November 2nd), probably to make people forget about the earlier heathen traditions. The feast we know as Hallowe'en today came to the US from Ireland (carried along by the great waves of emigration). The original festival on the Celtic calendar is Samhain.

> For now reflect on this: if the dead were used to receiving regular honouring, food and drink for centuries – how do they feel about most families in the 21st century no longer bothering with this? Go one step further: one day we will all join the ancestors – and then how will we then feel about not receive our fair share?

One group has gained notoriety in our history books: the berserkers. They were legendary Nordic warriors who possessed something akin to superpowers (making them much feared by other warriors). They had a special relationship to the god Odin or Wodan and a strong identification with certain animals. Using a term from shamanism one would say: they *merged with* animal spirits: they became bears or wolves and fought others in that ecstatic state of frenzy. Odin appears under many names (*kennings* and *heiti*) in the Eddas, too many to list here. Among other things he was *Drauga Drottin*, the Lord of the Dead and *Jolnir*, the Master of Jol (Yule, the midwinter feast).[19] He was also said to be the leader of an army of the dead, the Wild Hunt.

Large-scale conversion to Christianity

Conversion was a far-reaching phenomenon. It did not only mean honouring a new god, it also meant a complete break with both the ancestor cult and personal ancestors.

Frisian king Radboud (v. Redbad) famously came very close to being baptised, but he refused when he was told that his ancestors would not be waiting for him in Heaven after death (after all, they were heathens!) He responded eloquently that he much preferred spending eternity in Hell (really Hel with only one 'l' of course) with his pagan ancestors to hanging out in Heaven with his enemies.[20]

This is the familiar pattern of an incoming religion demonizing the previous practices and gods. In this case not only the earlier heathen gods were demonized, but the ancestors were demonized along with them. It was viewed as a form of idolatry, a worshipping of false gods. This was viewed as a *sin*, meaning that early Christians were told off by their parish priest for doing this.

Other common practices too now came under the heading sin: superstition, magic, dowsing, healing and divination. Essentially the Church resorted to two key strategies:

- *Demonization*
- *Assimilation (heathen practices were rebranded in a Christian form)*

Demonization involved pagan gods being portrayed as, or lumped together with, the Devil, to frighten people off and create a taboo.

Assimilation involved appropriating and rebranding heathen traditions, putting a Christian veneer on them. For example, temples become churches, the Christian calendar was imposed on the earlier farmer's almanac and the agricultural year was made evolve around the feast days of saints. Instead of Midsummer Eve people now celebrated St John's Eve and obviously the story of the Christ Child has dominated the winter solstice ever since, even though the story of his birth speaks of *the lambs in the field*, meaning that he clearly was born at a different time of year.

No one was allowed to drink to the *minne* (memory) of the deceased on their death anniversary any longer, which was a common practice. The custom was that beer or ale were brewed to mark different periods and occasions in the agricultural year and the brewing of it was a ritual act, with seasonal ingredients.[21] The practice of the so called *heildronk* or toast was a profound religious expression. For the Vikings a party or feast without a heildronk was inconceivable!

It was not just one toast or drink either, there was a ritual order to these toasts and at least three farmers were required to mix their festive beer or ale: one share was for the lord of the homestead (pater familias), the next for his wife, the lady of the house, plus on Christmas Eve there was to be a toast to Christ and Mary Mother of God. People who lived far from civilization were required by law to mix their own ceremonial beer and fines could be imposed on those people who neglected their sacred duties.

The Old Norse midwinter feast called Jol became the new name for Christmas in Scandinavia (Jul in contemporary Swedish), Yuletide in English. Yule used to be a festival that celebrated the change of seasons and it indicated a tipping point, where the cosmic seesaw starts moving the other way, the Sun (Rune SIGEL) returns. Abe de Verteller uses the Dutch word *scharniermoment*: hinge moment![22]

The Wild Hunt

The myth of the Wild Hunt occurs in many countries, ranging from England, Scotland, Germany and Iceland to the Netherlands and the Alps. The Wild Hunt (or Wilde Jacht) is a procession led by a supernatural being (or deity) roaming the countryside and reveling, hunting, killing or eating everything in their path. The name of the leader of the Hunt varies from place to place. Perhaps surprisingly the leader of this Hunt was originally female, a goddess. Her most common name was Perchta or Hulda, which was recorded by Latin authors as Diana or Herodias.

Seeing the Wild Hunt was thought to presage some catastrophe such as war or plague, or at best the death of the one who witnessed it. Mortals getting in the path of, or voluntarily following, the Hunt could be kidnapped and end up in the Land of the Dead. One girl who saw Wild Edric's Ride was warned by her father to put her apron over her head to avoid the sight. Others believed that people's spirits could be pulled away during their sleep to join the cavalcade.[23]

It has argued that the St. Nicholas festivities are the ritual counterpart to The Wild Hunt. There are many regional variations in the name of the leader, ranging from Odin/Wodan to Herne the Hunter or Frau Holle[24] or Berchta. The otherworld hunters are said to be the dead, elves; in the Northern Tradition elves are associated with the male dead ancestors[25] or even fairies (in the original meaning of the word: fae, habitants of supernatural realms).

In 1673 Johannes Scheffer, in his famous book Lapponia, recounts stories by Sami people about The Wild Hunt and the author Hélène Adeline Guerber wrote about Odin and his eight-legged magical horse Sleipnir collecting the souls of the dead, in her book from 1895: Myths of the Northern Lands.[26]

The concept entered the popular imagination courtesy of Jacob Grimm in 1835, when he published Deutsche Mythologie (German Mythology). Grimm suggested that this myth began life as a hunt led by a god and goddess, visiting the land during a holy period. They would have brought blessings in return for the offerings left out by people. Their voices could be heard in the howling winds but, due to the filter imposed by Christianity, this later became a pack of ghouls with malicious intent.[26]

In the Medieval period, after the ancient gods had been demonized and banned from collective consciousness, the leaders of The Wild Hunt were said to be characters based on real life personae, such as Charlemagne, King Arthur or Frederick Barbarossa (the Holy Roman Emperor in the 12th century).

In the 16th century, Hans von Hackelnberg was said to lead the Wild Hunt. The story recounts him slaying a boar, accidently piercing his foot on the boar's tusk and poisoning himself. The wound was fatal and, upon his death, von Hackelnberg declared he didn't want

*to go to heaven, but instead continue with his treasured avocation
– hunting. He was then forced to do this for an eternity in the night
sky, or, as recounted in alternate versions, condemned to lead the
Wild Hunt. Sources cite his name as possibly being a corruption of
an epithet of Odin's name.*[26]

In Wales we find a variation of the tale where Gwynn ap Nudd,
the Celtic Lord of the Dead, appears as the leader. He is said
to be followed by a pack of hounds with blood-red ears. Those
same hounds appear in England and they were called the Gabriel
hounds. Seeing them spelled doom. In England the leader was
Herne the Hunter of Herlathing, with a possible connection to
the mythical King Herla. The tradition of the Orkney Islands
speaks of fairies or ghosts coming out at night and galloping
around on white horses. In France we find a female leader of the
Hunt: Mesnée d'Hellequin, the Goddess of Death.[26]

The word *myth* has two opposite meanings: it can refer
to a timeless ultimate truth (such as the creation myths that
underpin many world religions) or it can mean a made-up tale
or falsehood. For that reason, it is easy to read up on the topic
with 21st century eyes and claim that it is 'pure fantasy', born of
the human imagination. However, consider the following:

*Clerics in 12th century Britain reportedly witnessed the Wild Hunt.
They claimed there were 20 to 30 hunters in the party and the hunt
continued for nine weeks. The earlier reports available of the Wild
Hunt generally represented the participants as diabolical, whereas,
in later medieval retellings, the hunters became fairies instead.*[27]

In Scotland, the Wild Hunt is closely linked to the fairy world in
many sources. Evil fairies, or fey, were said to be cast out from
the Sluagh or Unseelie Court, the noble fairy court. The Sluagh
allegedly flew in from the west in order to capture dying souls,
resulting in people in Scotland, well into the 20th century, closing

windows and doors on the west side of their houses when they had a sick person inside.[26]

In Scandinavia the Wild Hunt was not seen, only heard. In our time contemporary Heathen/Pagan/Shamanic practitioners actively work with the concept of The Wild Hunt and perform psychopomp work (escorting souls to the right destination in the afterlife). The aim of this work is to embrace (*not fight!*) the forces of chaos in a constructive way, meaning that old and stuck energies are cleared away. Seeds for new concepts and paradigms are planted. This is magical power in a very real sense! It must be married to the principle of right action. We must use it well on behalf of our community, not for our personal gain or egoic desires.[26]

The engagement with this type of work has brought a renewed interest in folklore because so many people are eagerly honouring and reconstructing the old ways of our ancestors. Once again, a reversal is at stake: the reversal of the sixth extinction, the accelerated loss of species, the pillaging of our planet. I am confident that Mother Earth will survive. It currently remains to be seen if the human race will.

The demonization of the dead

Why and how could this occur?
How does this affect our world today?

Christianity teaches about *original sin* and the need for *redemption*. In the Roman Catholic Church of my childhood the dead were commonly referred in Dutch to as *arme zielen* (unfortunate souls), implying that they are in dire need of spiritual assistance. The notion of the 'autonomous dead' operating outside the teachings of the Church contradicted this, and was squashed. As a child I would ask myself the same question that King Radboud asked: where did my pre-Christian ancestors go after death, if Heaven is not an option for them? Will Heaven split my ancestral lineage? That amounts to millennia worth of dead souls being denied entry to Heaven! Where is the Divine loving justice in that?

Norse mythology teaches that there are several realms where dead people go: Odin's hall Valhalla for warriors – the heroic dead, Freyja's hall Sessrúmnir located in Fólkvangr or Hel (also known as Helheimr). Hel is visualised as situated in the North (the direction of death and Winter), and is by no means a realm of punishment. The goddess Hel receives her guests well!

Some authors distinguish between a male or female leader of the Wild Hunt. The origin of a female leader is Mediterranean as the ancient Greek goddess Hecate had a ghostly army. She was called the Queen of Witches (and witchcraft) and also the Queen of Ghosts. Together with her sisters Artemis and Diana she was the godmother of witches.

The first full description of a procession of ghosts was written in Paris about a night in January of 1092 (Ordericus Vitalis). The priest Wachlin, coming back from visiting a sick person, saw a swarm led by an enormous warrior swinging a mighty club in his hand. The shapes that followed wept and moaned over their sins; then came a horde of corpse-bearers with coffins on their shoulders -- the priest counted some 50 coffins. Then women on horseback, seated on saddles with glowing nails stuck into them; then a host of ecclesiasticals on horseback. The priest knew many of these people who had died recently. He concluded at last that he had seen the "familia Herlechini," of whom many had told him, but in whom he had never believed: Now he had truly seen the dead.[27]

De Wilde Heir – The Wild Hunt in The Low Countries

We have accounts of The Wild Hunt from the southernmost and easternmost provinces in the Low Countries: Brabant, Gelderland and Limburg. In Gelderland, we find a hunter who was doomed to hunt forever, as a punishment for hunting on

Sunday, the holy day of rest. This is called *Berndekesjacht* after its leader Berndeke van Geulen (Beerneke van Galen). He is said to be out hunting in Spring especially.[28]

In Noord Brabant the Hunter is called *Wilde Jager Dirk*, or *Derk met de Beer* (Dirk with the Boar). He was a farmer who lost all his animals to the animal plague, which enraged him enough to point his rifle at the heavens to 'shoot God'. This sealed his fate. In Limburg we find stories of a ghostly army near the Mookerheide.

The Wild Hunt and its leader have many different names in Dutch: *Helse Jacht, Rebelse Jacht, Jacht van Hänsken met de hond (with the dog), Tilkesjacht, Telmsjacht, de wilde jacht van Tütü, de Kefkesjacht, De wilde jacht van Tüpis, Knuppeljacht, Turkusjacht, Jacht van de eeuwige Jood (the Hunt of Eternal Death), Tieltjesjacht, Juulkesjacht, Jacht van Hakkelbeernd en Jacht van Jakko.*[28]

Even Saint Hubert and Saint Martin were said to lead the Wild Hunt! This is most remarkable, as the named leader is Ruprecht (from Het Geuldal). This is the name of St. Nicholas's helper in Germany. In Twente we find the Wild Hunt of Tüpis at the winter solstice, rushing down the Haeckenberg[28]

Männerbund
In *De Germania* Roman historian Tacitus (in the first century CE) mentions the Harii, German warrior bands, and he associates this with the night and with the army of the dead.[29]

He describes them as using black shields and painting their bodies (*'nigra scuta, tincta corpora'*), and attacking at night as a shadowy army, terrorising their opponents. Some theories connect the Harii to Odin's Einherjar (his army of dead warriors in Valhalla).

The word Männerbund refers to young men bonding and forming bands. This phenomenon is often mentioned in the same breath as the berserkers because both have links to wolves and wild animals. Young men ventured out in the world by means of forming raiding parties or gangs. Some scholars say that this acted as a Rite of Passage or Coming of Age, for young men in Old Europe. It was a form of initiation, it turned boys into young men. Those bands often thought of themselves as wolf packs. According to the Rig Veda, an ancient Sanskrit text from before 1000 B.C., young men can only become warriors after sacrificing a dog at a winter ceremony and then wearing its skin for four years. They burn the skin once they return to society.

So why would they kill dogs, which were their own pets? I remember watching this B-level 80s or 90s action movie when I was a little kid about some child trained to be a super soldier assassin and he had to kill his own dog to show that he would listen to his commands. I'd say this is something similar. By having these kids kill their dogs, animals which they probably liked, they were prepared for the harshness of the outer world. If you can kill a man's best friend you can kill a man.[30]

Reversal

Herlequin[31] wore a costume with bells, intended to alert people to the presence of the fairy folk. His horned headdress became a template for depictions of the Devil. Over time he acquired a more human face. His famous checked outfit was originally a head covering with countless dangling pieces of cloth attached.

Both Devil and Jester signified the wrong world or upside down world, the reversed world, a world turning away from God. We have already explored this Christian filter. Originally this reversal indicates both the fertility of chaos and the upside-down-world that is the Land of the Dead, where the dead are sometimes perceived as walking upside down in the footprints of the living.

During confession people were asked by their priest: have

you seen Herlequin's family/army or caught a glimpse of The Wild Hunt? Someone who died a sudden death (without repenting his/her sins) was expected to join Herlequin's family or army, *the army of the doomed* (as the Church put it). Therefore, people dreaded a sudden or violent death.

Another real fear was that an infant would die without being baptised and end up roaming the world as a *dwaallichtje* or wandering light. Imagine the suffering of parents, having to live with that terror. Death in childbirth was common in those days and mortality rates in infancy were very high.

Hels Kabaal – Ketelmuziek – Charivari

Charivari processions were originally intended to expose and pile shame on unsuitable marriages. Young people wore devil masks to commit serious pranks yet escape punishment by staying anonymous. Acts performed included physical abuse and even homicide. This tradition persisted into the 20th century.[31]

In the 17th century Herlequin became Arlequino in Italian comedy. He gained a proper human face. Carried over from an earlier time, other than his acrobatic mobility and ambivalent character, was a black half-mask, only covering one side of the face. This costume is still used in some Austrian St. Nicholas processions.

Another interesting detail is that Herlequin rode a horse, (see Rune EH). Charivari was also used as a threat to extort money and alcohol: pay us X-Y-Z and we will leave you alone (for the time being anyway!)

Janssen links this to the era of pestilence, which considerably reduced the number of candidates on the dating market. A second marriage was considered unfair (you got lucky once already!) An older woman marrying a younger man was considered a waste of resources (no children will come of that!) And so forth. A time of scarcity sharpens the awareness of what is fair and unfair in society. We come full circle, we are back to the theme of scapegoats and people carrying the sins of their communities away by leaving or dying.

These youths have been connected with The Wild Hunt: they represented the army of the dead. The masked devils became young delinquents terrorizing members of their communities or people in their village. Charivari is accompanied by a lot of noise: horns, cow bells, whips. The Dutch term *ketelmuziek* implies a loud banging of pots and pans. Noise is said to have an atropopaic function: it wards off bad spirits or 'evil powers'. It can be used to drive out demons and so increase health, vitality and fertility.

The noise of the charivari proceedings can be viewed as a form of ritual violence, a deliberate aggression courting chaos and disorder. Noise and physical punishment can have a cleansing effect. The victim of the charivari is a scapegoat who may well be forced to leave the village because life there can no longer be endured after the charivari.

Another way of viewing the noise is as part of the reversal. In Dutch we have the phrase *hels kabaal,* which literally means a hellish amount of noise (in English we might say hells bells). The noise or 'anti-music' helps bridge a time of crisis, it purifies whatever is unclean, it interacts with a community scared of anti-social behaviour and norm-breaking.

When it comes to the dead and demons, their ambivalence lies in the fact that they could be either benevolent or malicious. In other words, they have the power to punish and bless or reward. In an agricultural society the interaction with the dead is seen as an energy exchange, one that needs to be balanced for optimal vitality and fertility to occur. The dead were buried after death and almost literally perceived as *seeds planted back in the earth.*

Folklore written down in Germany and Switzerland states that the more ferociously the Wild Hunt rages, the more fertile the land covered will be.[28]

Postscript

I often wonder whether we need to ritually and actively appease our warrior ancestors, our hunter forebears. I see fleeting glimpses of their way of life living on in our cellular memory and how this creates dysfunctional situations, out of sync with the Zeitgeist.

The Männerbund groups had an important function: they initiated young men and provided lifelong bonds. Today many young people self-initiate (through risk taking, drug use, self harm, gang violence etc.) to remain true to a primordial cosmic template that we no longer understand. Does the terror still come calling in the form of dysfunctional families and psychic attack/warfare, in the 21st century?

Activity #5 Apology Work for the Victims of Our Conquering/Colonizing Ancestors

Summer of 2015 I received an invitation from Susan Rossi to bring my sacred art courses to the US, to the Greater Philadelphia area. This may sound glamorous but I decided to investigate exactly *what was calling me there*. I discovered that Dutch and Swedish people had both committed atrocities in the area: the Lenni Lenape (also Delaware) People were pushed off their homeland by expanding European colonies. I am Dutch and my husband is Swedish. Our three children have both Dutch and Swedish ancestors. It soon became clear that I had exactly the right cultural background to do serious healing and apology work here, atoning for acts committed by ancestors. (Not necessarily my immediate biological ancestors but *ancestors nevertheless.)* Someone needs to do this work. If you are the one who becomes aware of such a situation – you are the person being called to do this work.

Dutch people colonized other countries and cultures too. Think of the Dutch Cape Colony (South Africa today), the Dutch East Indies (Indonesia), Dutch Guiana (Surinam) as well as islands in the Caribbean Sea: Aruba, Curaçao and Sint Maarten.

If you have Dutch ancestry, it is likely that you had ancestors involved in this process of colonization in some way or form. Do some research. Ask older family members, is anything known about this? Consult historical records. Monitor closely when something has *strong resonance for you intuitively*. Why does one fact or story hit you harder than another? Some say that we all have cellular memory holding ancestral memories. Failing that, our tutelary spirits will guide us.

Allow yourself to be led to an issue or situation you are willing and able to work on. Speak prayers, light candles, honour those who suffered. If you do not have personal names, speak the name of their tribe and homelands out aloud. Offer apologies. Be sincere and honest. Someone needs to do this, or the residue remains active in the ancestral field.

The Ho'oponopono Prayer is very effective (and I have provided the Dutch translation):

I am sorry – *Het spijt me*
(Please) Forgive me – *Vergeef me (alstublieft)*
Thank you – *Dankuwel/Dankjewel*
I love you – *Ik houd van jou*

I also make good use of Morrnah Simeona's prayer (a female Hawaiian healer). Please note that I substitute 'child' for 'son':

Divine creator, father, mother, son (child) as one...If I, my family, relatives and ancestors have offended you, your family, relatives and ancestors in thoughts, words, deeds and actions from the beginning of our creation to the present, we ask your forgiveness... Let this cleanse, purify, release, cut all the negative memories, blocks, energies and vibrations, and transmute these unwanted energies into pure light....And it is done.[32]

Continue working with this as you feel guided or nudged: apologise to ancestors for dying with unlived dreams, for being unable to feed their children, for never feeling good enough. Apologise unreservedly to every single being (not all of them human!) affected by the actions of your ancestors (even if they are long dead). Burn candles, sing songs, tell your ancestors the family news, make small offerings of food and alcohol... and so forth.

Chapter 6

The Matronae or Matres

"Modraniht id et matrum nocturnum" – The Modraniht is the Night of the Mothers"
(Bede, 7th century CE, *De Temporum Ratione 13*, about how the heathen Angles in England hold a sacrifice at New year on the Night of the Mothers)[1]

The Matronae

The one exception Caesar made in his castigation of the Germani was his account of the tribe which occupied the region between Colonia (Köln) and Gelduba (Krefeld-Gellep) – i.e. the original Rhinelanders. This tribe was the Ubii. According to Julius Caesar, it was the Ubii who had offered to ferry the Roman army over the Rhine to pursue any last survivors of the Gallic Wars.[2]

The Matronae (or Matres) are a collective of mysterious indigenous goddesses, of Germanic and Celtic origin, often appearing as a group of three, who were honoured in (Western) Europe at the time of the Roman Empire.[3] This raises some interesting questions:

- Was there (ever) a matriarchy in Old Europe before the patriarchy we know today?
- Was there an all-female trinity before the all-male Christian holy trinity conquered Europe?

We also find connections to Mother Goose, Holle and even links to the meanings of runes and themes in Northern European rock art.[4] Carlo Ginzburg links the Matronae to the 'nocturnal mistresses' led by Abundia, spirits appearing in the form of young girls or matrons dressed in white. Often encountered in the wood or in the stable, where they braided the horses' manes. These matronae dressed in white are a late echo of the Matrae, Matres or Matronae, found in the Lower Rhineland, France, England and Northern Italy.[5] A lot has been written about the Matronae, but mostly in German. There was a lively cultural exchange in the Rhineland between local culture and the Roman army.

The Germanic people of the pre-Roman era, the Ubii, worshipped their deities in the great outdoors. Nature was their 'cathedral'. Once the Roman army arrived in the Rhineland area and soldiers became involved in the Matronae cult, temples and shrines were built. The material we have today is from such shrines, as the Ubii left us almost no evidence of their spiritual life.[6]

The presence of the Romans created a market for stone masonry and artisans, local or foreign, but likely both, catered for the spiritual needs of troops and camp settlers. There was a great demand for votives to the Matronae, considering that 645 of the 1112 religious votive inscriptions in Lower Germany mention the Matronae. We have no stone depictions of the Matronae from the pre-Roman period because the Celts and Germans made religious votives out of precious metals, not stone.[7]

Soldiers and veterans had the funds to commission votives and highly wrought altars. They could accumulate considerable wealth before their service ended. This brought an economic boost felt by the entire Rhineland area. It also brought a much-improved infrastructure. Veterans may even have served as religious leaders of the Matronae, particularly in the camp settlements or countryside cult areas.From archaeological finds we know that an impressive number of Matronae were honoured but we know tantalisingly little about them. We have over 1100 inscribed plaques, altars and statues. We also have several temple sites dotted across the map of Europe. Those inscriptions speak of *Matronae* or *Matres*. In some places we also find inscriptions to goddesses called the *Nutrices,* who appear similar in nature. Sadly, no myths survive and we have no information provided by writers of that time.

No pan-European universal paganism ever existed. There was not necessarily even such a thing as a *pan-Germanic* or *pan-Celtic-Gaulish* paganism. There was never a coherent and unified belief system or pantheon that spanned all of Europe, instead, all tribes had their own pantheons. Pantheon may be too strong a word, implying a high level of organisation. They would have had a collective of deities and spirits that they honoured and made offerings to.[8]

My own interpretation is that their spirituality was local and closely tied to the land. It is likely that the spirits of the land were involved and that their deities were related to both features in the landscape and the local flora and fauna.

Even the more popular deities, some of them known to us today, would have had localized attributes and stories, which varied from tribe to tribe. Today we can still see glimpses of this when we compare, for instance, Donar or Thor to thunder gods in other pantheons from the same larger geographical area. We then find that the Norse God Thor (known as Donar in the Netherlands) has a counterpart in other gods from Northern Europe:

- **Perkūnas** *(Lithuanian: Perkūnas, Latvian: Pērkons, Old Prussian: Perkūns, Perkunos, Yotvingian: Parkuns)* was the Baltic god of thunder and the second most important deity in the Baltic pantheon after Dievas. In both Lithuanian and Latvian mythology, he is documented as the god of sky, thunder, lightning, storms, rain, fire, war, law, order, fertility, mountains, and oak trees.[9]
- **Perun** is the highest god of the pantheon in Slavic

mythology and the god of the sky, thunder, lightning, storms, rain, law, war, fertility and oak trees. His attributes are fire, mountains, wind, iris, eagle, the firmament, horses, carts, weapons (hammer/axe/arrow) and war.[10]

- **Ukko** ('old man') was the Finnish god of the sky, weather, and the crops. The Finnish word for thunder, 'ukkonen' (little Ukko) or 'ukonilma' (Ukko's weather), is derived from his name. In the Kalevala he is also called *'ylijumala'* (overgod, Supreme God), as he is the god of things of the sky. He makes all his appearances in myths solely by natural effects when invoked.[11]

- **Horagállis**, the god of thunder in Saami culture who was also known as a bringer of rain. He was seen as the protector of human beings and reindeer. It was believed that Horagállis cleans the air and washes diseases away.[12]

In Scandinavia Thor was the supreme deity in some areas while Odin had the same role in other areas. Today, we suspect that the god Tyr may originally have had the role of Odin as chief god and that this shift might be linked to the Precession of the Equinoxes and perpetual shifting of the night sky (really the cyclic wobbling of the Earth of her axis of rotation). Academics have suggested that Norse God Ullr is an older god who stems from an earlier, pre-Odin, era. In other areas Freyr was the main god. We find manifestations of Freyr when we speak of harvests, green gods and vegetations gods who face death and resurrection. It is all part of a larger Weave.

It is important to be aware of these regional differences because the Matronae/Matres were local and distinct, with specific attributes, responsibilities and or areas of influence. This is not so different from how, in a later period, Christian people will pray for intercession from specific saints, affiliated with specific causes and issues. Yet the Matronae had a large enough following to cross tribal lines and unite tribes in common devotion to deity.

They were well-loved and well-tended. The inscriptions we have (dating from the 1st-5th century CE) follow a rather specific formula where the altars were dedicated in gratitude for prayers that had been answered. They were of very high quality, clearly made by professional craftspeople and artists. The basic formula is:

Person x dedicates this altar to the Matronae and/or Matres in fulfilment of a vow for a prayer answered. As she puts it: *We have hard evidence of over 1100 definitively answered prayers over a roughly 500 year period of time.*[13]

Summary of facts

The Matronae, as they appear in texts from the period of the Roman Empire, were worshipped from the first to the fifth centuries CE. Some inscriptions have dates and other surviving inscriptions have been carbon dated. There are earlier inscriptions that may pre-date the Roman era cult. Those are written in Gaulish and located in Southern France. They don't have images, only words. The later altars nearly always included a picture of three seated women wearing the traditional clothing of the Ubii, which include large linen bonnets and crescent (or half-moon) shaped pendants.

The votive inscriptions celebrate *The Mothers* in their manifold manifestations[14]

- The Mothers of the Tribe.
- The Mothers of federations of Tribes.
- Mothers of Rivers.
- Mothers of Towns.
- Clan Mothers.
- Mothers of Land.

The functions of these mothers clearly overlap with the roles of goddesses, which is why they are often called *deae* (goddesses) as well: goddesses of healing/prosperity/justice/fate or fortune/ abundance/war/truce/pledges and so forth. Some of these 'Mothers' appear as both a deity in their own right and as a member of a collective of mothers.[14]

They often appear as a female trinity. Reading material in Dutch and German made me realise just how the close a connection there is between the Matrones and the Norns. Especially in Germany we commonly find a powerful triad of three women deities (who later become saints): the Betten, Bethen or Beden. *(Please see the sections about The Norns and Schikgodinnen in Chapter 4).*

In the Ogham Tree Alphabet the letter B is represented by 'white goddess' or ethereal spirit of Beith – Birch (rune BEORC). There does not appear to be any etymological connection and scholars have rejected the notion of a Birch Goddess but I sense a connction to the Betten or Beden.

The Mothers are referred to either as Matres or Matrones, the Latin word for Mother in plural (Old Norse Módir). Some inscriptions also have prayers.

The Night of the (Ancestral) Mothers: Modranecht or Modraniht

In the 7ᵗʰ century AD, the scribe Bede (born 673 D) wrote that the heathen Angles of England celebrated The Night of the Mothers as their New Year celebration. The cult is thought to be related to the Old Norse Viking Age cult of the Dísir ("goddesses), also appearing in collectives, and including both goddesses, giantesses and so called Fylgjur ('followers'), who are partly divine souls of ancestral mothers who follow their descendants as guardian and guiding spirits. Many Scandinavian tribes were also named after ancestral mothers, who were also often associated with rivers.[14]

An increasing number of people now joyfully celebrates this holy night again and nothing stops you from putting this feast on your calendar![15]

We are talking about archaeological finds from a very large geographical area, stretching from the Rhine River via Hadrian's Wall to Slovenia and even North Africa.[16] The Matronae cult provides us with tantalising snippets. Where did the concept of a collective of mother goddesses originate? Did people commonly worship divine mothers or an ancestral mother in pre-Christian Old Europe? Some authors interpret their existence as evidence of an Iron Age cult dedicated to deified Ancestral Mothers while others go as far as concluding that once upon a time Old Europe was matriarchal. It is a fascinating (and controversial) idea which has been neither proved nor disproved at this time. What we can say is that altars to the Matronae were raised by men and that the Matronae were clearly viewed as ruling all dimensions of human life. Both men and women requested their assistance and blessings through prayers and offerings.

The Matrones/Matronae or Matres/Matrae (Mothers) are Celtic and Germanic goddesses widely worshipped in Gaul and Britain; they were almost always depicted in groups of three. They are protectors of home, family and community, bringers of good fortune and providers of plenty.

Quite a few of the goddess triads had additional names as well, epithets sometimes referring to location or tribal affiliation. Whether these were considered to be separate sets of entities from one another is uncertain, but the iconography remained fairly consistent from group to group: three female figures, often accompanied by symbols of fertility, prosperity and abundance.[16]

The names for their collective: Matronae, Matres or Matrae are Roman in origin. The specific names of individual goddesses are surprisingly hard to place and analyse. Often, we cannot even tell whether they are Germanic or Celtic in origin.

Websites listing a comprehensive list of all Matronae, Matres or Nutrices we are aware of, their location and any information we have about them are easily found online.

For this book I have made a personal selection from the listings I could find, based on the following criteria:

- Matronae/Matres indigenous and specific to the Netherlands and immediate surroundings (Flanders in Belgium and locations situated on the German side of the Dutch-German border).
- Dedicated to causes highly relevant today.
- Matronae showing a connection to the runes of the Anglo-Frisian rune row.

The on-line listings by Hearth Fire Handworks[17] and Maria Kvilhaug[18] are invaluable sources of information and inspiration.

Directory of Matrones/Matres

Abiamarcae/Ambiamarcae (Borderland Mothers)[18]
Inscriptions: 'Matronis Abiamarcis', 'Matronibus Ambiorene-sibus'. Location: Floisdorf near Aachen, West Germany (near today's Dutch-German border) Meaning: Abiamarcae = Land Beyond or Borderland March). Ambiamarca means People of the Marches. Matronis Abiamarcis: Mothers to the March/Rhine people.

Abirenae (River Mothers)[18]
Inscription: 'Matronis Abirenibus'. Location: Deutz, West Germany. Meaning: Abirenae means 'Of the Rhine Borderland'. Matronis Ambirenae means Mothers of the Rhine People.

Ahinehiae (Mothers Of the River)[18]

Meaning: Ahinehiae – from OHG *aha* (water, River): The River Mothers. Location: Blankenheim, near Aachen, West Germany.

Ahueccaniae (Prophetic Magic Water Women)[18]

Inscriptions: 'Ahueccanis Avehae et Hellivesae': Prophetic Magic Water Beings. Location: Gleuel, Cologne, Germany (dated to 201 CE) .

- *ahwo, OHG 'aha' – 'Water', 'River'
- *wiccian, AngloSaxon – 'To Conjure', 'Do Magic'
- *wicken, MHG – 'To Prophecy'

Alaferhviae (Great, Life-Giving Mothers)[18]

Inscriptions: 'Matronibus Alaferhiviabus': The Great Life Giving Mothers. Location: Jülich, West Germany (several). *ferh (OHG)/*feorh (AngloSaxon) means life. Or else derived from *fereheih (OHG): tree or oak. So we arrive at: 'The Mothers Belonging to All Trees' (Trees are metaphors for people and lineages) or 'The Mothers Belonging to All Oaks' (Oak is a female tree, symbolizing woman, so that the meaning could even be The Mothers of All Mothers (i.e. The Mothers of Lineages).[18]

Bear in mind that different trees grow and thrive in different locations, depending on climate, soil, type of landscape, moisture levels, altitude etc. Yggdrasil was an ash tree (or possibly a yew) but further south the Oak is an extremely significant tree for Germanic and Celtic peoples. The people of the Low Lands allocated gender to trees: here Oak was male, Linden was female and therefore often associated with Mother Mary. Interesting to note that Maria Kvilhaug describes the Oak as a female tree based on Nordic sources (see *Alaterviae* and *Alhiahenae* – the Oak Tree Mothers).[18]

Alagabiae (All-Giving Mothers)

Inscriptions: 'Matronis Alagabius'. Location: Bürgel, Solingen, West Germany, fourth century CE. Meaning: 'Mothers Who Give Everything'. Thought to be a Germanic counterpart to the partially Celticized matron name *Ollogabiae*. It is possible that the same matrons were venerated under both names among the mixed Germanic-Celtic population on the lower Rhine.[18]

Alaisiagae (Venerated Mothers)

Inscriptions: 'Duabus Alaisiabis, Baudihillia et Friagabis' and 'Duabus Alaisiabis et Thingus'. Location: Housesteads on Hadrian's Wall in Cumbria, three inscriptions. Meaning: 'The Two Venerated Ones' (identified as Baudihilla/Beda and Friagabis/Fimmilena) and in one instance associated with Thingsus – Mars (the god of war). We met them as deities in Chapter 4.[16]

The names of the Two Venerated Ones, Baudihilla/Beda and Friagabis/Fimmilena has been associated with the Frisian law terms Bodthing and Fimelthing – Summon and Sentence, and even when studied on their own the names indicate that the Two Venerated Ones were closely related to a court of justice, and that they may have been goddesses of law and justice.[19]

Alateivia (The All Divine One)

Inscription: 'Alateiviae ex iussu Divos medicus'. Location: Xanten, a town in the state of North Rhine-Westphalia, Germany, in the district of Wesel. Meaning: 'To The All Divine One, on her own command, from the physician Divos' – possibly a goddess of healing.[18]

Alaterviae (All Loyal/Oak Tree Mothers)

Inscriptions: 'Matribus Alatervis (et Matribus Campestribus)'. Location: Edinburgh. Meaning: The All-Loyal Mothers (and the Country/Land(?)...(?) Mothers) or The Mothers of the Oak Trees

(Oak trees represent women or lineages).[18]

Early Celtic art depicted deities through images of nature, particularly trees, but later took on zoological and anthropomorphic features. The Matronae appear to have undergone the same change in iconography during the Roman period. Two large sacred enclosures from the 6th century BCE in Germany, one of which lies just south of Bonn, show rituals based around a tree or possibly an imitation of one. The sanctuary at Pesch appears to have incorporated that feature into the sanctuary with a sacred tree as a focus of the cult area. Tree imagery continued to appear even on Roman Matronae altars. Altars with sufficiently detailed images to specify the tree appear to be oaks, an unsurprising association given that oaks are durable and have long lifespans. The oak tree also serves as a non-anthropomorphic symbol of fertility.[20]

Alhiahenae (Temple/Oak Mothers)

Inscriptions: 'Matronis Alhiahenabus'. Location: Neidenstein, Heidelberg. Meaning: Mothers of the Temples/Mothers of Oaks.[18] Author's note: the lore surrounding Rune AC tells us that Oak Trees were later (or more commonly) perceived as masculine.

Almaviaheniae (Elm Path Mothers)

Location: Cologne, Germany. Associated with the river Elm (OHG: Elmaha) or to the tree-sort elm. Possibly a Celtic origin: The 'Matrae Almahae' – suggesting a Celtic origin to the name. (Elm=feminine tree=Woman, Ancestress, Lineage).[18]

Alusneihae (Beer Mothers)

Location: Inden-Pier, Kreis Düren, West Germany. From Gmc «aluþ» -- «Beer», «Intoxicating Drink» -- the second part of the name is uncertain, but is possibly the same as the mysterious 'neha' in the goddess name Nehallennia: Is it from LAT *nex, *necare – 'to kill', or from the verb 'helan' – to hide, or possibly from *neu –

associated with words for seafaring or approximation ('Mothers of Beer Approaching', 'Mothers of Beer Ships' or similar).[18]

Ambiamarcae/ Ambiomarciae
(Mothers of Fenced-in Marchlands)

Inscription (LAT) on votive altar at Deutz (dated 252 CE): 'In honorem domus divinae et genio loci, Ambiamarcis, Ambiorenesibus, Marti Victori, Mercurio, Neptuno, Cereri, diis deabusque omnibus': In Honor of the divine house and the protective spirits of this place, the Ambiamarcae (Mothers), Ambiorenis (Mothers), the victorious Mars (god of war), Mercury (god of divine messages), Neptun (god of oceans), Ceres (goddess of Earth), and all the gods and goddesses. Location: Deutz , Wardt, West Germany (dated 218 CE), plus one at Remagen: 'et Genio loci, Marti, Herculi, Mercurio, Ambiomarcis' (and the protective spirits, Mars, Hercules (Thor), Ambiomarcae), meaning: The name may be related to a particular place called Ambia (Embt today). The name seems to be a Celtic-Germanic mixed formation with strong Roman influence. (Author's note: *the names Mars, Mercury, Neptune and Ceres and Hercules would have been in use as Latin variant for Týr, Odin, Njord and Frigg/ Freyia and Thor).*[18]

Ambiorenses (Mothers of Both Sides)

Location: Deutz, Germany. Meaning: 'Mothers of Both Sides of the Rhine' (ancestral mothers to people on both sides, perhaps both Celts and Germans, or of two tribes).[18]

Amfratninae (Mothers of Success)

Location: Eschweiler, Germany. Meaning: OHG *frad – 'capable', *fradi – 'efficiency', 'success'.[18]

Andrusteinhiae (The Mother Followers)

Location: Bonn, Godesberg, Cologne. Meaning: Old Franconian

'antrustio' – follower, same meaning as ON *fylgja* – follower: a female guardian spirit and ancestral mother to a particular lineage or tribe.[18]

Annaneptiae (The Favorable/Generous Kinswomen Mothers)

Inscription: 'Matribus Annaneptis'. Location: Xanten (233 CE). Meaning: LAT Matres means Mothers, OHG 'Unnan' is to grant/Gothic 'ansts' (favour) and ON 'Nipt' is Sister, Female Relative or Kinswomen. Annaneptiae means 'Mothers Who Are Granting/Favorable/Generous Sisters/Kinswomen'. (In this context Kinswomen can also mean followers, spirit beings, ancestral mother souls who guard and protect and grant favors to their descendants).[18]

Arvolecia (Goddess of Quick Healing)

Inscription: 'Deae Arvolecie. Location: Brough, England (150 CE). Meaning: Arvolecia is probably a Germanic name and perhaps means The Quick Healer. The goddess votive altar was raised by one Maiotius in 150 CE England – his name is Celtic. Celtic-German overlapping was very common at this time.[18]

Asericinehae (Mothers of the Ancestral Reign)

Inscription: 'Matronis Asericinehabus', 'Matronis Aserecinehis'. Location: Odenhausen (Odins Houses) and Odendorf (Odins Place) in Cologne, Germany Meaning: Possibly related to the Germanic personal name *Ansu-rik, according to Simek's Dictionary of Northern Mythology. Thus they could represent the ancestral mothers of a person called Ansurik and his lineage. But the name Ansurik/Ansoricus means Ancestral Reign. The name of the goddess collective could mean Mothers of the Ancestral Reign.[18]

Audrinehae (Mothers of Divine Support
– Mothers of Destiny)

Inscriptions: 'Matronis Audrinehae', 'M.Auðrinehae', 'M.Auth-rinaheae', 'M.Autrinahenae'. Location: Hermühlheim, Cologne, Germany. Meaning: Proto-Norse *auja (divine protection), or ON 'auða' (destiny, fate).[18]

Aufanie or Matronae Aufania, Goddess(es)
of Sacred Abundance

Inscriptions: Nearly 90 inscriptions are dedicated to the singular 'Deae Aufaniae' (Goddess Aufania) or 'Sanctae Aufania' (Sacred Aufania) or else the plural 'Matronis Aufaniabus' (Aufania-Mothers). Location: They are found around Bonn, Nettersheim, Cordoba/Spain and Lyon/France, and at the Lower Rhine, dating between 164-235 CE and particularly numerous around the year 200 CE.

Meaning: Aufanie suggests 'generous ancestral mother' from Gothic 'ufjo' (abundance).[18]

The Roman veneration of the Matronae began at Bonn in Germany, where soldiers of various ranks participated in the cult. Here we find many votives addressed to the Matronae Aufania. Their name is most likely derived from and Ubian word meaning swamp. The local Ubian people were already worshipping the Matronae before the Romans arrived but by the mid-second century the soldiers at Bonn had adopted the gods into their own pantheons.[2]

Axisinginehae (Mothers of the Grain Ears)

Location: Cologne. Meaning: Related to Gothic 'ahs' (ear) of grain. Rune GER, think of fertility deites and the *Julbock*[18]

Berguiahenae (Oak Mothers or possibly
Mountain Mothers)

Inscriptions: 'Matronis Berhuiahenis' – '...rguiahenis' –

'...B..guinehis'. Location: Gereonsweiler, Jülich and Tetz near Aachen, Germany. Meaning: Possibly related to OHG 'fereheih' (oak), but of uncertain meaning.[18]

Burorina (The Provider Goddess)

Location: Walcheren, Netherlands. Meaning: From Anglo-Saxon 'byrele' (giver). The meaning of her name is cognate with Celtic/Germanic goddess Rosmerta (The Great Provider) and the Norse goddess name for Freyia, Gefion/Gefn (The Provider). Very common meaning of many important goddess names. (Rune GYFU).[18]

Matres Comedovae

These may have derived from the Proto-Celtic *medu (mead) connecting these goddesses etymologically with other Celtic deities of sacred elixirs, such as the Irish Medb and the Gaulish Meduna.[18]

Matronae Dervonnae

Derives from the Proto-Celtic *derwo (oak) suggesting the meaning of 'Mothers of the Oak.'[17]

Matres Domesticae

Literal meaning in Latin is 'Mothers of the Home (/Homeland).'[17]

Matres Eburnicae

Derives from the Proto-Celtic *eburo (yew) suggesting a meaning of 'Mothers of the Yew.' (Rune EOLH)[17]

Fernovinehae (Mothers of the Old Rivers)

Inscriptions: 'Matronis Fernovineis/Fernovinehis'. Location: Meckenheim and Cologne. Meaning: *fern-awi (old stream)[17]

Matres Frisavae (Mothers of the Frisian Ancestors)

Inscription: 'Matribus Frisavis Paternis' (To the Mothers of the Frisian Ancestors). Location: Wissen, near Xanten, Germany. Meaning: Matres (LAT): Mothers, Frisavae (of the Frisian (tribe), 'Paternis' (LAT) = Ancestors. May have been associated with the Germanic Frisii tribe.[18]

Matronae Gabiae or Gabinae (The Generous Mothers)

Inscription: at least ten votive stones dedicated to 'Matronis Gabiabus', and one saying 'Iunonibus Gabiabus'. Iunones is Latin and means the same as matrons (mothers or ancestral mothers).

Location: Rövenich near Euskirkchen, Germany. Likely to derive from the Proto-Germanic *geban (to give). Meaning: cognate with the ON goddess name Gefion (Gefn, Freyia): Generous, Giving, Providing. (Rune GYFU).[17]

Gamaleda (The Old Great Grandmother Goddess)

Inscription dedicated to the 'Ammacae sive Gamaledae' on votive altar. Location: Maastricht, Netherlands. Meaning: Gamaleda is related to ON 'gamall' (old) and ON Edda (Great Grandmother).[18]

Matronae Gantunae (The Goose Women)

Inscriptions: 'Gantunis Flossia Paterna' (Goose Women, Ancestral Mothers of the Flosi Tribe). Location: Cologne, Germany. May be derived from the Proto-Germanic *gans (goose) or *ganuto (gander). Meaning: *ganta is "goose" (associated with an ancient cult of water birds and water bird goddesses common in both Indo-European and Finno-Ugric traditions).[18](We meet Mother Goose in Chapter 12).

Gavadiae (The Goddesses of Pledges)

Inscriptions: Eight votive stones from around 200 CE dedicated to the 'Matronis Gavadiabus'. Location: Jülich, Mönchengradbach, Germany. Meaning: Related to Gothic 'wadi' (pledge) and 'gawadijon' (betroth). Goddesses of either vows and oaths or matchmaking.[18]

Gavasiae (The Clothing Mothers)

Inscriptions: 'Matronis Gavasiabus'. Location: Cologne . Meaning: Gothic 'gawasjon' (clothe), thought to refer to the making of swaddling clothes for a baby (midwifery). Women made all clothing at that time, so the name could refer to the (then) essentially female function of protecting and providing people with clothing.[18]

Matres Germanae (The Mothers of the Germans)

Inscription: 'Matribus meis Germanis Suebis', 'Matribus Italis Germanis Gallis Britis'. Location: Cologne . Meaning: 'German (and Italian, Gallic and British), Mothers of the People'.[18]

(Dea) Hariasa (The Ruler Goddess or the Goddess of Rulers)

Location: Cologne, 187 CE. Meaning: related to the ON word for 'ruler' (heri) or 'to rule' (heria), etymologically connected to a valkyria name: Herja (To Rule) [18]

Author note: I am working on this chapter on Holocaust Day, 27 January 2020. Concentration camp survivors are urging the world to choose peace and reconciliation, not war and escalation of conflict. Imagine a world where our global leaders seek sage advice from a wise Goddess of Rulers!

Havae (The High Mothers)

Location: Merzenich near Düren. Meaning: Semantically close to the ON word for 'High' (háva/hárr). Havamal, High One, Female High One.[18]

Hiheriaiae (The Jay Bird Mothers)

Location: Enzen near Euskirchen. Meaning: From Old Germanic *hihera (jay).[18]

(Dea) Idbangabia (The Hard Working Provider Goddess)

Location: Pier, Düren/Germany. Possibly derived from Idiangabia, ON: Iðinn means hard working, OHG Gabia and ON Gefia (to give/provide, as in in the goddess name Gefion).[18] Author note: Norse Gefjon was once an important goddess, connected to Rune GYFU.

Matronae Lubicae

Derivation uncertain; some connect them to the Proto-Celtic *lubo or "love" as well as to the Proto-Germanic *lubja or "herb, potion."[14] (Author note: the contemporary Russian verb to love is любить – lubit.[22])

Matres Magiseniae

May derive from the Proto-Celtic *magos or "field" and *seno (old), a possible reference to an ancient land or ancient piece of ground.[17]

Matres Menmandutiae

May derive from the Proto-Celtic *menman (thought, mind).[17]

Matres Nemetiales

May derive from the Proto-Celtic *nemeto (sanctuary, sacred grove) and may translate to 'mothers of the sacred grove.' Etymologically related to the goddess Nemetona (Chapter 4). Sanctuaries dedicated to a local goddess were often situated on an island in a swamp, lake or sea. It is likely that Waddenzee island Ameland was a sacred island, indicated today by an old abbey situated next to a well.[17]

Matronae Nersihenae

Derivation uncertain, may be connected etymologically to the Niers River, which is a river running through Germany and the Netherlands and a tributary of the river Maas. Its wellspring is near Erkelenz, south of Mönchengladbach, in North Rhine-Westphalia.[17]

Mahalinehae (Mothers of the Justice Court)

Location: Cologne. Meaning: Either from the place name Mecheln (in Belgium), or else to Germanic *mahal (place of justice, parliament). (Rune TIR).[17]

Dea Menmanhia (possibly Necklace Bearing Goddess)

Location: Rome, Italy. Meaning: Probably Germanic but of uncertain meaning. ON: Mén (Jewel, Necklace,) and Menia (servant girl), Necklace Bearer[18] (Author note: there is a possible connection to Mengloth).[19]

(Matronae) Ratheithiae (Mothers of the Fate Wheel)

Location: Euskirchen, Germany. Derivation uncertain but generally considered to be Germanic in origin.[17] Author note: proto-Germanic *raþa (wheel), the symbolic meaning is fate, Rune RAD).

Matronae Renahenae

Derivation uncertain but generally considered to be Germanic in origin. Could be connected with the Rhine River.[17]

Matres Rocloisiabo

May derive from the Proto-Celtic *klowsta (hearing). Might suggest a meaning of 'Mothers Who Hear [Prayers].'[17]

Saithchamiae (Mothers of Magic)

Location: Hoven near Zülpich, Germany. Meaning: Related to

ON seiðr= magic, divination, witchcraft.[18]

Dea Sandraudiga (Goddess of True Wealth)

Inscription: 'Deae Sandraudigae cultores temple'. Location: Zundert, Netherlands. Meaning: ON 'sannr' (true) and Gothic 'audags' (rich).[18]

Dea Sibulca (Sibyl Goddess)

Location: Bonn, Germany. Meaning is uncertain. (*Author comment: related to the famous Sibylla? For Germanic tribes the Veleda was the Sibyl or Völva*).[18]

Dea Sulevia (Goddess of Hot Springs)

Location: Trier. Uncertain meaning, possibly related to goddess Sulis from Bath, England, the Goddess of Hot Springs. (Rune LAGU).[18]

Dea Travalaeha (The Desired Goddess)

Location: Cologne, Germany. Connected with the name þrawija on the Swedish rune stone from Kalleby and with the Proto-Norse 'þrawo' (to long/desire).[18]

Tummaestiae (Mothers of House Constructions)

Location: Sinzenich near Euskirchen, 'Matronis Tumaestis': The Helping Goddesses of the House or the Building Site.[18]

Turstuahenae (Mothers of Troll Powers)

Location: Derichsweiler, Düren, Germany , 2nd and 3rd centuries CE. The meaning may derive from the Proto-Germanic *thurisa* (giant, think of Rune THORN). Probably from ON þurs (thurse, troll) and OHG 'duris' (thuris), also meaning 'mighty'. Some think it is from Gothic þaurstei (thirst).[18]

Udravarinehae /Udrovarinehae (Mothers of the Otter Dam)

Location: Lower Rhine region. Connected to otters and dams (associated with the many river mothers). The contemporary Swedish word for otter is *utter*.[18]

Ulauhinehae (Mothers of the Owl Grove/Mothers of the River Flow)

Location: Gleich near Füssensich in Germany . Meaning is derived from either *uwa-lauha* – Owl-Grove or else from *plau/pleu* – flow.[18]

(Matronae) Vanginehae

Possibly derived from the Proto-German *wanga* or "meadow."[15]

Fólkvangr (Old Norse for field of the host, people-field or army-field) is a meadow or field ruled over by the goddess Freyja where half of those that die in combat go upon death, while the other half are received by Odin in Valhalla.[24]

(Matronae) Vataranehae

May derive from the Proto-Germanic *watar* (water).[17]

(Matronae) Vatviae (The Clairvoyant Mothers)

Location: Rödingen, Morken-Haff, Germany. May derive from the Proto-Germanic *watar* (water), alternatively from the Latin 'vates' (seer).[18]

Author note: Rune LAGU. Most votives we have today suffered water damage from being placed in a well.[25]

The Stone Age inhabitants of Europe made offerings to bodies of water, such as swamps, rivers and streams. Most objects we have today were from the Bronze Age. Initially a whole region or complete body of water was perceived as sacred (indigenous peoples still do so today, and heroically try to pull Western people out of their money-centred destructive trance state) but over time smaller dedicated cult places or sanctuaries became the norm. We can tell from the scythes and weapons offered in such locations.

In former swamp regions in Northwestern Europe basic wood carvings of deities have been found, carved from large tree branches. Some were mounted on a foot of rocks and paired. Archaeologists believe they may have been used in fertility rituals. Common offerings were flax and white pebbles (*kiezelstenen*). Examples of such sites are Braak and Oberdoria in Germany, Assendelft in the Netherlands.[25]

From the Roman Era onwards people built small structures dedicated to deity veneration. Before that all rituals occurred in the outdoors. Building temples was a Roman custom copied by local people under occupation.

Matronae Vediantiae

May derive from the Proto-Celtic **gwedyo"* *(to pray)* and may have been associated with the Ligurian Vediantii tribe.[17]

Dea Vercana (Goddess of Works or Birch Goddess)

Location: Bad Betrich, Ernstweiler . Meaning: **werka* (work), or else the name of the B-rune, ON 'bjarkan' (birch). The birch tree played an important role in folk medicine. (Rune BEORC).[17]

Matronae Vesuniahenae

May be derived from the Proto-Celtic **wesu* (noble, excellent), may also be etymologically related to the goddess Vesunna (see Chapter 4)[17]

Matronae Saithamiae

May derive from the Proto-Germanic **saida* (magic, charm, spell) and is connected to the Old Norse term *seidh*.[18]

Matres Suleviae

May derive from the Proto-Celtic *su (good); alternatively, it may be cognate with the Old Irish *suil* (eye), which derives from the Proto-Celtic *sawol* (sun). They are not, as is sometimes thought, a multiple of the British healing goddess Sulis. (Rune SIGIL).[18]

Dea Vihansa (Goddess of Dedications or Goddess of Battle)

Location: Tongern in Belgium. A bronze plaque dedicating shield and spear to this goddess from a centurion of the III legion has been found. Meaning: Germanic *wihan (to fight or to dedicate).[18]

Viradecdis /Viradestis, Viratehis, Virodacthis (Goddess of Manly Virtue)

Location: Vechten, Birrens, North England, Lower Rhine, Trebur. Meaning: From the Celtic 'ferdaht' (masculinity).[18]

(Matres) Vroicae

May derive from the Proto-Celtic *wroiko (heath).[17]

Closing Comments

Zoomorphic images appear on Matronae altars as elements of local traditions. The most common animal motif is a snake, often combined with a tree. To me this seems connected to Yggdrasil and the serpent Nidhoggr forever gnawing on the roots of the world tree, but different scholars interpret this differently. Some altars depicts goats. I perceive this as an earlier horned god who later morphs into the Christian figure of The Devil – but I am not a scholar of this period.

The Romans introduced three new concepts to the local iconography: the cornucopia[26] (by far the most common image), the globe and the shell-shaped canopy. The cornucopia, or horn of plenty, comes from a Greek myth about the horn of the goat that sucked the god Zeus, which broke off and filled with whatever its owner most desired. The globe and shell are associated with water and reflect an association of many of the Matronae with water.

In the township of Nideggen, 25 miles west of Bonn, altars from a sanctuary suggest that veterans even had their own version of the goddesses for their own worship. The hilltop sanctuary near Pesch, 15 miles southwest of Bonn, was the largest of all known sites and included a large temple.[27]

Ovid's Metamorphoses show that the hero Pallas promises to place his arms on an oak tree for the Tiber river god in return for a killing blow to Halaesus. This common association between oak trees and divinity helped preserve the imagery among the Ubian and Roman Matronae cult communities.[28]

Along with many question marks and mysteries, a treasure trove of material remains available to us. I hope that this book encourages my readers to embark on their own quests and adventures. Please keep me posted of your discoveries!

Closing note: I highly recommend Rudolph Simek's Dictionary of Northern Mythology.[29]

Activity #6

Seek an encounter with Arvolecia (Goddess of Quick Healing) or another deity/matrona of your choice. Keep detailed notes and share with like-minded people interested in reconstruction work.

Those of you seeking skills in Magic: connect with the Turstuahenae (Mothers of Troll Powers)...

Chapter 7

De Witte Wieven The Mysterious 'White' Ladies or Wise Women

Witte Wieven [White Women] are nocturnal apparitions commonly found in the East and Northern parts of the Netherlands, most notably Drenthe, Overijsel and Gelderland, with the regions Twente, Achterhoek and the Veluwe in particular. But they're also known in Groningen as Widde Juvvers. They appeared all over the west of Europe. In Germany they were known as 'Weiße Frauen', the French called them 'Dame Blanche', the English 'White Women' and the Irish 'Banshee', but all of them are slightly different from the Dutch Witte Wieven. In the Netherlands they were otherwise known as Huede Holden, Joffers, Jomfers, Juvvers, Old Wiefien Platvoet, Olde Witten, Telewitten, Wiefkes, Widde Juffers, Witte Juffers, Witten or Witvrouwe. They always appeared as women in (dirty) white garments, oftentimes in groups of three.[1]

For easy reference

Wit Wijf (singular tense) = one 'White' or Wise Woman.

Witte Wieven or Witte Wijven = plural (several White/Witty/Wise Women, a collective).

In the Netherlands Witte Wieven are also known as: *Huede Holden, Joffers, Jomfers, Juvvers, Old Wiefien Platvoet, Olde Witten, Telewitten, Wiefkes, Widde Juffers, Witte Juffers, Witten and Witvrouwe.*

They are found in the following locations: *wetlands: bogs and marshes, forests, grave mounds, burial sites Hunebedden, lakes, moorlands, swamps.*

St Nicholas and The Witte Wieven

In the year 2015 many parents in the Netherlands became

outraged by a television program for children that featured the Witte Wieven. For Dutch children the most exciting day of the year is Sinterklaas (the feast day of Saint Nicholas). In the weeks running up to this event, children set their shoes by fireplaces and live in eager anticipation of the treats and gifts the elderly saint will bring, assuming they have behaved well this past year.[2]

Sinterklaas Season opens with a TV program for families called *Het Sinterklaas Journal,* the daily chronicles of the travels and preparations of Sinterklaas and his helpers, filmed documentary-style as a series of daily 'real life events' unfolding. This generally kicks off just after November 11th, the feast day of Sint Maarten (St Martin), when Dutch children perform the local variant of *trick-or-treating* (knocking on doors to receive sweets and treats).

Different provinces and cities take turns hosting the *Intocht van Sinterklaas* (the arrival and parade of St Nicholas and his entourage). In the year 2015 it was the turn of the province Twente, known for its ghostly ladies of the mists: the white or wise women. The Saint's ship sailed to Meppel and got shrouded in a dense fog. People tried to guide him in by starting a big fire in a church tower and one of Sint's helpers became the hero of the day by extinguishing this fire. His reward was being gifted one stone from a *Hunebed.*

This stone had magical properties and the Witte Wieven made a guest appearance on the TV show. This did *not* go down well with many families. Children as young as two or three years old watch the program and parents reported a rise in night-mares, panic attacks and children refusing to leave the house in foggy weather.[3]

In recent decades, due to Americanisation and all of us now living in a global village, some Dutch families have shifted these celebrations to Christmas instead. I have always preferred the clear separation of gift-giving and fun-for-kids and the profound symbolism (and spiritual darkness work followed by the rebirth of the Sun) at the winter solstice. However, raising three Dutch-Swedish children in the UK, I lost this battle a long time ago. Our children celebrate both Sinterklaas and Jul (the Swedish Christmas).

Witte Wieven

In Dutch myths the *Witte Wieven* (also Witte Wijven) are sometimes perceived as the spirits of wise women from ancient Neolithic times, or possibly elven beings, while others view them as ghosts or apparitions. Some authors connect them to the *Schikgodinnen* (deities of Fate): the Norns.

They are commonly found in the eastern and northernmost provinces of the Netherlands, most notably Drenthe, Overijsel (where the region of Twente is, known for both its Hunebedden and the Witte Wieven), the Achterhoek (literally corner at the back) of the region of the Veluwe (both in the province of Gelderland). They are also known in Groningen (as the *Widde Juvvers*).[1]

In the Netherlands they were otherwise known as Guede Holden, Joffers, Jomfers, Juvvers, Old Wiefien Platvoet, Olde Witten, Telewitten, Wiefkes, Widde Juffers, Witte Juffers, Witten or Witvrouwe. They always appeared as women in (off) white garments, oftentimes in groups of three.[1]

In some places they are known as *Juffers* (Groningen) or *Joffers* (maidens, the Dutch word juf means both unmarried woman and school teacher).

The fact that a Wit Wijf was sometimes known as *Old Wiefien Platvoet* is extremely interesting because that gives us a direct link to the figure of Vrouw Holle (Frau Holle in German). Old Wiefien Platvoet literally means *Old Wife Flatfoot* and Vrouw Holle reportedly has one large flat foot, from working the paddle of a spinning wheel! A related name for this figure is *Spinwijf*

(Spinning Woman), often observed working her spinning wheel by moonlight.

The shadow manifestation (or lower octave expression) of anything is never far off, so farmers used her as a figure of terror to keep children off their fields. The threat used was that Old Wiefien Platvoet would spirit them away and cut all the hair off their scalp to use it for spinning. Some threats were even more severe: a woman dressed in white (sometimes called *Spin-An*) was said to slaughter anyone who trampled the rye or harvest, and quite possibly burn children alive.

Spinwijf

Spin-An or Spinnen-Annechien was mainly seen in Zuidwolde, an area in the South East of Drenthe. She appeared as an old woman in white garments, working away at her spinning wheel as she basked in moonlight on top of a hill. Some have claimed to hear the sounds of a spinning wheel at work on top of the Hekelenberg, and some have seen her. She was also said to work on top of the Schottershuizerberg. The excavations that took place there revealed remains of an actual spinning wheel.[4]

The literal translation of Witte Wieven is 'white women' but this is no reference to skin colour, originally this means *wise women*. Etymology informs us that the word *wit* here is cognate with the word witty in contemporary English. The association of wise women with the colour white might have been a translation error, or an association between wisdom and the colour white may actually have existed. Some people who self-identify as druids wear white robes in rituals today. The reference then is to colours used in ceremonies and magical workings (not to skin colour). They are often associated with mist and fog as well, hence the colour white.

In pre-Christian times these women were healers and herbalists, people who administered medicine to their communities and looked after the sick, the dying, and women in childbed. Before the Christian filter of demonic witches was imposed, these people were held in high esteem (remember that the medical profession as we know it today did not exist in those days and most people could not afford specialist 'medical' care). One theory is that even after their death, rituals were performed at their grave sites to honour them.

According to the Poetic Edda, the god Odin (Wodan) has a habit of visiting grave sites of dead *"vǫlvas"*, (the correct plural in Old Norse is *vǫlur*. The *vǫlva* is a seer and prophetess who performs divination work on behalf of her people, the word is said to mean 'carrier of a magical wand'). Odin/Wodan raises *vǫlur* from their grave and asks them questions about the destiny of the gods and the ultimate nature of the cosmos. Based on that piece of Old Norse intelligence, it seems possible to me that people visited the graves of powerful *witte wieven* to perform necromancy: to receive guidance from a powerful dead person.[5]

Another theory is that Witte Wieven made the decision to stay on earth after death in energetic form and became spirits or guardians of both land and communities. Mist appearing on or near a grave mound was then perceived as the Wise Women appearing. People would bring them offerings and ask them for guidance and assistance with community matters, such as illness, crop failure, threats from another tribe or community, and so forth.

In the Northern Tradition there is a long-standing Germanic belief in both spirits of the land and ancestors remaining after death to keep an eye on land, people and property. In some sources de Witte Wieven are referred to as Elven (Alfen or Alven).

The term is not limited to the Netherlands. Jacob Grimm uses the German term *Weisse Frauen* in his book Deutsche Mythologie (1835). In France they are called *Dames Blanches*. English people refer to *White Women* who can predict when a human life will begin or end.

There are several places in the Netherlands named for the Witte Wieven:[6]

- *Wittewievenbult* (Wise Women Bump or Mound), near de village of Eefde, where Witte Wieven are said to appear every year on Christmas Eve and dance on this hill.
- *Wittewijvenkuil* (Wise Women Pit), situated near the village of Barchem, is a pit between two local hills where, according to local legend, three white or wise women live.

We demonize what we fear

The Witte Wieven were said to play pranks and tricks on local communities. Folklore offers many stories about this.[7] Speaking as a teacher of seidr and shamanic practices, I would say that this occurs only when such beings do not receive the respect they deserve. It is likely that these stories have been misinterpreted in the Christian period.

The stories we have hail mostly from the eastern and northern regions in the Netherlands (Gelderland, Drenthe, Groningen).

Once Christianity had established itself as the new dominant religion of Europe a number of things happened to older customs and beliefs:

- A Christian spin was put on them (plants named for heathen gods received new names involving saints).
- The 'old' deities and spirits were demonized and blamed for all things that went wrong in the world. People were actively encouraged to fear and avoid these beings.
- The filter of the wicked or malevolent witch was projected onto healers, herbalist and wise women and men and this conception ultimately led to the witch hunts and trials in the fifteenth, sixteenths and seventeenth centuries.

In studying and discussing this material, we need to be aware of those filters. We have already established that Witte Wieven knew when people were fated to born and die (meaning that in Old Norse terms they have a close connection to the Norns, *Schikgodinnen* in Dutch). This dimension of their being is easily twisted or misunderstood, meaning that these mysterious figures are perceived as figures of doom and damnation.

The general understanding is that, when handled with respect and receiving the appropriate offerings, these women would support community life and sometimes arrive in the dead of night to finish house work or farm work (e.g. spinning). We often encounter this aspect in fairy tales: supernatural beings help the protagonist at night to get an impossible task done on time. The flip side of this was that they might lash out if they were not honoured and treated with respect, meaning that they might hurt or harm people, property and livestock.

They have also been known to chase people who displease or offend them. Dutch storyteller Abe van der Veen recounts one of the most famous stories about de Witte Wieven, from Lochem. A young man sets out for the Wittewievenkuil in Zwiep. Upon arrival he speaks the following words:

> 'Witte wieven wit, hier breng ik oe het spit, zie moar dat je het gebroad erbie kriegt!'
> 'Witty White/Wise Women, here I bring you the roasting spit, better see to it that you receive the roast along with it!' [6]

Immediately three mysterious beings materialize out of thin air and the young man runs for his life with the Witte Wieven in hot pursuit.

When a person acted greedy and grasping, there was a big chance that the Witte Wieven would come calling. Generally speaking, they would leave you alone as long you did not bother them but they were ruthless when it came to breaking promises. In the story about the *Witte Wijf of Montferland*, one farmer got drunk and asked a Wif Wijf to dance with him. She would not stop dancing until the man dropped dead.[7] Once again this is not an uncommon occurrence in fairy tales. *Object lesson*: never breathe alcoholic fumes in the face of a *Wit Wijf* or approach her disrespectfully while you are under the influence. Making an offering of alcohol or spirits at the appropriate site is a far better way to proceed and maintain mutual goodwill!

Are Witte Wieven ghosts?

In England we find White/Wise Women described as ghostly figures haunting burial sites. Over time (meaning as Christianization proceeds) they become closely associated with elves and witches. They were said to live in grave mounds and till fields at night. They expected a reward for their work, and farmers would often leave out a dish of pancakes on their land, then find all farm work completed the next morning. They were said to sometimes spirit away a human child and leave a changeling or *fairy child* instead. They often stole milk and beer as well.[8]

I am no changeling and I never believed I was really a princess lodged with an ordinary family. However, from childhood I have felt a huge yearning to 'go home' to Scandinavia. I also have had dreams about 'being of giant lineage' and others have confirmed this (saying they often see the Jotunn Skadi walking with me). We find many nuggets of spiritual truth and wisdom in folklore!

Dwaallichtjes – Will-o'-the-wisp

In the province Overijsel some people believed that *will-o'-the-wisp* flickering over the land lured people into hot pursuit and led them astray, never to be seen again. Others claimed that they were the ghosts of witches and the wandering souls of women who sinned in this life and continued to sin in the afterlife. In some places it was believed that the Witte Wieven came from de Witte Wievenkuil (a pit) while others said they lived in grave mounds and hunebedden or terpen.

The Witte Wieven had a knack for finding lost objects or valuables and some believed that they stored large sums of money underneath the Hunebedden. In their most demonized form, they were said to sexually assault men at night (who died in a state of euphoria) and people also claimed to hear the haunting sound of crying, stolen, infants coming from the Hunebedden at night.

There are stories of Witte Wieven knocking on village doors asking for a *balkenhaas,* a cat, which they would roast and eat. They also told people secrets and showed them miraculous things, not to be shared with a living soul.[1]

Until today Dutch people use the phrase Witte Wieven to describe tatters of mist *(nevelflarden)*. British people call these atmospheric ghostly lights (the scientific name is bioluminescence) *jack-o'-lantern, friar's lantern, hobby lantern* or *hinkypunk.*[9]

Another common belief is that these lights are the souls of children who drowned in the bogs.[1] People try to follow them and get lost. Some people recommend casting holy water at them to fix the problem, but it is preferable for a specialist to perform psychopomp work.[10]

Monsters or 'child terrors' invoked by parents

It is clear that parents resorted to frightening children to keep them well-behaved and safe in a very watery country long before organised communal swimming lessons. Farmers did not hesitate to invoke them either, to keep children off their land. The monsters invoked to frighten children *(kinderschrik,* not a parenting technique anyone recommends today!) give us a historic insight in to the collective Dutch imagination. Here is a list:

- De *Bietebauw*, synonym for *Bullebak,* refers to a ghostly apparition or crude person.[11]
- De *Bloedkoets*, from Belgium, was the coach from Hell (literally *hell on wheels*). Blacked out and sealed, blood was seeping through the cracks and masked men walked on either side, abducting any children they could find (playing outdoors after dark) and taking them to the gruesome Tenenkappers (Toe Cutters).

There exists an alternative version of a posh lady travelling in a horse carriage, luring children inside by offering them candy and abducting them to a large castle where a sick king needed to bathe in the blood of children for his cure. (It is likely these tales were linked to the rumours that had spread all over Europe about Hungarian countess Elizabeth Báthory, who has made it into the Guinness Book of World Records as the most prolific female murderer ever)[12]

- De *Bloedpater* (also Tenensnijder, Korenpater or Korenmenneke), is a frightening being frequently mentioned in Zeeland, Limburg and Vlaanderen, said to live in wheat fields. If children went there to pick flowers (Bloedpater is a Dutch synonym for the blood-red poppy) de Bloedpater (or *Korenpater*, Wheatfather/Wheatman) would torture them. (This figure was most likely invented to protect children from rapists – stay clear of isolated places where a paedophile may catch you).[13]
- De *boeman*, (also known as *Boevent, Boekaros, Boezejeude, Beukel, Boozenkeerl, Malle Kerel, Donkere Vent* or *Den Padderen*) is the Dutch version of the Bogeyman. Said to kidnap misbehaving children late at night or pull them into bodies of water. Others describe him as a malicious house spirit. In Limburg he is described as a tall man wearing a chain making a clanging sound, similar to the

Pikkepoot (a 'child hunter' from Utrecht).[14]

- De *Boezehappert,* a child-eating water demon from Friesland, (*bûzehappert*). A very tall monster with scales, horns, sharp nails and green eyes lighting up. *Bornes,* (Henricus Bornius, 1617-1675), was once a steward, put in charge of the Zeeland region by Willem III. He had a dog named Ossaert and was infamous among the townsfolk for his cruelty. After his death he could not find peace in the afterlife and he still haunts the area of Hulst.[15]

- *Elf-rib,* also known as the *Tientoner,* hails from the northern part of the Netherlands, Westfriesland (where I was born). He is said to be a water demon who takes the shape of a dog. Some believe that is the lingering spirit of King Radboud (or Redbad) being punished for his refusal to be baptised. He lives in wells, canal and ditches, is heard barking late at night and spirits away children.[16]

- *IJzeren Veulen,* the Iron Foal was a ghost appearing at the witching hour in the province of Utrecht. It was filled with iron and its joints were made from rusty hinges, so it produced a strange sound running up and down a bridge in the town Cabauw.[17]

- *Kladdegat,* is a beast from the town of Hattem in the province of Gelderland. He freely roamed the streets at night during the 19th century. No one dared go out after dark but a brave baker called Jan Vischer captured the beast and chained him up within the walls of a local castle ruin and sealed him in with masonry. The dungeons of these ruins extend under all of Hattem and parents told their children to avoid being dragged down into this creepy netherworld.[18]

- *Loekenbeer,* from Belgium, abducts children playing outside after dark. It is possible that his name is derived from Norse trickster god Loki but more likely that his name related to the Dutch verb *lokken* (to lure). The beer-part comes from the Dutch word *beerput* (cesspit). *(Here I note that some people connect Loki's name etymologically to the English verb to lock: tricksters lock and unlock or unleash possibilities).*[19]

- *Lorrenboer,* literally means Rag Merchant (or Rag Farmer). He started off as an ordinary ragman, going from door to door with a large burlap sack, shouting "Lorren!" (Rags!) Parent turned this figure into a bogeyman to frighten their children into behaving well.[20]

- *De Man Met De Haak*, the Man with the hook is a water demon with green eyes, a beard made of seaweed and webbed feet. He captured children venturing too close to water and fed on their blood. He kept the souls of children inside nefarious urns.[21]

- *Takkenmann,* this Twig Man or Tree Branch Man resembles some creatures from Germanic mythology, most notably the Lange Man. Most likely he is a made-up urban legend. His name sprouted from a thread on a Something Awful bulletin board where people were invited to post fake photoshopped pictures accompanied by a fictive background story. One figure gained popularity, the so called Slender Man (Slim Man or even Elongated Man). A Wikipedia page dedicated to the misinformation was created and then deleted again (but now back up legitimately! The double nn is the original misspelling, in Dutch the word 'man' is spelled with one n).[22]

- *Tongesnaier,* an ugly figure called the Tongue Slasher, said to cut off the tongues of children. Used to frighten children off from sticking their tongues out at each other.[23]

- *De Flodder*, (also known as "Flodderduivel, Watervlodder or "Flodderduûvel")[24] is a nocturnal tormentor from Brabant and Zeeland. He hooks his big and slimy frog-like claws over the shoulders of his victims and carries them off. He is said to live in polders (land reclaimed from the sea). He appears in animal form and the way to frighten him off is to cross socks or stockings after taking them off. *(I realised only while writing this book that the 1986 Dutch comedy movie Flodder, about an anti-social and socially disruptive family must have been named with this creature in mind!)*[25]

We have already heard about the Spinwijf and Zwarte Piet, also de Duivel. Dutch parents also used witches and wizards to frighten their children:

- *Alruin,* (also known as *Aardmannetje, Pisdief, Galgemanneke, Geluksmanneke* or *Geldmanneke*) is the Dutch name for the poisonous Mandrake plant (Mandragora Officinarum). Its root can resemble a human being and it was used for its magical properties. Some believed the Mandrake was made by God, before he decided humans should look differently![26]
- *Bloedende Wind,* (Bleeding Wind), is the name of a witch. One stubborn farmer decided to go haymaking in the middle of storm. The farmer stabbed at the storm with his pitchfork and blood trickled down the prongs. He had killed the witch causing the storm. This story comes from villages in Zuid Holland and Utrecht.[27]
- *Heggemoeder or Heksenmoeder,* (Hedge Mother or Mother of Witches) is a nocturnal ghost who brings illness, especially fever. She has the power to remove illness as well (a less common occurrence). She was said to live in dense hazel hedges and was notorious for her hot pursuit of pregnant women. As a safety measure women often kept their stocking on in bed, one worn normally and one turned inside out. The fevers could be stopped by carving in peat and burning the relevant segment. The Heggemoeder would sit on the peat and this would break

the spell. People would carve their name in the peat or they would carve out one strip for each sickness day.[28]

- **Olde Marolde,** is both a witch and nightmare, from Drenthe, Overijsel and Gelderland. She flies naked through the air and steals children from their cradles. She gives people the flu. People would speak this verse to release her spell:

> *Olde Marolde,*
> *ik hebbe de kolde.*
> *Ik hebbe ze now.*
> *Ik gève ze ow.*
> *Ik bind em hier neer,*
> *ik krieg em neet weer.*

(Old Marold/I have the cold/I have it now/I give it now/I bind it down /I won't get it again)[29]

This verse would be recited circling an oak tree (or poplar, elder tree). The tree will shake as the illness is transferred and may even die. Another option is tying a piece of fabric to the tree.

Yet another way to transfer the illness is by making an incision in the bark of the tree and another under the nail of the patient. The blood of the person had to mix with the sap of the tree. Alternatively a nail was hammered into a tree – once the bark grows over the nail, the illness is cured or the broken bone mended.

In Gelderland sick people placed three knots in the branches of a willow tree. Before running off as fast as possible they would say:

> *Goé morgen olde,*
> *Ik geef oe de kolde;*
> *Goé morgen olde!*

(Good morning Old One, I give you the cold; Good morning Old One!)

The illness could also be transferred to an animal.[29] The name of the sick person could be carved in the peat before burning it. Other times the peat was carved with one tally for every day of sickness. Some burned the peat rather than burning it. Often the following words were used:

Koorts, koorts, ik ben niet thuis,
Ga maar naar een ander huis.
(Fever, fever I am not at home/ Go visit another house!)

There is an obvious resemblance to the English rhyme:

Rain rain go away,
Come again another day.

- *Tante Cor,* (Aunt Cor), was a 'white' (or virtuous) witch who lived on a street called Driehoekstraat in Amsterdam. She hid her black piercing eyes behind dark glasses. She offered services in fortune telling and dissolving evils spells (*curse unravelling* in contemporary shamanic terminology).[30]
- *Vaar-Köbke* was a man who sold his soul to the Devil, so he could work magic. His real name was Jacob Martens from Sittard in Limburg.[31]

White Woman, Wise Woman, Witch, Priestess, Prophetess

In 1660 a priest from Drenthe published a book titled '*Antiqueteiten van Drenthe*' and provided a fascinating description of the Witte Wieven. People visited them in their grave mounds to request healing, divination, assistance at childbirth or help in finding lost objects. This closely resembles the Nordic figure of the Volva or the Germanic Weleda (Veleda). Both sat on a raised platform and provided community services of a spiritual nature. Abe de Verteller[6] points out that there is also a close association with cats: Witte Wieven requested *balkenhaze* and the Vǫlva wore catskin gloves. He also links them to the Norns or threefold Goddess of Life and Death (maiden, mother, crone), as the Witte Wieven often appeared as threesomes. We now see connections to Mother Holle, the Queen of Witches and also to the Queen of Elves, to the Sidhe and other traditions of Northern and Western Europe.

Closing comment: *Geurkens* (Vorden, Gelderland) is a local name for the Witte Wieven. There was a figure called *Schele Guurte* (Cross-eyed Guurte), in Ulken, Gelderland. She was said to inhabit a grave mound called *de Guurtjesbelt*. Ceramic urns have been found here, called *ulkenpotten*.[32]

Activity #7

Undertake a journey or meditation to connect with the Witte Wieven. Use soul travel to visit a Hunnebed. More about Hunebedden in Chapter 8.

Chapter 8

Hunebedden: Giant Tomb or Cosmic Womb

Hunebedden, dolmens and passage graves

I am passionate about visiting Stone Age sites and will I travel long distances to visit them and sit out there, to gain spiritual experiences and revelations.

Speakers of Northern European languages are not always going to agree on words for the mysterious stone structures or megalithic monuments we find in the landscape. The following information was taken from the book *Een Paleis voor de Doden* by Herman Clerinx.[1]

The deliberate formation of large rocks that Dutch people call a Hunebed, are called een Riesengrab (Giant's Grave) in German.

Breton, the Celtic language of Brittany in France, gave us the term *menhir* (maen = stone + hir = long, long stone). It also gave us the word dolmen (taol or tol = tafel and maen or men = stone, therefore "table stone" or table-shaped stone formation). Essentially dolmens create an enclosed space.

When we find several menhirs together, often arranged in a geometric arrangement (most commonly a circle), Dutch people will speak of a *cromlech* (this is a contraction of two Old Celtic words: crom = bent or curved, lech = stone, curved stone). That is to say: to Dutch, French and German people it is!

However, English people refer to megaliths arranged in a round formation as "a stone circle" and to a *cromlech* as a *burial chamber*.

English people refer to hunebedden (plural) as *passage graves*. Check out my Rune Drum video at Lutra passage grave in Sweden.[2]

Origin of the word Hunebed

Over the centuries people have come up with an impressive list of possible explanations. The Dutch word hunebed literally translates as 'bed of a Hun'. One explanation is that they were created by The Huns (and therefore the 'beds of the Huns'). This leaves open the question whether that refers to a bed for sleeping or if it is a euphemism for a grave or final resting place.

The Huns were a nomadic people from Central Asia. They moved westward from Mongolia and established a vast, if short-lived, dominion in Europe, just outside the borders of the Roman Empire. They conquered the Goths and many Germanic peoples, under the leadership of King Attila. After his death in the year 453 CE they ceased to be a major threat and lost much of their empire. However, in folk memory they lived on as larger than life, in other words as *giants*.[3]

The English word giant (*reus* in Dutch) is a translation of the word Jǫtunn (Old Norse). There were the first beings to live in Midgard and are among the oldest beings we encounter in myths; they were there before the gods. Donar/Thor is often found 'in the East' fighting them. In many ways this is a poor translation because it evokes an image of beings large in size. Their powers are immense but their physical size isn't necessarily.

The German-Dutch preacher and medical doctor Johan Picardt[4] was the first classicist to write extensively about the hunebedden. He was one of the founders of the discipline of archaeology in the Netherlands.

He spoke of:

[*…gemene, barbaarse and wrede Reuzen, Huynen, Giganten…*] … "*mean, barbaric and cruel Ogres, Huns, Giants (…) who fear God nor human beings and were born solely to lead the human race to its demise.*"

-Johan Picardt (1600–1670) quoted by Herman Clerinx[3]

Dutch folklore offers many tales of giants using earthbound rocks as marbles and pelting huge rocks at each other. If you use your imagination some rocks appear to show the fingerprints, fists, or footprints of giants.

The discovery of *human* bones in the Hunebedden was explained as 'human beings having frightened off those giants/ Huns'. *(This contradicts the giant lore, but human beings like tidy explanations!)*

Some hunebedden are clearly visible but others are buried and form part of underground burial chambers. Sometimes they were buried under burial mounds created from stones piled on stones. (Such constructions are sometimes called cairns – here note that English cairns can also refer to far smaller piles of stones, often waypoints and route markers in the landscape).

[Voorst zijn in deze landen geëerd Lahra, Welda (. . .) Freja, Wodan: een schoon gezelschap....]

Once upon a time Lahra, Welda (...) Freja, Wodan were venerated here: fine company indeed! Satan must have 'laughed in his fist' (Dutch expression referring to gleeful laughter hidden by putting a hand in front of one's mouth, meaning: Satan must have gleefully congratulated himself) when he squeezed this filthy and wicked motley crew into the Netherlands and surrounding countries in order to be honoured with devotion, offerings and great respect. Velda (also known as Veleda or Weleda) is that darned witch, who made a big name for herself practising the black arts of divination and fortune telling as well demonic exorcism.[4]

-Passage from the Annales Drenthia (the annals of the province Drenthe in the Netherlands), 1660

The Danish author Saxo Grammaticus, one of our (biased) informants about Norse cosmology, already wrote about Danish passage graves in the thirteenth century. He posed the theory that they were created by giants and his theory remained in vogue until the eighteenth century. The German term: *Gräber für Riesen* means Graves for Giants.

In the area of Emsland, in Lower Saxony in Germany, hunebedden are known as Hünengräber, where gräber means graves and the word Hün means black, therefore "black graves". A synonym for *Hünengrab* (single) is *Großsteingrab* (Large Stone Grave).

Many cosmologies speak of giants walking the earth even before gods and humans arrived on the scene. Alternatively, they are linked to natural phenomena such as ice, mountains, rivers and lakes etc. The features in the landscape are then explained as have been created or caused by the activities and movements of giants. Sometimes giants are said to have played a ball game with rocks, or have engaged in a fight throwing boulders at each other – this explains the odd formations of earthbound rocks in Northern lands.[3]

In Norse cosmology we are told that the world as we know it was created from the body of primordial giant Ymir. His skull became our celestial dome, his blood our rivers, his bones our mountains – and so forth.

An alternative etymology for the word Hun exists. Some Dutch people claim that a hunebed is really a *henbedde* as *henne* is an old Dutch word for death. (The term *henneklaid* comes from the Dutch province Groningen and means *lijkwade* or *doodshemd*, both refer to the robe a dead person is laid out in). In that case Hunebedden are a place where we find ghosts and spirits but not giants.[5]

The hunebed by Steenbergen is called *Kalstenen* in one source. The word *kal* (which in the annals of Drenthe appeared as *kol*) could refer to a woman or witch. The Dutch word *toverkol* means witch and is the closest translation the Dutch language offers for the Swedish word *trollkvinna*, a woman who practices magic (and either *is* a troll or hangs out with trolls). This is a strong indication that the hunebedden were associated with supernatural women, (remember the *Witte Wieven*).[5]

Yet another interpretation is that *kallen* (perhaps related to the verb *calling* in English) means talking or speaking. The Hunebed of Eext used to be called De Stemberg or The Mound of Voices. This was during a period when the entire hunebed was situated underground. One stone mason pierced the ground with an iron staff in 1756. Spooky hollow sounds emanated from the burial chamber below (quite possibly acting as a sound box) The mason thought these sounds were voices. He stayed well clear after that and no more stones were collected from that site for decades.[6]

From the sixteenth century onward giants were demonized, along with heathen gods, elves, cobolds and related otherworld beings. When people spoke about giants – they were talking about demons or devils.

Some people viewed the cover slabs (table top stones) as altars. It was claimed that human sacrifices were made there. Especially strangers or foreigners were, we are told, forced to crawl down the narrow passageway under the 'altar stone'. While they did so they were groped and covered in excrement. There was animosity between the people of Drenthe and Brabant, meaning that de *Brabanders* (people from Brabant) lost their lives in the process. We may need to read the information more symbolically as describing an initiation or rite of passage instead. The accusation of human sacrifice is a sure-fire way of demonizing and discrediting another tribe or culture.[5]

Folk belief in Twente claims that babies came from the Hunebedden, posing a very interesting link between the Witte Wieven and Norns! It also paints an evocative picture of a passage grave as a womb or vulva.[5] On a related note, the name of the Dutch city of Hellemond means 'Mouth of Hel', indicating a portal in the landscape.

The hunebed of Gasteren appears on medieval maps as *Duvel's Kut,* literally: Devil's Cunt, in Latin Daemonis Cunnus.[7]

It is also claimed that Saint Boniface put a stop to such 'Heathen human offering rituals'.[8]

Things get even more fascinating and mysterious. The writings of Sicke Benninge from Groningen (around the year 1500) show that the Hunebed of Gasteren already then had the name 'Duvels Kolse'. This term refers to the *male* genitals.

The solution to the riddle is found in the field of etymology. Initially people thought that the word *kolse* was derived from *kul* (also the rude word *lul*, is cock or penis in Dutch). However, it is more probably that the word *kolse* is related to the Dutch word *kous*, meaning stocking. The word kous was, in the eastern provinces of the Netherlands at that time, also used to refer to the female genitals. In other words: Duvels Kut is exactly the same thing as Duvel Kolse and it refers to the hunebed at Gasteren.[7]

The Dutch word *kut* need to be interpreted in a broader sense, as a portal, an opening to a cave. The Dutch word spelunk is directly related to the contemporary English word spelunking, which means exploring caves. This portal or cave opening was seen as access to underground realms, the world of demons and evil spirits. The name was, possibly, allocated while the hunebed was only partially submerged in a mound and a small opening remained. According to archaeologists it is perfectly possible that several hunebedden had the name *Duvels Kut* or *Duyvels Kutte*, we only know this for sure about Gasteren.[7]

Mystery schools and other ancient wisdom traditions teach that liminal places such as grave mounds are places where the mysteries of Death meet the mysteries of Rebirth. These are dark places of transformation where Rites of Passage were often performed. This is why this chapter has the subtitle *giants' tomb or cosmic womb*. The heathen peoples of Old Europe perceived the earth literally as the body of a great goddess who is our Ultimate Mother, who births all beings and reabsorbs them back into herself at their time of death.

The Greek goddess Persephone was said to have been abducted by Hades, the ruler of the Underworld. Mystery school work I have done with groups of students indicates that Persephone had chosen to visit the underworld because she needed to leave the realm of her mother and be initiated into the mysteries of sexuality and death.

In a much earlier time entrances to caves and, indeed, graves, were seen as sacred openings in the body of the Great Goddess. In the human anatomy the pubic mound, especially in females, is the Mons pubis, Mons Venus, or Mons Veneris even today. However, in the medieval era even the goddess Venus was demonized. At birth we leave our human mother's body through the birth canal and in the moment of death we leave this human body behind and we are said to journey to the Afterlife 'moving through a tunnel'. Our body returns to Mother Earth, especially when we are buried but even when we are cremated and our ashes are spread in a location, we have a strong connection to.

Mystery schools commonly staged a symbolic death experience, just as tribal peoples do the same thing in the training of their shamans. When I started my own shamanic training in the UK,[9] I had to dig my own grave and I was buried alive for a night. This proves that this ancient tradition lives on in the twenty-first century!

Might it be the case that people ceremonially spent a night in a passage grave or hunebed to face death and emerge reborn the next day? That is the key principle: by looking Death in the eyes while we are still alive, we lose the fear of our personal death. We learn that Death is our sacred ally, because Death brings both focus and the courage to live life to the full. It punctures the illusion that we will live forever and therefore we can afford to put things off.

In this case the Duyvelskutte is a portal to the Other World. Christian priests worked hard to eradicate all references to heathen rituals and places. They often did this by substituting a Christianised version instead: churches were literally built on the sites of pagan temples or outdoor holy sites. Heathen festivals were replaced by Christian festivals in the wheel of the year: Christmas rather winter solstice and Yule. The feast of St John (In Dutch: Het St Jan's Feest) rather than the summer solstice. All Saints Day rather than Samhain or Hallowe'en –and so forth.

Het hunebed van Eext is also called *trutteveentie*. The contemporary Dutch word *trut* is a rude word or swear word. It refers to the vagina and it is used to denote an unpleasant person (not unlike calling a woman a *bitch* in English). Things get even more interesting: in addition to vagina, the old Dutch word *trut* also means *witch*![5]

Even the repulsive folk memory of covering people with faeces may be an echo from a long time ago when ritual humiliation was part of initiations and fertile 'dark goddess rituals'. We will never know if people were really put to death at Hunebedden because the accusation of committing human sacrifice is a tried and tested technique for devaluing and demonizing old religions that the conquering new religion no longer approves of.

Working with this material will always involve a meticulous stripping off, of layer after layer of Christian interpretation and demonization, not unlike using paint stripper to reveal the true shape and colour of an antique piece of furniture.

At a later time in Drenthe people claimed that babies came from Hunebedden. Perhaps this was something parents told their children, like babies being delivered by a stork or found in a cabbage patch. However, even such stories contain precious kernels of much ancient wisdom. The stork is related to Finno-Ugric myths that link the migration paths of swans and other birds to the journey of the soul made after death and a mysterious Summer Land. If babies were said to come from

Hunebedden this is a strong indication that fertility rituals were performed in these places once upon a time.

Up to the seventeenth century Dutch hunebedden were said to be haunted and people stayed well clear of them at night. Just as holy trees were cut down and the wood used to build churches, many of the cover stones of hunebedden were used as foundation stones for churches. Alternatively, they were used to build the brick wall enclosing a churchyard.

The same thing happened in Sweden. My husband and I often see rune stones cemented into church walls (e.g. at Bogsta Church, Södermanland) or leaning against dry stone walls in church yards. Abe wonders whether some of the power held in those stones was deliberately absorbed into the new cult places (Christian churches). I myself have wondered about a Wit Wief moving into a church along with an ancient slab![5]

At the time of writing there are two different theories about the original purpose of hunebedden. They are said to be passage graves, dating from about 5400 years ago, which hosted entire families. The problem with this interpretation is that some hunebedden have been excavated and no human bones have been found. Instead, we find a large amount of shards of pots.

The second theory is less popular. This makes the hunebedden Chambers of Initiation, community cult places for tribal Rites of Passages. If this theory is right people were not literally buried there, instead they had a mystical (symbolic) death experience, such as people experienced in dream incubation chambers (or asklepions) in Greece. In that case people spent the night there to receive visions and do intentional dreaming. They emerged wiser after having overcome their fear of death. This allowed them to take a new role and new responsibilities in their communities. A similar thing happened during the Eleusinian Mysteries.

There is a story, written down in 1845, from Wapserveen in the Netherlands. Here two old women are found, busy operating two golden spinning wheels. One farmer's hand wanted to provoke those ladies. He rode there on his horse and hollered:

Old wiefien platvoet, Komstoe mar oet; As 't kwaad doet.
Little Old Wife Flatfoot, come out if the (bullying) does any harm!

The old wives got very angry indeed. The farmer's hand rode off but they chased him and threw green bones at him. He reached the stable just in time but one of the green bones paralysed his unfortunate horse. Had the green bone struck the lad –he would not have lived to tell the tale. To modern ears this sounds nasty and disrespectful but remember that filters of misinterpretation may have been imposed. In its original form this story may well refer to an initiation or test of courage. By visiting a hunebed after dark a young man demonstrates his manliness and bravery.[10]

Following what we know about tribal initiations of teenage boys: this is how a boy proves himself an adult and gains privileges as well as responsibilities, such as the right to marry and start his own family. Here we can also observe closely how the White/Wise/Witty spinning woman becomes a haunting figure of night terrors over time.[11]

Activity #8 Sitting out!

Practice an ancient 'Nameless Art'[12]: visit a Megalithic monument or stone circle and sit out, for a few hours – or if you are brave, for a whole night! (If the thought makes you nervous, take a friend).

Make notes. Did you catch any glimpse of a spirit or supernatural being? Failing that, some whisps of mist?

Chapter 9

Heks – Hex – Sex

[In Friesland wordt verteld dat een heks zo koud als een steen in bed ligt, terwijl haar ziel op reis is. Verder heeft zij geen schaduw...]In Frisia stories are told about a witch lying stone cold in her bed while her soul is away travelling. Furthermore, she has no shadow.[1]

'I am she that is the natural mother of all things, mistress and governess of all the elements, the initial progeny of worlds, chief of powers divine, Queen of heaven, the principal of the Gods celestial, the light of the goddesses: at my will the planets of the air, the wholesome winds of the Seas, and the silences of hell be disposed; my name, my divinity is adored throughout all the world in divers manners, in variable customs and in many names, [...] Some call me Juno, others Bellona of the Battles, and still others Hecate. Principally the Ethiopians which dwell in the Orient, and the Egyptians which are excellent in all kind of ancient doctrine, and by their proper ceremonies accustomed to worship me, do call me Queen Isis.'
Lucius Apuleius, The Golden Ass[2]

The notorious period of witch-hunts in Early Modern Europe and Colonial North America occurred during the Early Modern period, meaning from about 1450–1750 CE. It spanned the upheavals of the Reformation and the Thirty Years' War and resulted in an estimated 35,000–100,000 executions. No one knows the exact death toll and historians do not appear to agree on estimates.

Some authors point out that the killing of witches started well before the year 1300, indeed, we have documented cases. It did not end in 1700, though the numbers had dropped significantly by then. Author Greg Laden says that a figure of 600,000 people would not shock him.[3]

The Wild Hunt was often mentioned in written accounts of witchcraft interrogations and this allows us to see variations in local beliefs.

In France the fertility aspect of a female Leader of the Wild Hunt was more evident, with the names Abundia and Satia on file. In Italy she was known as Befana, Befania or Epiphania, the latter name probably coming from the Christian festival of Epiphany, where ancient New Year's rites were still celebrated. In some places, including England, the leader of the Hunt was male, and known as Herne the Hunter (in Windsor), Herlechin (sometimes spelt Herlequin, Harlequin, Hellequin or Hillikin), Herla, Berchtold, Berholt, Berndietrich and sometimes Hackel, Odin or Wuotan.[4]

One brutal but little-known fact is that an admission made, even under torture, allowed the local law enforcers to confiscate all your property, which appeared to almost act as a 'bonus' or bounty for a conviction in so far as people profited from it.

Over the centuries, the Witch has stood accused of many things: committing acts of black magic (against human beings, animals and crops alike), nocturnal flights in order to attend witches Sabbaths, making a pact with the Devil, perverted sex or orgies and last but not least cannibalism (eating the corpses of new born babies). It is an impressive list of accusations.

However, it is not true that witch hunts or trials did not exist before the year 1350. The following account is related in Charles MacKay's Witch Mania: The History of Witchcraft:[3]

This passage describes the genocide of the people living in a particular part of northern Europe. They were the people of Stedinger. "The Stedinger were settlers, mostly from Holland, who opened up marshy land next to Friesland, on the Weser. For refusing to pay tithes to the Archbishop of Bremen, a crusade was preached against them and they were wiped out in 1234.

The Hebrew Scriptures addressed witchcraft, including Exodus 22:18 and various verses in Leviticus and Deuteronomy, before the Christian Era. In about 200-500 CE. the Talmud described forms of punishments and execution for witchcraft.[4]

The general idea was (or became) that powerful magic could only be worked with the assistance of the Devil or demonic beings. Through a pact with the Devil special powers and favours could be obtained: sex, riches, worldly power and knowledge.

One Dutch word for witches is *nachtvrouwen*: women of the night. In folklore they were perceived as elves or faeries who came visiting at night.[5] Like all supernatural creatures they could choose to either bring blessings or do harm, so they needed appeasing with offerings.

The Witch as 'a Sexy Bitch'

As soon as we start talking about witches, we enter an ambivalent realm of opposites and blatant contradictions:

- Healer – Person who intentionally harms others.
- Ugly old woman – associated with ecstasy and mind-blowing sex.
- The cast-out or loner, living on the edge of the village – supposedly one of many attending witches' sabbats together.
- Miracle worker – someone who kills people, animals and blights the harvest.
- Medicine Woman or Herbalist (forerunner of our modern doctor) – Poisoner.
- Midwife – Said to use the fat of dead babies in her foul salves.

Reading the transcripts from the period of the Inquisition of witchcraft trials the modern mind reels with disbelief: flying on broomsticks, sleeping with the Devil, performing miracle cures? Yet women, as well as men, in a smaller number, and even children as young as seven – nine years old, were burnt at the stake for these actions or socio-religious crimes. *What is going on here?*

A very brief history of witchcraft

The period of witch hunts and executions that we have all heard about occurred in Europe from the 1500s to the 1700s. This could give the impression that a fear of witches, witchcraft and black magic did not exist until Christianity became the dominant religion in Europe. This impression is far from correct.

> *Magic, involving sacrifices, symbols and incantations, was seen as necessary in sustaining the equilibrium so essential to human survival. Many cultures used it in rituals to placate or enlist the help of supernatural forces. In the wrong hands, however, magic was deemed to have terrible potential for causing human suffering and cosmic disturbance.*[6]

The issue of *wrong hands* is primarily a matter of perspective. Psychologists commonly recommend that we see people and their behavior as separate things. Others will say that actions speak louder than words and that we need to 'walk our talk'. In many spiritual belief systems radical and far-reaching responsibility for one's own thoughts/actions and impact on others and the Earth is a key principle.

Magic, here defined as *working closely with spirits to gain greater control over nature, the weather, animals and human beings (and therefore our own destiny),* was for millennia closely entwined with the fields of both medicine and religion.

Our youngest son asked me recently: 'What exactly is the

difference between witches and shamans?' That is a good question! Shamans use altered states of consciousness and soul flight to access the spirit world and bring back healing and guidance for their tribe or community. They merge with animals and often wear sacred costumes to facilitate this work: antlered headdresses were common in the Neolithic period (c. 10,000 – 7000 BCE). I explain this in a 2019 TV program about Mesolithic site Star Carr in the Mystic Britain series for the Smithsonian Museum.[7]

In that period agriculture replaced hunting and people started leading more settled lives. Where shamans may have been the leaders of the tribe in an earlier time, a larger number of people permanently living close together in settlements necessitated a different kind of leadership. This set the scene for structures we have today: organized religion, politics and law enforcement.

People in ancient Babylonia believed in witchcraft. The word alchemy, still used today comes from *Kemet* (Black Land, an old word for Egypt referring to the fertile black soil of the Nile Valley).[8] The German word for witch, Hex (Dutch: Heks) may just be related to the ancient cult of the goddess Hecate. The Old Testament informs us that Egyptian priests could cast down their staffs and have them transform into serpents.[9] The Oracle of Delphi had a priestess called the Pythia or Pythoness.

The Ancient Greeks believed in *daemons,* meaning spirits acting as intermediaries between deities and humans. Our word demon is derived from this but has acquired an exclusively sinister meaning over the centuries. Thessaly in Greece became a hotbed of witchcraft and the Thessalian witches remain notorious until today.

Arabian mythology speaks of ghouls as evil spirits said to haunt cemeteries and eat human flesh. The bible describes Jesus driving out a group of demons at Gadarenes, described in the Gospel of Mark. Possession by demons is often associated with witchcraft, where both witches and their supposed victims are described as *satanically possessed*.[10]

> *The New Testament, Galatians 5:19 – 20 includes witchcraft among the 'works of the flesh'; alongside fornication, uncleanness, lasciviousness, idolatry, strife, sedition heresies. This might seem to place witchcraft in the sordid and outlandish context of the 'satanic orgy' as denounced by later Christian writers.*[10]
>
> *Bishop Peter Binsfield, a sixteenth-century German theologian and demonologist identified the seven demons corresponding with the seven deadly sins: Lucifer – pride, Mammon – greed, Asmodeus – lust, Leviathan – envy, Beelzebub – gluttony, Satan – wrath, Belthegor – sloth*[10]

The Latin word strix, meaning owl, was used by classical writers for a type of witch possessing the ability to shape shift into an owl. It lives on as *strega* in Italian.

It is clear that there have been magical practitioners for as long as there have been human beings.

Of miracles and magic

When I first started my own training in core shamanism and did case studies in shamanic healing, I encountered the magic of miracles. Healing work was not something I was planning to dedicate my life to (I did the training because I wanted to become a better painter of other worlds!) but observing so many miracles occur definitely changed the direction of my life. (It also changed my social life because some people decided I had lost the plot and gone off with the fairies while others could not stop asking me questions about the ultimate nature of the universe).

The church fathers and priests of early Christianity in Europe faced a great dilemma: how were they going to explain the difference between Jesus performing miracles in the gospels, including miracles performed by legitimate priests in the name of Christ, and the magic worked by pagan witches and wizards, cunning women and sorcerers. Ever since, they have worked hard to eradicate perceived pagan superstitions and the belief in the supernatural power of witches. Not just that, they imposed a filter of perception which remains active today: those magical workings were said to come *from the Devil*.[11]

This in turn meant that curative magic (healing) underwent a process of Christianization. Churches were built on ancient and long-venerated sites. Many monks and nuns became learned herbalists and monasteries had medicine plant gardens. Magic talismans, charms and amulets were banned but a thriving trade blossomed in *relics*: objects associated with saints who had performed miracles. Pilgrims could now purchase bottles of holy water or stone scrapings from statues. Churches took pride in gruesome trophies: bones of martyrs, vials of blood liquefying and coagulating again on special occasions.

If a person deeply embedded in non-Western culture looks at all this, I am sure that they will not see much, if any, difference between pagan magic and church magic.

Witches' Sabbats and/or Wild Tales

Any person who has experience of working with altered states of consciousness (albeit through drugs, transcendental meditation or using shamanic techniques such as drumming and journeying/intentional dreaming) will understand that these accounts describe experiences *narrated from states of magical or altered consciousness* rather then from everyday consciousness and events).

To achieve ecstasy a person needs to either fall asleep or enter an altered state of consciousness. This allows the soul to leave his or her body. The obvious problem is that when a soul really and fully leaves our body, *we die*. Therefore, this must be an over-simplification. The Northern Tradition (working with students I refer to this body of work as *the Old Norse Anatomy of Soul*) is more specific about this: the human soul is viewed as having four, seven or nine aspects, of which the physical body (*lik*) is one, the soul encloses the body – not the other way around, and the *hamr* is the energetic or astral body. When this "is moving about", in either the dream state or through deliberate intention, this is called *hamnfarir*: shape travel or astral travel, considered a sacred art and highly skilled activity. Dutch authors will sometimes refer to this as De Dubbel (The Double)[1] because it looks just like the everyday self, to people with the gift of sight. It can also be manipulated to appear in a different way, often in animal form. There are many examples in the Norse Eddas and sagas about magical people walking around in animal form.

[Een vrijer op Terschelling krijgt van zijn vrienden te horen dat zijn lief een kol is...]
A boyfriend on the island of Terschelling is warned by friends that his girlfriend is a "kol" (toverkol: hag, witch). He decides to drop in late at night and finds her in deep sleep. He can't rouse her. He observes a mouse climbing into her mouth and a moment later she wakes up. Another time he finds her asleep in her chair and a huge spark from her firepan leaps into her mouth. She sighs deeply and awakens. The boyfriend has seen enough: she is a wicked witch! [1]

These are just examples. Witches commonly take the form of a dog, frog, fly or even a spider. We all know that witches have familiars, most famously a black cat. The animal is perceived as a helper and exists, in corporeal form, in everyday reality. Witches are also said to send animals out on tasks, often a hare, for example, to steal milk or butter from the neighbours. If someone shoots the hare – a witch is found dead the next morning. Here remember de *balkenhaas* – really a cat.

The soul of a witch could get into the milk churn and work her magic on the butter. She could then steal the butter and ensure that the milk in the churn did not turn to butter. A tried and tested remedy is to then stick a red-hot scythe or horse shoe into the churn. The next day the witch will be marked by burns or stabbing wounds.[1]

These missions are not always benign: a cat falling asleep on the face of a baby can suffocate the child (but was the cat really sent by a witch or is the family looking for someone or something to blame?) This example shows how a more magical collective consciousness has its own shadow side: *superstition and accusation*, pointing a finger because someone must be responsible for the fatal accident or blighted harvest. In modern times we attribute such experiences to bad luck, an accident, a highly unfortunate constellation of circumstances or bad weather, being in the wrong place at the wrong time and so forth.

In Dutch we also find the concept of *Kattendansen* (Cats' Dances) where a group of witches gets together to make merry, feast and dance. In the stories these feasts often end very abruptly, because a brave farmer or boyfriend appears and hurts the cats with either a knife or boiling water. The next day certain women and girls in the area have wounds in the places on their body where the cats were hurt.[1]

Dutch folklore informs us that witches can even be found in inanimate objects. The notorious toverkol Grietje Hollemand uit Broek in Waterland took up residence in a candle. Someone made a cut in the candle with a knife and the next morning Grietje sported a deep cut on her nose.

The most timeless image of a witch on the move is of course of her flying her broomstick to a Witches' Sabbat. Often, she is said to use flying ointment and to leave the house through the chimney on her night flight.

Carlo Ginzburg coined the term *oneiric events* (events happening in the realm of dreams) and points out that we possess only 'hostile testimonies', originating from or filtered by demonologists, inquisitors and judges. And that with the end of the persecutions, the Sabbath dissolved.[12]

> *The attempt to attain knowledge of the past is also a journey into the world of the dead*
> -Carlo Ginzburg[13]

Christianity was not always the dominant religion in power: as the second century CE proceeded, Christians were accused of horrible crimes: bestial cults, cannibalism, incest, infanticide[14]...

Abe de Verteller points outs that the means of transport used by witches is not limited to broomsticks along: egg shells, mussel shells and butterdishes, to mention but a few. To this I myself will add that art from Scandinavia and the Baltic states commonly shows witches flying on a distaff.[1]

[Over varen in eierschalen wordt al geschreven in de 17e eeuw. In een schrijfsel uit 1657 staat ...]
Sea journeys where eggshells are used as boats are described in the 17th century. One text from 1657 informs us that: "Many people believed that witches could cross the English Channel, from Calais to Dover, using eggshells and a fine needle. This belief lived on in the area called De Groninger Ommelanden well into the 19th century. This is the reason why eggshells always had to be crushed – to stop witches from using them to sail to England. [Author's note: the needle was used as a quant pole, think of punting!][1]

In Flanders (Belgium) we even find a story about a wicked witch paddling across the North Sea in an eggshell. Unfortunately, her eggshell vessel was destroyed by a crowd, meaning that the hag could not leave and that is how Evil reached our country! Lesson learned: do not throw out eggshells – burn them instead to make them useless to witches!

In Friesland, hekses were called *tjoensters* and said to sail all the way to the East Indies in eggshells. Therefore, if you are afraid of witches, throw eggshells in water and they will (hopefully) paddle off. Frisian witches from Molkwerum were said to gather and sail in milk cans to Spain to attend a feast or Sabbat, once again using a needle as a quant pole to propel themselves.

One woman from Schiedam was burned at the stake because she sailed around in a mussel shell and ensured that the fisherman caught stones rather than herring in their nets.[1]

Witches were said to gather at former execution sites in the form of cats; to fly on a large wheel, in a nutshell (which turns into a full-sized ship as soon as it reaches the water) or even on a small bunch of straw!

The most common destinations for Dutch wayfaring witches were Spain, England and Cologne in Germany (for its wine cellars). Wine cellars as destinations also appear in the accounts of the *Benandanti* in Italy. Spain was seen as an exotic country where oranges dropped off the trees and in this context, we need to remember that St. Nicholas (Chapter 11) arrives from the same magical place! England may have been associated with angels and heavenly beings across the water. The Dutch word for England: Engeland, translates as the Land of Angels.[1]

Children's song about sailing to England
Witte zwanen, zwarte zwanen
wie gaat er mee naar Engeland varen?
Engeland is gesloten
de sleutel is gebroken.
Is er dan geen timmerman
die de sleutel maken kan?
Laat doorgaan
laat doorgaan
wie achter is moet voorgaan!

White swans, black swans
Who joins us sailing to England?
England is closed
The key is broken
Isn't there a carpenter
Who can fix the key?
Let others pass
Let others pass
Those at the back now need to lead from the front!

The Byzantine historian Procopius of Caesarea[15], wrote, arguably, his most famous passage in the Gothic Wars, around 552–553 CE. He describes an island called Brittia, where the inhabitants of certain fishing villages, located on the ocean's shore right opposite Brittia, perform a sacred service. The destination of souls of the dead is the island of Brittia and the inhabitants of coastal villages face the task of ferrying them across:

> The men who know that they must go and do this work during the night, relieving those who did it before them, as soon as darkness falls withdraw to their houses and go to sleep, waiting for someone who will come and call them for that task. Later in the night: knocks on the door. They jump out of bed and go to the edge of the sea.
> On the shore they find special empty boats. When they climb into them, the boats sink almost to the surface of the water (as if heavily laden). They begin to row and after +/- 1 hour they arrive in Brittia (normally the voyage lasts a night and a day). After disembarking their passengers they depart with light ships. They have not seen anyone, save for a voice that informs the boatmen of the social rank of the passengers, the names of their fathers, and in the case of the women, the name of their husband.[15]

This is an extraordinary passage: did common people, not trained 'shamans', commonly perform psychopomp work in a more magical era? Does that mean that we all carry the soul conductor archetype within our psyche and that there were more psychopomps in our ancestral lineage than we realise?

Christian magic

I have, over years of reading in about twenty languages, developed the following view:

Before Christianity became the dominant religion in Europe, a process followed by both secularization and advent of the contemporary scientific worldview, evolving over several centuries, a more magical (from our 21st century point of view) collective consciousness was the norm.

This had beautiful aspects: people commonly believed in miracles and, arguably, miracles were more common because the collective mindset was open to this! It meant that many people believed in healing and divine intervention at a time when people had no access to anything *resembling* medical care as we know it today You could say that it was more common for people to be engaged in a *collective visionary experience.*[16] We can also argue that modern life still offers many miracles – but we have been conditioned not to recognize them as such. Both an airplane and a washing machine, for example, are miracles, and so is the gigantic drop in infant mortality, the percentage of women surviving childbirth, in Western culture.

It also had a shadow side, which was equally powerful: superstition, finger pointing, blaming and shaming, lynching and execution of scapegoats.

Things came to a head when Europe became Christianized because the Church actively and forcefully decided to stamp out any and all manifestations of magic and magical thinking. At the same time, confusingly, the Church very much practiced its own forms of magic: from teaching transubstantiation to creating a pilgrimage culture of holy relics and people seeking the intercession of saints (who replaced earlier pagan deities, and often with only a thin gloss of veneer).

The consequences of this were *not only bad*. There was a time where the medical profession, as we know it today, did not exist. There was also a time when law enforcement, again as we know it in democratic countries today, did not exist. Law was an unpredictable thing: meted out by local land owners or chieftains. These people were rarely impartial because their top priority was guarding their own wealth, status and privilege in the local community.

One fact is that the Church built churches on ancient sacred sites. This made them keepers of both wells (the water now used for baptism), sacred trees etc. As the collective mindset shifted and people forgot about these places of pre-Christian worship, the clergy became the keepers and caretakers. All over Northwestern Europe such sites have a mix of heathen and Christian memories and energies today. We don't know whether those sites would have survived without Christian guardians.

A related issue was the earlier heathen concept of feuds and revenge. The Viking Code of honour (but please note that this was not only a Viking phenomenon) demanded that people seek restitution. Here is where our phrase 'an eye for an eye', or 'a tooth for a tooth' comes from. This principle is called the Law of Retaliation and it means that a person who has injured another person is to be penalized to a similar degree, and the person inflicting such punishment should be the injured party.[17]

The problem is that the cycle of violence never ends (in our day think of Mafia or gangland killings) because there is always a new injured party: you killed my sister, therefore I kill your brother – but then your sister feels forced to save her honour and take action by ordering her husband to kill... etc.

The Church was desperate to put a stop to these cycles of violence. This is in part where our concept of forgiveness comes in. It is also where our modern concept of law enforcement dawns. A neutral and impartial body takes care of crime solving and punishment so the collective can step back and trust that (at least that is the concept in its utopian form). However, in some cases a convicted serial killer or paedophile have served their sentence and are released back into the community. Some people argue that 'a person who has taken a human life' should never go free in the community again. Not only because they will almost certainly re-offend (no one ever *heals* in prison or from psychopathy) but also because they are enjoying privileges their victims will never have again: breathing, walking the earth, food and drink, sex, freedom of choice and movement. Not just that, they will almost certainly re-offend.

This brings us to another controversial topic at our own time: the death sentence. Some hardline people feel that once a person has killed another person in cold blood (no self-defense and no mitigating factors) that person has forfeited their right to live.

Please note that I am not promoting these viewpoints, I am only saying that I observe them around me today. And now I ask my readers to take one moment to connect that way of thinking to the era of the witch hunts.

Another shadow piece is that the Church, the very institution speaking for forgiveness and breaking cycles of violence, has been responsible for the execution of a mind-boggling number of people – so even the Church has presented a double face. There is also an undeniable connection between the Church and child abuse: pederast priests committing crimes with the children in their spiritual care.[18]

My point is this: unless we time travel and 'climb into the mindset' of the period we are discussing/studying, insofar as we are able, we are not going to get to the bottom of what was going on there. I offer the following *personal* reflections to get this process rolling for my readers:

- At a time of a more magical collective consciousness (and therefore a time of superstition) people (especially poorly educated people who may have been illiterate) did not think the way people with a Western education do today.

- In the magical world perception there is not the clear-cut delineation between 'this world and other worlds', or 'external world and internal fantasy world' we apply today. People were not taught, in school, to make those distinctions.

- Psychotropic substances we classify as drugs today (e.g. poison plants, psychedelic mushrooms) were in common use. There was not yet a clear distinction between herbalism and mainstream medical care. Healers routinely used potions, salves and ointments made from plants, some of them baneful.

- The collective worldview (shared cosmology) heavily promoted a belief in witchcraft. The sudden death of a (previously healthy) cow or a blighted harvest must be someone's fault – we must identify that person and make him or her pay!

- Along with magic and the belief that magic could be used to cause harm, or even death, to people, animals or property came the belief in ways of countering this. In Dutch accounts of witchcraft we find many references to a witch in jail being asked to *onttoveren* a person or animal. This means lifting the magic, cancelling it out, so the person/animal/situation returns to normal. Obviously, there were limits: a blighted harvest could not be returned to a good harvest by a witch speaking a formula of *onttovering*.

- Disenfranchised and marginalized people often had no recourse to settle matters or seek a primitive form of justice, other than resorting to witchcraft, spells and cursing, often referred to as Maleficium: An act of witchcraft performed with the intention of causing damage or injury.[19]

- In a collective mindset where everyone in the village thinks along similar lines, the threshold for magical conversations is much lower. In our time many 'spiritual' people tell me that it is a relief to be with kindred spirits, because they can speak freely about their beliefs and experiences without being ridiculed. The flip side of that is a culture where everyone is always looking to identify witches as scapegoats for the occurrences in village life: a stillborn baby, a cow dropping dead, a hail storm destroying a field of wheat. This would create a permanent and pervasive atmosphere of suspicion and gossip. Those of us who enjoy the anonymity of big city life today cannot begin to comprehend the mindset of malicious village gossip. We may not even know our neighbours by name! Yet, in a different era, having a black cat might have marked us as a witch and the comings and goings of our cat would be observed as closely as our own movements.

Dutch witches were said to train up their daughters. Some accounts of Dutch witch trials are, frankly, hair-raising: a mother and her twelve-year old daughter (Heylken Brycken) travel to a witches' Sabbath together where they both engage in *boeleren met de duivel* (having sexual intercourse with the Devil). The girl describes in lurid detail how the penis of the devil is as cold as metal. Our modern mindset offers no lens of perception for mollifying or reframing this.[20]

What I will do, therefore, is apply a shamanic lens of perception. At a time where no legal line had yet been drawn between healers and doctors, between poisons and medicine, many women with large families were their own family doctors and nurses: they picked herbs, dealt with injuries and accidents to everyone from family members to farm animals. They would, indeed, have trained up their daughters as healers and midwives (we cannot project the 21st century ambition to erase sexism and value gender diversity onto those days) in these medical ways and been assisted by them. I can quite easily image a scenario where mother and daughter make ointments together involving psychotropic plants (and other substances) and entering a joined altered state of consciousness.

My third book[21] explores how the human imagination is our interface with other worlds. Not only that, we participate in the co-creation of those realms through our thoughts, words and mental images. Now imagine a magic-focussed village culture where even children are steeped in supernatural tales. Someone died unexpectedly – who did that? You all know H.; you hear adults whisper about her attending a Witches' Sabbat. On Sundays you attend Church and you hear the priest rant against witchcraft and all things wicked. Of course, you and other children work out what the women talk about when they think the kids are not listening. Rural children living in crowded hovels would grow up with sex happening in close quarters, not enjoy their own bedroom, as many Western children do today. Could all of those things together create an atmosphere were mother and daughter 'get high' together and entered a shared alternate reality where both accounts match? Without a modern education (likely without *any* modern-style education) they would not necessarily make the distinction between 'real' and empirically proven or having happened in a trance state.

Here we also need to remember that those times lacked an Age of Reason, laws against child labour, child detention facilities (as different from adult prisons or jail) etc. The Western concept and privilege of giving children a proper carefree childhood has always depended on wealth, social status and education. Then, as now, underprivileged parents are less able to guard their children from the harsh realities of life. We must not project our concept and ambitions of modern childhood onto those times. Children worked from a young age, older children looked after younger children while parents did paid work, and so forth. Some families may just have considered hiring out their teenage daughters for sex a more acceptable fate than starvation for the whole family. We cannot judge people as long as we have not faced their ordeals. Also: the statistics for occurrences of child sexual abuse are staggering today. Tragically, we have no reason to believe that they would have been lower throughout other periods in history.

The idea that the witches' potions induced hallucinations seems worth considering, accounting as it does for some of these strange beliefs. Some plants sometimes associated with such potions, like deadly nightshade (belladonna), henbane, mandrake and jimsonweed, are indeed known to contain hallucinogenic chemicals called tropane alkaloids.[22]

In his fascinating book, Veneficium, Daniel Shulke explains how certain poison plants are associated with specific phenomena:

Henbane's pharmacology, application for sorcery: it is indeed more suited to shape-shifting spells involving the transmogrification of man into beast.[23]

Aconite, along with poison hemlock and nightshade plants such as belladonna, is also frequently identified with medieval witches flying ointments[24]

Chemical experiments have proved that the poisons of the two hemlocks [C. maculatum and *Cowbane*, Cicuta virossa] especially coniine, taken in small doses and rubbed into the skin, can produce the sensation of gliding through the air.[25]

Common Accusations leveled at witches

- *Necromancy*: raising the dead. Divides into two different kinds of magic:
  - Sciomancy means raising the disembodied spirit of the

deceased by mediumistic means.

- Necyomancy is the re-animation of dead tissue (less common than sciomancy).[26]
- Night flight or night travelling, of which the most famous example are the Italian benandanti, who waged a magical battle for the fertility of crops (this work is closely related to The Wild Hunt).
- Attending nocturnal rites, such as a Witches' Sabbat, also known as a 'Satanic Orgy'.[27]
- They were said to gain their powers from a personal pact with the Devil.
- Cannibalism and child sacrifice, "passing newborn babies through a fire and using the resulting ashes as a magical ingredient".[28]
- Lustful witches would put spells on men to win their affections – they also took revenge by making men impotent and women infertile.
- They worked against Christian society by inspiring lustful thoughts, causing storms, plagues, sickness and death.
- Causing crop blighting or crop failure, of cornfields, vineyards and orchards – Schulke speaks of a curious relationship between witches, grain and the Devil and a so-called Devil's Tithe, also known as the Devil's Portion in rural England.[29]
- Making flying ointments and other salves or ointments with psychotropic properties.[29] Shulke speaks of an Inverse Field, where shadow grains exist, meaning the sinister or toxic plants of field or meadow (and add to the witches' pharmacopoeia). Think of Darnel or Ergotism/ St Anthony's Fire). Here one also needs to make a mental link to the sacramental loaf in the Christian mystery tradition, which clearly builds on fertility traditions of a much earlier (Neolithic) time.[29]
- Impure, licentious, scandalous behavior, using a

human body in ways that society forbids through both social control and larger controlling (ruling/authority) structures as well as using the bodies of others (especially body parts of corpses exhumed at cemeteries) in ways that violate all social rules.

- Antisocial behavior: breaking rules and social boundaries, challenging or disobeying authority figures (Swedish accounts from the Trolldom or folk magic tradition offer rituals for actively placing oneself outside the reach of the Church).[30]
- Playing the Insider-Outsider card: appearing to be loner living on the periphery of society yet being a secret member of a coven or collective attending sabbats and *Cats' Dances*.
- Deceiving people, by pretending to be something they are not, or even moving one step beyond that: actively affecting (changing) other people's perception on reality and take on events.
- Seemingly being in service to the forces of chaos, or worse, being guided or possessed by evil spirits.

Albrecht Dürer

It has been claimed that the German artist Albrecht Dürer painted witchcraft scenes, for instance 'The Secrets of the Witch Riding the Goat Backwards'.[31] However, please note that Albrecht Dürer did *not* give the artwork this title, it was assigned by some historian (the artist in me shudders!) Dr. Elizabeth Garner explains that this woman is *not* a witch and that Witches in medieval prints were not depicted nude at this time except by one of Dürer's apprentices, Hans Baldung Grien, who built his reputation based on printing erotic themes.

Sabbath

Shulke's describes the Witches' Sabbat:

In addition to crossroads, caves and forests, the meadow, as a general feature, is mentioned in medieval witchcraft lore as a place where the Witches' Sabbat itself takes place. According to the Spanish Inquisition, Aquelarre was both the name for the Sabbat of the Basque witches, and the place of their gathering. Inquisitors derived the word from aker, a male goat and larre, a meadow, but it may originally have been alkelarre, or 'the meadow of alka', the local name for the Dactylis hispanica, a poisonous cock's foot grass known in the area. Likewise the notorious Swedish witches of Mora held their assembly at Blåkulla, a place described by their inquisitors as a 'delicate large meadow, whereof you can see no end'.[32]

Wise woman or wicked witch

In our day and age many attempts have been made to put a different gloss on witches: they were wise women, medicine women, herbalists, midwives saving the lives of mothers and babies. Before I did a vast amount of reading on the topic, I too idealised my 'witch ancestors' (and still *honour* them but I am better informed today).

It has become popular to self-identify as a witch. A spiritiual teacher colleague once reminded me that a few decades ago huge debates raged in the US about *who is actually entitled to call themselves a witch* but some Moon Books author colleagues have started a literary genre called Witchlit, sparked off by a Twitter post (of all things)!

I admit that I dream of living in the forest in Sweden as full time Forest Witch. Of working with the materials presenting themselves: plants, trees, bark, animal bones, berries and skulls[32] –but can anyone call themselves a witch? Today's answer is yes! We live in a democracy with free speech but *calling yourself a witch will not make you a witch!* The equivalent in the field (controversially) known as *shamanism* is someone attending a weekend workshop, calling themselves a *shaman*, then making themselves a website to promote their services. (Even worse, I get regular emails from strangers saying: 'unlike you I did not need to train in shamanism, I just know what to do intuitively! But could you please answer some burning questions I have...')

These examples immediately flesh out a timeless continuum active until today: absolutely any field or profession has practitioners ranging from the sublime to the downright dangerous. This is why we need to operate discernment before we put ourselves in the hands of any professional. Therefore, we can neither say that the witches of the past (any time in the past) were *all wise women who had no desire other than healing and benefiting their communities* nor that *all of them were wicked witches breeding evil and spreading chaos, harming and killing.* Witchcraft has the power to do both. At any one time in human history witches have resorted to doing all of those things. There is no such thing as a binding Code of Ethics all witches subscribe to.

Horned God or horny Devil

In the Neolithic period a transition occurred from hunter-gatherer tribes to agriculture and larger groups of people living together in permanent settlements or villages.

Reading any description of the Devil always brings to my mind images of an earlier Fertility God. In the Stone Age this was a Master of Animals responsible for releasing or if taboos were violated, withholding, game. With agriculture a new set of deities arrived, embodying the seed and harvest. Animist thinking understands that Life requires exchange and reciprocity. Taking without giving back creates imbalances. In that respect western culture can learn a very great deal from earlier or more 'primitive' societies. We have reached a dangerous level of imbalance. Our planet is teetering on the brink of mass destruction. Mass extinction is already occurring and, at the time of writing, Australia was burning, closely followed by Covid-19 shutting down the Western world.

The people of Old Europe would undoubtedly have perceived events and people as either 'good' or 'bad', just as we do today. However, the Church imposed a very heavy overlay of duality with divine personifications: an omnipresent good God and a Devil out to destroy Creation.

The green man or vegetation god of a previous era had to be killed and resurrected. The grain is harvested to feed the community and new seeds are sown. The Norse god Freyr is said to be a fertility god (often depicted with an erect phallus) but he was also given Alfheim (the realm of the elves) as a tandgåva, Swedish for 'tooth gift' (when he cut his first tooth). The elves are intimately connected to the Cult of the Male Ancestors.[33]

Just as every single mother goddess also has a death goddess manifestation, even Aphrodite has her dark counterpart in the Dove Goddess of Dodona,[34] every male fertility god has both a horny side and death-followed-by-resurrection aspect. The moment that the sacred cycle of life-death-rebirth was no longer understood, a more sinister and dualistic perception comes into being: an 'only good' son of God who is crucified on a cross and the saviour of human beings, matched by a Devil who is 'darkness personified' and who leads human beings into temptation and sin.

Just as the sacrament of the host carries echoes of an earlier grain cult, Jesus dying on the cross carry's echoes of earlier vegetation gods who died so our world would have nourishment and seeds for another harvest. And the force that tribal or pre-Christian people refer to as Spirit or spirits becomes The Holy Ghost.

The best-known of night-travelling sorcerers in European history are the benandanti of the Italian Friuli, who waged magical war for the fertility of the fields. According to Ginzburg the Ossetian burkudzauta maintained that they fought on the 'meadows of the beyond' to 'wrest the shoots of wheat from the souls of the dead'.[35]

The role children played in European witch trials

In the year 1669 a staggering 85 people were executed in the small town of Mora, in central Sweden, for allegedly seducing 300 children and spiriting them away to Satanic Sabbats. The hysteria was started by teenagers, a 15-year-old boy who accused a 17-year-old girl of stealing children 'for Satan'.

The teens and their circle were interviewed individually and all gave the same account of being snatched from their beds. Some children spoke of a white angel appearing to rescue them and explaining that 'this was happening because of the wickedness of people'. Those children named 70 witches in all and 15 of those witches were *children*. The accused were rounded up and interrogated under torture.

The witches said they would meet at a gravel pit by a crossroads where they put vests on their heads and danced "round and round and round about." They went to the crossroads and summoned the Devil to take them to an imaginary place called Blockula. According to one account the Devil "generally appeared as a little old man, in a grey coat, with red and blue stockings, with exceedingly long garters. He had a high-crowned hat, with bands of many-colored linen enfolded about it, and a long red beard that hung down to his middle."[37]

The witches said the Devil carried them all away on the backs of horses, asses, goats and monkeys, over the tops of houses, to Blockula, a house with a gate in an infinite green meadow. In a pledge to service of the Devil, the witches cut their fingers and wrote their names in their own blood in his book (see Devil's Pact).[36]

The Mora case remains notorious today and similar things happened in the Low Countries. The role children played in all this is deeply disturbing. Today few people read any material in its original form and opinions are often based on trends and posts, often biased personal opinions, featured on social media. To understand the matters at the heart of this book, we need to read transcripts of witch trials, academic papers and well-researched books.[37]

It is worth pointing that that people feared witches even beyond their physical death. This is why stories abound of driving stakes through a heart (more commonly applied to vampires) and performing rituals to keep the witch *out* of the community and *gone forever.*

A Dutch recipe for Flying Ointment

For those of you who speak Dutch, Abe de Verteller offers a 15th century recipe for flying ointment, possibly written by Johannes van Alphen (Latinised to Joannes Alphensis), written in Middle Dutch.[38] He explains that this recipe does not contain any psychotropic components really. However, he does suggest that the ritual described will guard and guide people in the passing seven different planets (known at that time) on their night flight!

Activity #9 Make your own flying ointment

Someone once gifted me a pot of home-made flying ointment. I feel strongly that psychotropic ingredients should only be handled by people who have years of training and experience. However, the most powerful ingredient is, arguably, the human imagination. There is a reason why my third book is called Medicine of the Imagination!

I invite you to consider making your own flying ointment. It could consist of local herbs mixed with butter, or beeswax. Add an intention to your ointment by praying or chanting over it. Empower it further, if you wish, by leaving it out under a Full Moon or Dark Moon. Keep experimenting, try different things. Fasten your seatbelts and keep a dream diary or vision file!

Chapter 10

Kabouters: of Kobolds, House Spirits and Fertility Gods

The kobold (occasionally *cobold*) is a sprite stemming from Germanic mythology and surviving into modern times in German folklore. Although usually invisible, a kobold can materialize in the form of an animal, fire, a human being, and a candle. The most common depictions of kobolds show them as humanlike figures the size of small children.[1]

Yn 'e bosken wenje de kabouters. Troch in holle beam komme se ta de groun yn. Dêr yn 'e groun ha se har paleis.
In the forest live cobolds. Through a hollow tree they reach their palace under the ground.[2]

Sometimes we surprise ourselves. I never thought I'd write an essay about *kabouters*! However, in Sweden last week I was busy at sunset on Christmas Eve, setting out a bowl of porridge and a glass of whiskey for our Gårdstomte! (The spirit of our home and plot).

Just as popular fiction presents fairies as dainty beings with butterfly wings, we now have a popular genre where cobolds and hobgoblins are depicted as cute creatures living in the forest (de *boskabouter*). This chapter is about the origins and older significance of these beings in European folklore and myth.

What is a *kabouter*?

In the Roman era people venerated household gods, called the Lares and Penates. The old Anglo-Saxon term for these beings is Cofgod, plural Cofgodas. The word was probably invented to translate a Latin concept.[3]

The Dutch word *kabouter*[4] is etymologically related to the English word kobold (or cobold). The word originally means spirit of the house/homestead or spirit of the stables. In Chapter 9 we already met the *Alruin*: in 13th century Germany people carved humanoid figures from mandrake roots, to represent these powerful spirits. They often had a phallic appearance, related to beliefs around male ancestors playing a role in the fertility of the land.

Core shamanism commonly presents most supernatural beings as *kind helping spirits just waiting to be in relationship with human beings* but, based on northern European cosmology, this is a dangerous simplification. There are many worlds (the Poetic Edda speaks of twelve worlds) and not all inhabitants of those worlds rate human beings very highly. Maintaining a relationship then becomes a matter of treading with care, making appropriate offerings at the right times and communicating plans and intentions, seeking permission. If this is not done correctly, we may anger those beings and they might turn against us. It is not so different from dealing respectfully with fellow human beings.

Another English word is hobgoblin and hob means hearth. Hobgoblins are said to resemble human beings and perform domestic tasks while people sleep (as long as they receive food offerings) but they will turn against families who don't honour their presence. In contrast Goblins are described as small green-skinned creatures who enjoy causing trouble.[5]

In Scandinavia we find the tomte. I first met Tomte in Sweden as a human-size Father Christmas figure delivering the Christmas presents for children!

In Swedish the word Tomte (capitalized) most commonly refers to Jultomten ("Father Christmas"): the elf dressed in red, associated with delivering people's *julklappar* or Christmas presents. Some authors have linked his red costume to the fly agaric mushrooms which proliferate in Scandinavia.[6]

When I started learning Swedish, I was puzzled about the connection between the Swedish words *tomte* and *tomt* (plot of land). People told me then that there was no connection – but today I know better!

The Gårdstomte (tomte of the homestead) is a very different creature from the Jultomte (Christmas tomte). He wears grey clothing and goes by different names, for instance: tomtebisse, tömtvittra, nisse, goanisse, lillnisse, tomtpyssel, tussen eller tomtebese. He is an old man and he doesn't like new-fangled modern things. He likes to see a farm or homestead run the traditional way. When people give him his due, he will help with all activities, from milking cows and haymaking to the caring for horses. One of his hobbies is braiding the manes of horses. Finding the manes of your horses braided one morning is a sign of his presence and goodwill. He is a guardian and custodian of the property. As there is a strong connection, in the traditions of Northern Europe between elves (in the Norse sense I just described,) and male ancestors, he may well be an ancestor, or at least ancestor-of-place. Our Gårdstomte is an ancestor-of-place, the first person who lived in this location and cleared our land for human settlement in the 17th century.

The Swedish word for property, as in the parcel of land that a property sits on, is tomt. Folklore reports that from pre-Christian times people have known that any such tomt has its own Tomte (dedicated spirit) who watches over family life, the buildings and the animals. At Christmas time the Gårdstomte traditionally receives his helping of the Christmas porridge and a glass of whiskey. I set this out for him on a table by our barn, where I also place other offerings for him during the year. (He gets whiskey when I host large groups on his turf!)[6]

Klabouterman
German, Dutch and Flemish ships had a protective spirit called the Klabouterman. His name is derived from the verb *klabastern*,

making a noise. He would knock on the walls of a ship to issue warning about rotting wood. In a similar way the *mijnkobold* (mine cobold) was said to knock out a signal to warn the miners that a shaft was about to collapse. This being is related to the notorious poltergeist (*polteren* also means making noises). The general idea was that the the ships cobold was the in-dwelling spirit of a ship's figurehead (or alternatively a statue attached to the mast).7

A legend from Kempen (Germany) informs us that the name of the King of Cobolds is Kyrië, meaning Lord in Greek. He lives in a mound inside one of the grave mounds on the heath at Hoogeloon in Brabant. Unfortunately, a hunter killed him. We can sometimes hear a kabouter exclaim that Kyrië is dead! After this incident the kabouters collectively left Kempen and surroundings.[8]

For Dutch-speakers among you, Abe has compiled a list a list of 142 supernatural beings he has found in Dutch and Flemish stories – please check out his book.[9] I will offer a description and translation for only a selection of them.(I have also included some beings found in other sources, those are referenced by separate footnotes).

- **Aardmannetjes** is another word for kabouters (literally *small earthmen*). Dressed in green they swap human children for changelings and some enjoy dancing in wheat fields.
- **Alven** (Gelderland, Zeeland, Vlaanderen) is a general word for elves. They travel in egg shells and sieves. They live in hills or mounds called *alvinnenheuvels*. Getting lost on the way home means an elf led you astray. They like dancing in wheat fields and sometimes leave a crop circle. They play tricks on human perception.
- **Assepoesters**, (literally Cinderellas), are the shades of children abused by their stepmothers. They will mess

around in the hearth and throw ashes around.

- **Barende vrouwe** (Varende moeder, Bjernavra, Windsbruid – literally a woman in labour) refers to a whirlwind moving up and down and is the soul of a woman who died in childbirth, doomed to bounce between Heaven and Hell because she did not go to confession.
- **Biesbout**, (Noord-Brabant): a creature mentioned in an (unfinished) magical prayer spoken by a witch called Griet from Lierop in 1595 during her witch trial. It is said to be an invocation for calling the Devil and ask to be lifted into the air and transported to a Witches' Sabbath:

> ['s morgens als ik opsta,
> in mijn groene gordel dat ik ga...]
> *In the morning when I get up*
> *Get going in my green girdle*
> *High, low, mountain and dale*
> *Biesbout multiplied*
> *By that wild woodland...*

- **Blauwe Gerrit** (Blauw Garrit, Blue Gerrit), Sinninghe – Gelderland, is the name of an invisible sprite who would sit on horses and carriages and make them freeze. He had glowing eyes and a luminous flapping blue cloak. Reportedly he once came to the rescue of an abducted girl.
- **Het Blauwe wolkje** (The Little Blue Cloud), Enschede, is the form the pestilence demon took as it spread across the land. Here we need to remember that the witch hunts were (in part) sparked off by the mass deaths caused by the bubonic plague.[10]
- **Bokkerijders** (Billygoat Riders), Limburg and Belgium, are ghosts flying around on billygoats, in service to the Devil.
- **Dún(n)aters** (Duineters, Dune Eaters), Schiermonnikoog

and Ameland, are small brown hairy men (about 5 cm high), who can make themselves very large at will. They live in the dunes (of the Dutch Waddenzee Islands) and look after the souls of babies before they find their mums and dads. When they are in a foul mood, they push the little ones under the sand until they eat the sand. One girl became a humpback from eating so much sand.

- **Dwaallichtje** (wandering light, also: *stalkaars*), generally perceived as the soul of either a criminal or an unbaptised child. Can lead people astray and cause them to drown. The solution is baptism but people attempting this are warned that they will be busy all night, with a clouds of small blue clouds swarming around them.

- **Griepke:** (Uddelermeer, Veluwe, Zeeland) Malicious water spirit who will attack people by jumping on their back. Also known as Ossaert.

- **Haspelvrouwtje** (Reel Woman), Brabant: a female kabouter, said to help women in childbirth and tend sick women, they also finished the work of overburdened women. If angered they would scratch people with their nails or abduct them to their underground homes.

- **Heggemoeder** (Witch Mother or Heksenmother, literally *Hedge Mother*): a nocturnal apparition, who resides in hazel shrubs, bringing illness, especially to women in childbirth.

- **Jipenessen (Vlaanderen)** Female cobolds or gipsies who reside deep in the earth and in mounds. Will do the laundry at night in return for a bowl of porridge. Loved eating cats. Were known to seduce farmers' sons and even kill women.

- **Kludde (untranslatable),** Brabant and Vlaanderen, is tormenting spirit and shapeshifter. Can appear as a cat, frog or bat. Can even turn into a tree growing all the way to heaven, disappearing into the clouds. Can be a dog attacking people or a skinny horse catapulting his rider into a lake. He wears iron chains and inhabits hollow trees. He is born from the body of witch or wizard burned at the stake.

- **Koolhaas,** (Cabbage Hare), is the spirit of cabbage seeds hiding in the seed pod. Farm workers copy this in straw and hide it in the soil of the field.
- **Lodder or Loeder,** Vlaanderen, is a shapeshifting tormenter wearing chains. He loves frightening people (by turning himself into huge black dog and staring them down) and even abducting them. (This word is used in contemporary Dutch to refer to a malicious person. My elderly mother will use this word to refer to a serial killer or child sex offender).
- **Maanje Klop** (Groningen), is a helpful cobold with a hammer who repairs fishing ships at night in Delfzijl.
- **Mare,** a bad spirit in the shape of an old woman who climbs on the chest of sleeping people and paralyses them, so they have a nightmare. This same being is said to ride horses at night in energetic form (while the actual horse is in the stable). She also appear as a beautiful woman and cause wet dreams.
- **Nachtwerkertjes,** (Night Worker Spirits), Utrecht, spirit working hard in a workshop at night doing the work of human beings. To be distinguished from *Werkgeesten*: spirits forcing people to repeat work already completed once asleep, meaning they are too exhausted to work the next day.
- **Pygmeentjes** are humpback dwarves very skilled in sorcery and magic. Can be helpful or malicious. The like shapeshifting into a bluebottle or blowfly and one of them buzzing around you is a bad omen. A very famous pygmy is *Keutelduimke*, better known as Tom Thumb *(Klein Duimpje)* in Grimm's fairytales.

- **Reuzen** are giants, primordial beings who walked the land before the Germanic gods did. It is said that they created the landscape as we know it by carving out rivers and creating hills from the earth thus shifted. Legends claim that often they accidentally created features in the landscape by shaking out their clogs. They were said to wear animal skins and have more 'brawn than brain' and to have created the Hunebedden.

- (De) **Roggemoeder** (Rye Mother) or **Korenmoeder** (Corn Mother) with the local name *Antsje Pluk*, (Groningen): is the spirit of the Rye or Corn who drags off children trampling the harvest. Has been known to chase women. She becomes visible whenever we see the wind moving the grains. However, if she pinches a sheaf of grain, it turns toxic. (This is a local explanation for ergot, a fungal disease of rye and other cereals in which black elongated fruiting bodies grow in the ears of the cereal. Eating contaminated food can result in ergotism. Interestingly ergot was used in small amounts by wise women/midwives after childbirth to expel the placenta and contract the uterus).

- **Spinwijf** (also Spinjuffer, Groningen), old lady dressed in white, who does her spinning by moonlight in a remote location. A famous one lived in the Spinberg of Jipsinghuizen. She was said to spin extremely long threads to catch young men.

- **Sommeltjes (or Sammeltjes),** Texel and Wieringen, earth spirits living in the dunes and on the Sommeltjes mountain (a grave mound, please note Holland does not have mountains and any slight hill may be referred to as a mountain!) They are active at night because they cannot tolerate sunlight, become petrified by sunbeams. Children were told that babies were delivered by Sommeltjes.

- **Spook** (also schim, geestverschijning), is a dead person appearing in the form of a translucent shape, often because of unfinished business with the living.

- **Tsjelwijf or Wielwijf**, Friesland, is a witch flying around on a large wheel, up to no good!
- **Trijewiif or (Driewijf)**, Friesland, are ghostly figures appearing from the sacred woods of Trynwâlden in the shape of a white, red and black woman with their hair flapping in the wind. They dance above a black altar stone to create a whirlwind, so the women cannot be distinguished from each other. The three of them together are the Trijewiif ("Three Wife")
- **Trintjes (English: Moss Maidens, German Moos Leute):** were otherworld people inhabiting the ancient primordial forests of German (also known as Wilde Leute, Wild People). Most of them are female: Wood Wives or Moss Maidens and associated with trees, perceived as guardians of trees. They are helpful to human beings who show a deep respect for the forest. Lucky humans can learn healing skills and magic if a Moss Woman is willing to befriend them. We find descriptions of them in accounts of The Wild Hunt, where the Leader of the Hunt is said to chase them. They could hide out in safe trees marked with a cross. For this reason, woodsmen would often leave a stump marked with a cross to create such sanctuaries. Trintje is short of Catherine (Katrina/Katrijn)
- **Wanne Thekla** (Flanders) was the Queen of Elves, Witches and Air Spirits. She descends at night to dance on Earth and drink on the Pottelberg. By morning she sails off in a magnificent ship on the river Leije.
- **Waterveulen** (Water Foal, Volendam), was a foal that climbed ashore from the Zuiderzee to court a beautiful girl. He brought her small fishes as a gift. One day she mounted him and they swam off, never to be seen again.
- **Wisselkind (Dikkop, Krielkop, Wechselbalg in German),** changeling or elven child swapped for a human child.

Often an older elf taking this shape, screaming non-stop and eating an unnatural amount of food without growing larger.

- **Witte Vrouwe** (Friesland, Gaast): is a white lady who appears to float or fly and is said to be the guardian of fishes, birds and even "juttersgoed" (meaning ship's cargo that washes up on beaches).

- **Wolf (Korenwolf – Corn Wolf, Roggewolf – Rye Wolf)**, found in Germany and Limburg), the spirit of the grain is found in the last sheaf of wheat harvested and takes the shape of a wolf. Often the farm hand who found it acted like a wolf. This wolf is invisible and it can only be seen, just like the Corn or Rye Mother, in the way the wind makes the grains move. That is when the wolf fertilises the corn. Children roaming the fields are eaten by the six-legged Corn Wolf.

- **Zeeridder**, Sea Knight, (Friesland). In the year 1305 a Sea Knight was caught out at sea. He wore a harness and helm. He had a big moustache and lush flowing hair, both made of seaweed. After being captured he refused to eat or drink. He was displayed in many villages and towns in Friesland but after three weeks he died in Dokkum.

- **Zwarte juffer, black maiden** (also Zwarte wijven – black wives or cichorijwijven – chicory wives), Groningen, is a malicious spirit in the form of a woman in mourning, with her apron pulled over her head. She will reside in a hedge or float above a road and bring ill back luck. Seeing her means that someone in your family will die soon. (She appears to be the shadow version of the *white/witty/wise* Witte Wieven).

Closing comment: angels only make a *very* rare appearance in Dutch sources and folklore. Occasionally one guards a priest or an Angel of Death appears to collect a soul.

Closing thoughts about the circular nature of things

Writing this book was a circular process. Everything is connected. Every topic cycled back to other, related, subjects and triggered lightbulb moments. Below are some examples.

We know that witches often used the chimney to leave or enter a house. We also that Dutch children set out their shoes on the hearth in the hope of receiving treats from Sinterklaas. If we compare a house to the human body, the chimney would represent the airways, the passage between the lungs and the mouth, between the inside and the outside of the body. It is the most natural place to access otherworlds. A hearth is a natural portal and the chimney acts as a tunnel or interface between worlds.

Abe suggests that the witch's familiar may well a remaining version of the imp or hobgoblin. The witch is said to have a third nipple, used to feed her familiar milk or blood, in return for the services of the kobold or imp. This was the so called witches' teat that witch hunters looked out for.[11]

Kobolds have a connection to both mines and ships. In cosmology both mines and the sea are associated with The Great Below or netherworld realms deep in the Earth. The chemical element Cobalt (Co) was named for the kobold. I know it as a pigment that gives a distinct blue hue to paints. On a related note, the chemical element Nickel (Ni)[12] was named for a misschievous sprite (cobold) of German miner mythology and its name is related to Old Nick (so we are back to St Nicholas and the Devil) It received its name from the German word Kupfernickel (literally Devil's Copper) because the ore was believed to contain copper, yet no copper could be extracted from it.[7]

When we speak of kabouters, many Dutch people will immediately think of garden gnomes wearing red pointy (or Phrygian) hats. The town Brienz in Switzerland was know for its production of wooden house dwarves. These garden figures became conflated with the cobolds inhabiting farms and mines and the fashion for garden gnomes soon spread all over Europe. The 1930s Disney film Snow White and the Seven Dwarves made them even more popular. In 2008 there were a (staggering) 25 million garden gnomes in Germany alone.[13] The gnomes/kobolds/imps/hobgoblins have staged a comeback!

Activity #10

Were any otherworld beings mentioned during your childhood? Write down what you remember. Do some research for the place(s) where you grew up. Talk to older family members such as (grand) parents and aunts/uncles. Ask questions. Keep a journal of their answers.

If you are up for it: tune into any otherworld beings sharing the land you live and work on. Also ask questions about 'missing' people in the family tree (miscarriages, stillborn babies, those who died young, those who were locked away in asylums). In your prayers make everyone feel included, even the ones whose names you do not know. That is a simple form of ancestral healing work.

Print off this list and make a habit of connecting to some of these beings. Keep a journal and share experiences with others!

Chapter 11

Sinterklaas – Saint Nicholas as Soul Conductor

Sinterklaas Kapoentje, (St Nicholas Kapoentje)
gooi wat in m'n schoentje, (Cast something in my shoe)
gooi wat in m'n laarsje. (Cast something in my boot)
Dank u, Sinterklaasje. (Thank you St Nicholas)[1]

Please take a moment to listen to this classical song on YouTube and see representations of the ever-popular saint in contemporary Dutch culture!

As my quest to uncover the pre-Christian spirituality of the Netherlands continued, I came face to face with many *home truths* (to use an English expression). Many discoveries moved me to tears, shook me to the very core and brought a complete evaluation of cultural landmarks I never questioned in childhood.

For Dutch children the Big Day of the Year is the birthday of Saint Nicholas. He arrives from Spain on a steamboat in mid-November, a few weeks before his birthday and feast day. He is accompanied by his tribe of *zwarte pieten* (black Petes). He rides a white horse called Americo. Dutch children set their shoes by the hearth or near a chimney (failing that, in the hallway of their house) and sing traditional songs to honour the saint. They leave a carrot in their shoe as a treat for Americo. The next morning, they wake up to sweets and treats deposited in their shoe. The carrot is gone, proof that the Saint and Americo have really visited in the night!

His actual birthday is celebrated in different ways, depending on the age of the participants. For young children, the parents and teachers weave a web of enchantment. Sinterklaas will bring them treats and toys, but they must behave, because Zwarte Piet (Black Pete) spies on them and keeps track of their behaviour in his Big Book.

Families of older children (who no longer 'believe') will organise an event called *Pakjesavond* (Gift Night or The Night of Opening Parcels). Often everyone pulls one name out of a hat (not unlike *a Secret Santa*) and is responsible for creating a gift and personal rhyme for this person. This involves something called a "surprise" (pronounced the French way), meaning that the gift is wrapped in a very creative way, so it arrives in a shape that makes benigne fun of some passion, quirk or special interest. For the owner of a pet the surprise may look like a cat, dog, rabbit or parakeet. A more enterprising child might create a giant dog turd out of paper mache and include a poop scoop as a bonus 'gift' (just to make the audience laugh). A bald person may get a *surprise* with a shock of curly hair or wearing an abundant wig (a bit like the British habit of calling a bald person Curly or a tall person Tiny!) The same thing goes for the personalised rhymes: one takes (gentle) pot shots at the recipient:

As you are so obsessed with this//It is time to take the piss!
Sinterklaas was watching you// As you stepped in your dog's poo
However not all is lost// Because at some cost
Sint actually bought you new shoes
From now on use the scoop and avoid those poos!

Teenagers are ribbed ruthlessly about a crush they have on someone, their habit of spending hours in the bathroom, the amount of time they spend on-line chatting to friends and so forth.

Here is a box// It used to contain socks// Now it will house rats and chats…

For a year
You may disappear
Into your own personal chat box
(But make sure you don't contract chickenpox!)

Obviously, I just knocked these out in English, to give the flavour of things: some teasing and loud laughter followed by opening the *surprise* and receiving a gift from Sint! There are often deliberate impossibilities hinted at, as well (such as contracting chickenpox while you are self-isolating in a cardboard 'chat box'!)

The tradition of gift-giving predates St Nicholas. In many cultures it represents the principle of sacred reciprocity, connected to the New Year. The reasoning was that people who showed generosity at the beginning of a new calendar year would be generously rewarded with good fortune and, what is called in Swedish 'return gifts' (*Varje* gåva kräver en gengåva – every gift requires a return gift!) This principle lives on in the Gifu/Gebo rune, which looks like a cross. However, the Church opposed this concept, because it violates the principle of being kind out of sheer love for Christ, without necessarily getting or seeking anything in return.

I am not a great fan of material gifts (either giving or receiving them) because our consumerist society has driven this to dangerous excess. However, I love it when people make me something or find the perfect item I actually need! However, after a strict Roman Catholic upbringing, with its heavy emphasis on self-sacrifice and martyrdom, for me the principle of *fair energy exchange* was a revelation: I no longer needed to exhaust and endanger myself by giving pieces of myself away to whoever asked. It was empowering and liberating – but that is an aside!

Demonization of the Dead

It may surprise some people to hear that the Feast of St. Nicholas was going strong in the Netherlands already in the Medieval times. According to author Louis Janssen, who wrote a seminal book on the topic of St. Nicholas, there were three tiers of celebration that evolved over time[2]:

- The nocturnal home visit for small children (toddlers and pre-schoolers).
- A feast for school age children.
- A masquerade for tweens and teens.

Until well into the nineteenth century there were masquerades in both the Netherlands and Flanders. Those gradually faded out as our modern version of the feast took shape.

Here it must be noted that on the Waddeneilanden (the Dutch Islands in the North Sea) so called *Oude Sinterklazen* also known as *Klaasomes* still do the rounds today, meaning that the inhabitants of those islands have preserved an older tradition. These Dutch masquerades appear to be connected to wild pagan events in Austria and Switzerland called *Perchten*.[3]

It is tempting to think of Sinterklaas as an innocuous or *light-hearted child-centred celebration.* The dimension we have lost track of in modern times is that originally St. Nicholas was a *soul conductor* or *psychopomp,* a *zielengeleider* in Dutch. The troop of people that accompanied him were, originally, *the dead.* This links him to the phenomenon of The Wild Hunt. As Christianization made inroads, the dead were demonised and perceived as 'devils' or demonic beings.

From a spiritual point of view this is a hideous fact (and undoubtedly not the fate or treatment we desire for ourselves the day we die!) On another level it can also be argued that this demonization still allowed the dead their place in the larger constellation of Sinterklaas phenomena and on our calendar – and this may well be why we can still unearth the true story today.

Demonization was one of the most powerful and most devastating tools employed by rulers within the Christian hierarchy. It was used to change forever ordinary people's perception and frame of reference (altering people's perception of events is a powerful form of magic in its own right!) so wise women became witches, heathens or pagans became heretics, the Jews and the Moors became scapegoats. The field of comparative religions teaches that when a new dominant religion arrives often the old gods become the devils and demons of the new faith. Old Norse sources tell us that this is the period where old texts lump Odin, Freyja and Satan together. The Christian Devil arrives at heathen Valhalla and Odin becomes a demon.

Roman goddess Diana (often equated with the Greek goddess Artemis) suffered the same ignominious fate. She was said to make nocturnal visits to homes, accompanied by Good Women (think back to the Witte Wieven for a moment). If they were received well and generously, they would bless the inhabitants and bring them good fortune. After Christianity conquered Europe, women who had any form of contact with Diana were branded as witches and in Church literature Diana was branded *des duivels moer* (the mother of the Devil).

Historians tell us that rather than conveniently evaporating, she may just have lived on in folklore and folk traditions under localized names such as Holda (Holle), Perchta or Befana. (See Chapter 12). The suggestion has been made that St. Nicholas, conveniently male and a respectable saint at that, was the successor of Diana and carried on the nocturnal visits – and took responsibility for the collection of the souls of the dead.

A key point made by Janssen in his excellent exploration[2] is that *the solidarity between the living and the dead was a crucial aspect of early medieval Christianity.* Janssen makes a plea for what he calls *continuity of change.* In other words: change is the way that life lives itself and nothing is static but modern phenomena contain with them the kernels of earlier manifestations of the same thing. You could view this as a set of nested Russian dolls: when you peel off one outward manifestation, deep inside it you find another, older, model.

The Boy Bishop

Already in the 12th century the child-loving saint was associated with the punishing of bad behaviour and rewarding of good behaviour. Over time the punishment element was delegated to his helper, meaning that one important dimension of St Nicholas faded from view.

One hymn from the eleventh century puts it this way: 'You frighten to death those who deserve this'.[4] In this period St Nicholas was venerated by adults and children, the rich and the poor, traders and vagrants, judges and lawyers but also thieves and prisoners. This indicates a degree of contradiction or even controversy.

There was a tradition in operation on the *Dag van de Onnozele (of Onschuldige) Kinderen*, on December 28th. (In our day this occasion lives on as the International Day of Innocent Children Victims of Aggression). One choirboy was elected as the Boy Bishop. In the 13th century this tradition was shifted to December 6th (the birthday of our Saint). This was a typical festival of role reversal, where the real Bishop stepped down and the Boy Bishop ruled the roost. This soon derailed into boys messing around: scandalous ditties being sung in church and boys playing pranks around town.[4]

Such festivals of role reversal (here we can also think of the Saturnalia and Bacchanalia) open the door on chaos and disruption. Those forces actually serve renewal by shaking up the established order. The issue will always be how much mayhem the adult leaders will tolerate for that sacred window of time.

Historical facts, myths and legends

For a time, there was a theory that St Nicholas was a manifestation of Wodan (Odin): a kind of Janus figure with one face being the adorable saint while his flip side was Wodan, who could be terrifying and deadly, a trickster and oath-breaker. This theory has been disproved but St Nicholas is definitely connected to the European phenomenon called The Wild Hunt – and so is Wodan/Odin.

St Nicholas was *thaumaturge* or miracle worker.[5] Perhaps more surprisingly he was also the patron saint of lovers and people courting. In the fourteenth century star-crossed lovers gave each other *vrijers* and *vrijsters,* literally the words mean male and female lovers, in the form of large gingerbread men and women. Another popular gift were sugary hearts made from marzipan or candy.[5]

The flip side of this coin were the *Zwarte Klazen* (Black Klazen) who went from door to door rattling chains and frightening people, on the same evening (and it is unlikely that they left the girls alone!)

Not all of these phenomena were decent. There were many songs with sexual innuendo. Sinterklaas was referred to as a *hylicksmaker*[6] (marriage match maker) and apparently things often went too far. One song tells a fatherless child to have a chat with the Saint about his origins. Boys born out of wedlock were often called Klaas (as a reference to being fathered by the saint) while *girl of Sinterklaas* was a term for a promiscuous girl or woman.

Christianity performed another appropriation: the tradition of giving and receiving gifts was moved to Christmas and the gifts were now attributed to the Christ Child.

In the earlier days of Christianization, St Nicholas was perceived as being accompanied by the Devil, but now the Devil 'starts his own business', and ended up operating under many different names in many different guises. Some of his names, at the time of Luther, still reveal the earlier connection: *Hell-Niklas* in Germany, *Klaaskerel* in the Netherlands and *Old Nick* in England.

The helper of Sinterklaas has three classical attributes: a chain, a large sack and the rod. The chain refers to the *chained-up devil* of an earlier time. (Compare this to Norse god Loki). The rod marks him as the person doling out punishment and the sack reminds of his function as the *zielenvreter* or 'soul eater'. He puts all doomed souls in the sack so he can take them to the Christian realm called Hell.[6]

The name of the Christian realm of eternal punishment: Hel, was taken from Norse cosmology: the goddess Hel and her realm by the same name. This is the Land of the Dead in Norse cosmology but not a realm of damnation or punishment in the Christian sense. Goddess Hel treats her guests well in her great hall. So, what we see here is a complete travesty of the non-heroic dead being welcomed with food and drink in the Hall of the Norse goddess Hel.

Friesland

The province Friesland knows a phenomenon called *Klaasjagen*. This is different in essence from the traditions on the Waddeneilanden (Dutch islands in the North Sea). Here masked people bang on doors, hunt down naughty (or misbehaving) children, fling gingerbread coins (*pepernoten*) around and of course they carry the rod, the sack and the chain. The guise is often improvised: a coat turned inside out[7], a sheepskin, a white bedsheet, a mitre made from old newspapers or some kind of tatty hat. The mystery ingredient is the *mombakkes* (no explanation provided). To me this sounds like a mask or face-covering.

The people going guising are called Klaas, Pieter (Peter) or simply Duivel (Devil). They go around in small groups of two or three individuals. Sometimes they are children singing songs in return for some spare change or treats. Once again, we find dirty songs with sexual innuendo. Those ditties promise Saint Nicholas *'een nieuw wijf'* (a new wife, the word *wijf* here meaning a woman, not a married woman). In Venray St Nicholas actually had a woman with him, that is to say: a man in drag. In some locations teenage boys carried large sacks and caught girls they then put in those sacks (the courting or lovers motif again). One implication in the source material is that guising facilitates unlicensed behaviour (not unlike the Venetian carnival) where people could behave in ways, without being recognised and held accountable, that the everyday rules prohibit.[8]

If we take one step back, we realise that we are back to the rejuvenating and fertilising powers of chaos and disorder: this type of behaviour brought new pairings and the resulting cross-fertilization and yes, also babies born out of wedlock!

Here we also inch very close to the cultural archetype of The Trickster. In the Northern Tradition this is Loki, who does get tied up in a cave by the goddess Skadi, with a serpent dripping venom on his face. Think of the chain carried by Zwarte Piet. The job of the Trickster is to bring reversal, to upset the apple cart, to tilt the established order on its axis – so something new can come into being. The Trickster is the father of cultural renewal.

Racism

We are living through an era of culture wars and political correctness, calling out, being woke, bias training and always checking our privilege status. We are also living in an era of educating ourselves (we cannot be a member of the global village with 24/7 access to information, yet claim ignorance of contemporary issues).

In this context privilege could be defined as *anything you don't need to worry about but seriously affects others* or alternatively *anything you don't need to worry about because you can pay another person to take care of the matter.*

I have lived away from the Netherlands for thirty years now but I have been told that the figure of Zwarte Piet (Black Peter) has attracted accusations of racism, as evidently being deeply woven into Dutch culture. Apparently, some people want to do away with Zwarte Piet altogether and there are also postmodern manifestations such as *de Regenboog Piet* (Rainbow Pete).

This chapter hopes to explain that Zwarte Piet is not supposed to be black in the racial sense of skin colour. He represents a white man blackening his skin to represent a dead man. Reversal is a key theme in many cultures when it comes to dealing with the dead. Traditionally this was done using shoe polish but today everyone has easy access to face paints which are, at least, kinder on human skin.

In today's world I agree that a tradition hailing from another era, (a white man blackening his skin to represent either a dead man or, according to a different school of thought, the Devil), is highly unfortunate and inappropriate. Due to large-scale immigration the population of the Netherlands is far more ethnically diverse today than it was in previous centuries. This may be why it has taken so long for this tradition to be perceived as a problematic or even downright offensive.

On the other hand, I am an avid collector of books about other cultures and I have certainly seen photographs of African and Australian Aboriginal people painting their faces white (sometimes white bones, a skull or ribs are painted on their skin as well) in order to represent the dead in ceremonies. Seeing those images transports us into the mystery teachings of tribal cultures.

Today I observe a related phenomenon where authors from another era get trashed for their tone. I have seen this done to, for instance, the Danish author Vilhelm Grønbech (14 June 1873 – 21 April 1948).[9]

He was a Danish cultural historian and professor of the history of religion at the University of Copenhagen. He did most of his writing during and after World War II. In Heathen groups I have seen women aggressively slag him off as 'a sexist pig' (and worse), telling other pagans and heathens not to bother reading his work. To my mind this is wrong. He was an extremely intelligent man and had he had lived today, I have no doubt that his awareness of sexism and gender fluidity would have been in gear. However, his writing needs to be dated correctly and viewed as a product of that period. Projecting our cultural obsessions onto him seven decades later is not helpful. I was reading quotes by him out to my students in Sweden and people loved his words. He was a contemporary of C. G. Jung (26 July 1875 – 6 June 1961), another pioneer who today stands accused of sexism and dated attitudes. I personally think we are throwing out a lot of babies along with the bath water if we dump and disregard people who made a significant cultural contribution decades or even centuries ago. I also feel that we cannot wipe out their contribution even if on a personal level they behaved badly. We know that Jung seduced a young woman and patient called Sabina Spielrein.[10]

My personal opinion is that deleting his life's work from our cultural heritage is not the way to go. Other people are welcome to disagree with me.

Ameland and the 'Klaasomes'

Ameland is one island in the chain of Waddeneilanden. Here the Sinterklaas celebrations take a very unique and more indigenous form, a less commercialised form than on the mainland. The following information was adapted from Louis Janssen's book.[8]

The tourist season is over for the year and the island has gone quiet. Outside observers or spectators are not welcome. The festival spreads across two nights. Between 5–7pm the *baanvegers* (or streets sweepers) appear, their job is to sweep the streets clean. They retreat to costume up at 7pm and reappear as *Klaasomes*. Apparently de *baanvegers* used to be masked as well.

At 5pm the *baanvegers* appear, shrouded in white sheets. Street lamps are switched off and there is no artificial light those evenings, which adds greatly to the otherworldly atmosphere.

Everyday reality is suspended and ghostly figures flutter around. A kind of game unfolds and it involves contradictions or opposites: inside-outside, house-street, light-dark, male-female, adults-children, menacing-entertaining, and so forth. Boys under the age of 18 are excluded from participation, meaning that they will try their hardest to robe up and get involved!

De Klaasomes need to conquer the world, in a way. The non-initiates are swept away by the *baanvegers*. Young people will harass the *baanvegers* and end up being chased. Gentle the proceedings are not, the youths can count on gaining bruises or even a thorough beating, if they are too cheeky.

At 8pm the masquerade starts. People spend weeks secretly working on their costumes. Even their own families are not allowed to see them. A classical costume consists of white trousers, a white shirt, a fantasy cloak and a headdress. The mask used to be made from white mesh in the past but today they are shop-bought.

The Omes (abbreviation of Klaasomes) operate in groups of two, three or more people, all dressed in identical costumes. A lot of time is spent on creating the cloaks and headdresses. On the back are images or depictions that poke fun at local or national situations. They also carry a decorated stick, as power object and symbol and a horn (in the past this was a buffalo horn or cow's horn). They will even make sure to buy new shoes for the occasion as small details such as familiar shoes can give the game away!

The Omes honk their horns (here think of vuvuzelas at football matches!) When groups of Omes come face to face they will shake hands. This is called *voesten* (a verb derived from the word *vuist* – fist, "fisting") and it serves to weed out the underage boys. It is a test of masculinity. What the Omes do not like either is seeing light creep through a crack between the curtains. This event never passes without windows being smashed.

In the *open huizen* (open homes) women, girls and children await their arrival. The Omes can enter any home they like at will. They enforce the rules but are above the law themselves. This means they will take liberties such as sitting in the lap of a woman or demanding a girl dances for them. They will bang the floor with their stick and the girl concerned will hop a few times in front of them. Disobedience is punished with a tap of the stick on their legs. The idea is that the Omes visit all open homes. The atmosphere is tense, menacing.

A more lightweight aspect is that the women employ clever ways of figuring out who is behind the mask. If they succeed the spell is broken the man concerned stands humiliated. Around midnight people drop their masks.

One final comment is that the people concerned do not dwell on the deeper meaning or mythic origin of these medieval traditions. Hollum is a good Christian village! Similar traditions are observed on nearby islands.[8]

Related festivities in other European countries

The countries with St. Nicholas celebrations[11] most closely collected to those of the Netherlands and Belgium are Switzerland and Austria.

In Northern Germany, Sankt Nikolaus is usually celebrated on a small scale. Many children put a boot called *Nikolaus-Stiefel* (Nikolaus boot) outside the front door on the night of 5 December.

Nicholas is often portrayed in Bavarian folklore as being accompanied by *Knecht Ruprecht* who will ask the children if they have been saying their prayers. If not, he shakes his bag of ashes at them, or beats them with a stick.

In France and the French-speaking part of Belgium, the whole family greets the saint and grandparents tell children stories about St. Nicholas. A small donkey carries baskets filled with small treats and biscuits for the children. There is a popular, if gruesome, story about three children who got lost. A wicked butcher lured them into his shop and butchered them, salting them away in a large tub. Thankfully the children were revived through an intervention of St Nicholas and returned safely to their families. This event made St. Nichols the protector and patron saint of children. The evil butcher still follows St. Nicholas around in the form of *Père Fouettard*. In France, statues and paintings often portray this event, showing the saint with children in a barrel. In Luxembourg *Kleeschen* is accompanied by the Houseker a frightening helper wearing a brown monk's habit.

In Austria, Bavaria and Tyrol St. Nicholas has a demonic companion called Krampus (or Krampusz)[12], a frightening and hairy beast or animal-man. The job of Krampus is to catch naughty children and carry them of to his lair. Krampus has a Germanic origin but his influence has spread beyond the German borders into nearby countries and territories. December fifth has become Krampusnacht, where the hairy devil roams the streets and frightens people with his chain and bells. He also visits homes and offices, sometimes with the saint and sometimes on his own.

The Albanians know Saint Nicholas as *Shen'Kollë* and here he is venerated by most Catholic families. His feast is celebrated on the eve of December sixth, known as *Shen'Kolli i Dimnit* (Saint Nicholas of Winter). It is interesting to note that there is also a day dedicated to the commemoration of the interring of his bones in Bari. This happens on the eve of May ninth and this event is known as *Shen'Kolli i Majit* (Saint Nicholas of May). An interesting point is that Saint Nicholas of Winter resonates with Frau Holle as the Winter Goddess.

In Serbia Saint Nicholas is the most widely celebrated patron saint of families, celebrated as the feast day of *Nikoljdan*. Since Nikoljdan always falls in the fasting period preceding

Christmas, it is celebrated according to the Eastern Orthodox fasting rules.¯

In Bulgaria, Saint Nicholas Day is celebrated on the 6 December as *Nikulden*. Families invite relatives and neighbours for a meal of fish, usually *ribnik*, a carp wrapped in dough, and two loaves of ceremonial bread, all of which are blessed at church or at home.

In the Czech Republic and Slovakia, *Mikuláš*, (in Poland *Mikołaj* and in Ukraine *Svyatyi Mykolay*) is often also accompanied by an angel who acts as a counterweight to the ominous 'black' helper.

In Hungary, Croatia and Romania, children typically leave their boots out on the windowsill on the evening of 5 December and Mikulás (or Szent Miklós) leaves them sweets and small toys. Naughty children might receive a small rod from Krampusz, the frightening helper of the saint.

In Slovenia Miklavž (or Sveti Miklavž) and in Croatia, Nikolaus (or Sveti Nikola) visits on Saint Nicholas day (Nikolinje in Croatia and Miklavževanje in Slovenia) and brings children gifts. Good behaviour is praised and children behaving poorly are threatened with a visit from *Parkelj* or Krampus who traditionally leaves them a rod, to be used by their parents for disciplining them.[11]

Activity #11

If you are second or third generation Dutch in another country, or on another continent, I invite you to organise a small scale Sinterklaas celebration, as described in this chapter.

Invite your (grand) children, or even a friend's or the neighbour's children, to set out a shoe (with carrot offering) and then fill those shoes with treats, at your house.

Listen to some popular Sinterklaas songs on YouTube and try to sing along for a line or two (the lyrics can generally be found on-line).

If enough people are up for it, shift the major gift-exchange away from Christmas for one year and organise a *Pakjesavond!*

Helpful links (see links in the Notes)

Celebrating Sinterklaas *(article about celebrating the feast of St Nicholas)*[13]

De Leukste Sinterklaasliedjes compilatie (the most popular Sinterklaas songs)[14]

Fijf Makkelijke sinterklaas surprises (five easy hacks for making Sinterklaas 'Surprises')[15]

Chapter 12

Vrouw (Frau) Holle en de Vroneldenstraet
(Mother Holle and her Celestial Road)

Vrouw Holle klopt haar beddengoed uit!
Vrouw Holle is shaking out her bedding!
(In my childhood this was said when it started snowing)

During the persecution times in Europe, some women suspected of witchcraft were said to 'Ride with Holda'.

Who is Vrouw Holle
When we start researching pre-Christian Germanic material and how it interacts andintersects with Norse cosmology, Vrouw Holle (globally better known by her German name Frau Holle and sometimes called Mother Holle or Hulda) is a key figure.[1] She appears in many locations and in many guises. She sometimes also travels incognito as *Aunt Maehlen*, begging for food and shelter, always magically rewarding generosity and charity.

The first mention of her appears around the year 1200, meaning that about seven centuries of active Christianizing/ converting have occurred, as well as a general mingling of beliefs from all wind directions.[2]

Modern spirituality often calls her a *goddess* and manifestation of an old (even primordial) Mother. Scholars view her differently. Lecouteux perceives her as having a strong connection to the fairy realms and spirits (guardians) of place.[2]

The advent of core shamanism and counter-cultural appropriation of the Tungus word *shaman* from Siberia have contributed to the contemporary phenomenon of Alpine shamanism, where 'Core' techniques such as shamanic drumming and even crystals are combined with hikes to significant mountains, 'pilgrims to peaks'.[3]

It is likely that Holle represents a much older figure than the Norse gods (as we know them today). As such she is linked to the Celtic Cailleach, the Icelandic Beinakarling, The Bone Crone, the Swedish Kärring, the Russian Baba Yaga and Louhi in the Finnish Kalevala. She is a personification of land and seasons. She is the life-bringing, death-dealing goddess. She often lives in a mountain cave, deep in the earth[4] (Rune PEORTH).

In my opinion author (and practising Heathen) Cat Heath provides the most comprehensive perspective on this matter.[5] She says that Frau Holle cannot be written off as only a folkloric figure. She may have had her origins in the fifty century bogs but her provenance is likely to remain a mystery. She points out that 'scholarship is an ever-changing beast' and that Holle has a connection to Frija and Frau Freke (see Chapter 4). There are tentative connections to both Nerthus and Norse goddess Hel. There are indications that Wodan usurped the position of an earlier female divine being in the late heathen period.

I value scholarship immensely, and I read as many books and papers as I possibly can to stay informed, but ultimately for me it is a matter of relationship and personal revelation. In the year 2019 I had one teaching moment in the US where my students were engaged in a Seidr practice on the land. Two vultures were circling overhead and I suddenly 'saw' an earlier powerful female deity standing behind Odin. I also saw that she is related to, or has evolved from the Neolithic Bird Goddess described by Marija Gimbutas in her books. I cannot prove that I am right about this but as the author of this book I will give my own take, along with other perspectives.

Holle has been linked to Hel, the Norse goddess whose eponymous realm was culturally appropriated by the Church as Hell (note the double 'll', a realm of doom and eternal damnation).

She is an ancient Germanic being connected to both

agriculture and women's crafts. She is most active around the time of the winter solstice and some call her a 'Winter Goddess'. In 2017 I made an art video dedicated to her, with a special focus on her role as a psychopomp or soul conductor for children.[6]

Holle has a strong connection to the Frau Holle Pond on the Hohen Meiszner mountain range in Hesse. Since at least 1641 the landmark has been carried her name but it was probably a sacred site long before that. Evidence of sacrifices, medieval potsherds and 1st century Roman coins have been found there.[7]

The argument has been made that she should be called 'Unholde' instead, meaning unholy or monstrous, linked to the supernatural. The word Holde in contemporary German means graceful, charming or dear.[7]

Philologist and folklorist Claude Lecouteux[8], from his studies of the word in Early and Middle High German contexts, concludes that the word *hold(e)* is related to the realm of the fairies, a world where both benevolent and malevolent beings can be found.-

Based on personal encounters with her, I feel that Holde/ Holle definitely is the right name for her. She is formidable but not monstrous! She performs a crucial holy office in the liminal space between the worlds. She may frighten some (and she takes no nonsense) but ultimately, she is benevolent.

Ridenour reports that by the mid-17th century most of the elements of the Holda myth had fallen into place. There is a strong connection to Diana, Herodias and, in legends of the Venusberg, to Venus. Holle then also acquires an intercessor or chamberlain, a psychopomp figure with a white beard and staff: *Loyal Eckhart*.[9]

We need to understand her entourage as 'the souls of people who died violent or premature deaths, who must wander the earth until the day that fate has fixed for their passing'. (The concept of an un-fated – as opposed to ill-fated, death is an interesting one!)[10]

Because Holle magically blesses and bestows gifts on generous good-hearted people, a danger arose of greedy unscrupulous people seeking access to this 'boundless source'. This is, likely, why Loyal Eckhart appears. He warns off onlookers and guards the gate to 'the Venusberg'. The Hörselberg is presented as a grim abode of lost souls while the Venusberg is the place of endless feasting and erotic pleasures. (Once again, I point out a possible connection between Perchta and Rune PERTHRA or PEORTH, the rock or mountain rune).

However, there is a catch: the Venusberg is a realm of pleasure from which there is no escape! As such it has many parallels in folk tales and legends. It may appear as a gold-filled subterranean hall of dwarves, enchanted fairylands or a kingdom under the sea: a *land of no return*. Folklorists have interpreted these references by folklorists as pointing to death and eternal reward. Entering this realm, the soul may never again participate in mortal life, but instead partakes of immortality and the immortals' power to know and control man's fate.[9]

The food offerings left for Holle-Perchta and company is a ritual 'transaction'. It attracts and nourishes the dead so that the dead may feed the living in turn. The impoverished mortal connects with immortal abundance, in this way.

In cosmologies from all over the world we find a general terror of contact with the dead and the notion that any interaction might be lethal or fatal. The spiritual explanation for this is that dead people often take a piece of our soul with them, when they die, grief causes soul loss and we feel that motion as 'death pulling on us' before our time. Many African cultures teach that 'the dead pull on the living' and the dangers of that.

We find many reports of Holle roaming both land and sky as a leader of The Wild Hunt, accompanied by her Heimchen, the spirits of dead children. She sometimes appears as a huntress blowing her horn, followed by a pack of dogs. Some scholars point out that Odin replaced her when a shift occurred to a venerating sky gods, warrior gods, a predominantly male pantheon.

Iceland, of course, has Gryla, an Ogress living in a cave who descends from the mountains in mid-Winter. She has 13 sons (The Yule Lads), and a giant, black cat.[11]

Holle was said to collect the souls of dead children, children who died before being baptised, or who passed in pre-Christian times. New-born children were said to have been pulled wet from *Holda's pond*. At that time people named children at nine days old and believed that the souls of children were not yet attached to the ancestral tree during those dangerous nine days. Her death goddess aspect makes her a frightening and easily misunderstood figure, but do we really want the souls of dead infants floating between the world? (No, we don't!) She was said to travel in the guise of an old woman in a wagon, accompanied by a troop of spirit children.[6]

In later Christian times Perchta-Holle also welcomes into her entourage those people who have not earned a place in 'either Heaven or Hell': suicides, witches and wizards.

Both Vrouw Holle and Norse goddess Hel were associated with the Elder tree, *Hollebier* and *Holantar* in German, whose spirit, also perceived as a dignified old woman, is said to guard the road to the Underworld. In Danish she is the Hyllemoer or Elder Mother. This tree is connected to sexuality and birth and it has erotic connotations in folk songs.[12]

In German the elder tree is named for Frau Holle: Hollerbaum. The Elder Tree was known as 'the medicine chest of common people', because all its parts (berries, leaves etc.) can be used to treat various ailments. I like sitting by our Elder Tree in Sweden. I catch glimpses of Vrouw Holle there. I sometimes seek her guidance, but only fools rush where angels fear to tread. She is formidable!

When Europe became Christianised, Holle became feared, even demonised, along with all pre-Christian material and beings. Her crucial role: patrolling the liminal zone between Life and Death was no longer understood. Her profound compassion for Life, especially new life in all its tender and fragile manifestations, was no longer fathomed. Instead, she became the Goddess of Witches and was said to lead an army of witches riding their distaffs (a tool used in spinning) in her life-giving aspect or she appeared armed with sickles (in her death-bringing aspect). The troop accompanying her is often called the Furious Host. In Dutch: Het Wilde Heir.

She keeps a close eye on the women doing their spinning and weaving. At the time of the winter solstice women were supposed to clear their distaffs and put their spinning tools away. She would visit and run inspections. When she was pleased, she would gift women and girls spindles and if not, she'd mete out punishment

Some people, therefore, refer to her as a goddess of housekeeping 'with OCD tendencies'. However, working with her directly brought me the revelation that the clearing of distaffs and drop spindles is of a magical/shamanic nature: it involved unwinding the Threads of Life of those who had died that year, along with any imprints or attachments to the Earth realm still active for them. It also means the unbinding of that all that serves no more (old stories, pain, perceptions and paradigms). Therefore, she is the great goddess of ancestral healing work, as well as psychopomp work.

In Old Europe this work of disentangling and freeing was built into the yearly calendar as a sacred task. This means that the problems did not stack up for generations or centuries, as they do today! Therefor I urge people to work with Holle again in this vital area of compassionate community service: healing and soothing the ancestors, helping them cross over, healing long-standing imprints destroying families, reaching out to those who have had a miscarriage, lost a child or desperately long for a child.

De Vroneldenstraet or Milky Way

In Middle Dutch the name of the Milky Way was Vroneldenstraet: the street or highway of Frau Holle. This may have referred to the Milky Way, which the countries of Northern Europe perceived as a celestial highway. It was also linked to the migration paths of birds (as Frau Holle is often depicted as having one goose foot) and is called The Pathway of Birds in Finnish and Lithuanian.[13]

As a truly ancient Old European being, Holle is a shapeshifter who takes many different forms, ranging from beautiful young woman to an old witch or hag (the indwelling spirit of the HAEGL rune). She is said to have silver hair, crooked teeth and a big nose (yes, the standard description of a witch, my children were measuring my nose the other day!) Like Odin's wife Frigg she is said to carry a bunch of keys hanging from her belt and to be a patroness of housewives and housekeeping skills. She insists on hard work and high standards! Some scholars have posed the question whether she might actually be a more southern manifestations of Frigg, as Odin's consort. (Others think Odin usurped her!)

She shares with Frigg a connection to bodies of water, such as wells, springs, bogs and fens. Frigg's realm is called Fensalir, the "halls in the fen". Children are bathed in her well, to make them "good" and healthy, their lives sprinkled with good fortune by Holle.

Others link her to the Scandinavian Huldra, who is a mysterious Forest Spirit with a tail. Some call her the Queen of the Huldrefolk, forest spirits or Faery Folk.

It has been claimed that one race of faeries, the Huldrefolk, may be named after Holle. In Scandinavia they are often described as wood wives, beautiful maidens with cow tails (which they try to hide from their human suitors!)[14]

In one German legend a woman dressed in white appears from a

*lake and introduces herself as Hertha, Lady of the Earth. "I have
come from the island of Rugen in the North to visit this part of
my realm" She says that Holle has won her favour and that she
appoints Holle as her representative in these lands. She gives Holle
a bell and a beautiful house, where all housework is done perfectly
by magic and invisible hands.*[15]

The Brothers Grimm famously told a tale about Frau Holle.
A widow had two daughters, a lazy girl (Pitchmary) and a
virtuous one (Goldmary). The industrious girl falls down a
well in an attempt to retrieve a dropped spindle. She lands in a
magical place where bread asks to be taken out of the oven and
apples on a tree ask to picked. She assists an old woman with her
housework (and indeed the shaking out of bedding, making it
snow in the everyday world). As a reward she is showered with
gold. Her mother then also sends the lazy sister down the well
but things don't end well, she ends up being tarred instead (in
another version toads drop from her mouth as she speaks). One
could also say that one girl represents the return of Light and the
golden sun while the other girl is darkness and inertia. Author
GardenStone uses a phrase used by medieval philosophers: 'Evil
or the Devil can only ever be God's Ape' and imitate Good, but
fail'.[15]

The Hollen[16] gather at New Moon in a place where a birch
tree grows near a spring. They dance in a circle around the tree
while Frau Holle rattles her bunch of golden keys. The Thursday
night before Christmas is called Holle Eve in the Westerwald
Forest. Vrouw Holle doing her washing is said to create rain,
fog is smoke from her chimney and fire, and lightning is her
scotching the flax. Snow is caused by her shaking out her
featherdown bedding. During winter people turned the wool
and flax from the summer's harvest into clothing for everyone
on a homestead.

Folk Wisdom from Germany[17]

- When mist covers the mountain: Frau Holle has a made a fire in the mountain.
- Newborn children are fetched by midwives from Holle's pond.
- Like Berthe (Berchta) Holle is the Queen of Elves and Holden.
- In some local versions she appears as a hunchback mother.
- Bad spinners were threatened with The Enchanted Woman.
- During the strawberry harvest any strawberries that had dropped on the Earth were left there for Holle.

Mother Goose

Some authors connect Holle to Mother Goose, because she was said to have a flat (webbed) foot, from pressing down the pedal of the spinning wheel for hours a day. She is described as wearing a red goose down cloak on Christmas Eve (in earlier times of course the winter solstice), while delivering presents. This links her to St Nicholas, the Germanic template for Santa Claus today.

There are stories about Holle turning a spinning wheel to gold and the thread on it too. However, if women in the Harz mountains do not empty their distaff, Holle brings chopped straw instead.

My own intuition tells me that she is connected to Mother Goose and that both are linked to an earlier Neolithic goddess, possibly a bird goddess, who embodies the Earth and all weathers and seasons, but does not yet divide into the hypostases we find later (such as Frigg-Freyja). And of course, even later one male god and his son take center stage and their Judeo-Christian male priests turn all ancient powerful goddesses into wicked witch figures.

Neolithic and Bronze Age iconographic evidence points to bird and snake female figures: these include birds and snakes with female attributes, and hybrids of the two.[18]

The Norse goddess Freyja is often called a witch as well and said to ride a large feline, ancestor of the stereotypical witches' cat and familiar.

In conclusion, the witch and the beneficent and monstrous goddesses were transmutations of the Neolithic European goddess of life and death. Whereas the powers over both life and death were natural to the prehistoric goddess, her powers over death were feared by many of the assimilating historical cultures. The new patriarchal peoples, because of their fear of the life continuum of birth, death, and rebirth, were taught to fear and dishonor the death aspects of the goddesses instead of worshiping them as totalities. The unified goddess became fragmented. Later, when in Western culture the religion of the goddess, and of gods and goddesses, was replaced with male-centered Judeo-Christian religion, and spirit became honored over matter, the deity became removed, distant from mortals. The mortal could no longer directly partake of the divine.[18]

The Slavic witch Baba Yaga is often portrayed as a bird or snake[19] and depicted as living in the forest. Her house notoriously stands on chicken legs (another bird!) She was said to eat any mortals who got too close. This is the archetype behind the story of the Witch who tries to eat *Hans en Grietje* (Hansel and Gretel).

It has been said that Life is a conjugation of the verb *to eat*: we eat to live until we ourselves become food for other species (generally after burial). Cremation makes us *food for fire.*

Freyja is said to have a falcon cloak and to fly over the battle fields, accompanied by Valkyries, as the Picker of the Slain. The Irish goddess Badb was a crow goddess who brought death (think back to Frisian goddess Baduhenna). She may have been synonymous with The Morrígan. Some authors say that she morphed out of an earlier deity who was really a personification of the land. Celtic people call her the Cailleach.

This figure is found in traditional cosmology as 'the personification, in divine female form, of the physical landscape within which human life is lived and also of the cosmic forces at work in that landscape'. [] Placenames and physical elements of the landscape are frequently associated with the death and burial of divine females who can be considered derivations of a generative female divinity. These include mountains, mounds, coastline, rivers, lakes and caves. This cosmology included the weather and the fertility of the land, which later developed into the sovereignty principle. Jungian analyst, Sylvia Brinton Perera refers to this as 'the sacred and natural order of the unus mundus *– the primeval unity before the opposites are separated'.*[20]

Holle too represents this primordial unity, this divine state of Oneness. Only later do splits occur between mother goddess and death goddess, Nerthus divides into Frigg and Freyja, later worshipped by 'upstanding women and wicked witches' respectively. In this context, please remember how many *matronae* represent features in the landscape (Mountain Mothers or Mothers of Rivers etc.)

Vrouw Holle was said to rock the cradle at times when exhausted new mothers slept. Just like Odin she has a strong connection to the wild storms that sweep the land. The winter storms are linked to the final outbreath of the dying and to Odin as the god of Divine speech and poetry; also to Norse goddess Hel receiving into her realm Helheim the people dying an ordinary "straw" death in bed and not a warrior's heroic death. Some call Holle *The White Lady*, or *The Winter Goddess*, because of her connection to Winter and snow.

GardenStone on Holle's connection
to trees and plants

German author GardenStone claims that new research shows a strong connection between Frau Holle and Nerthus or Hertha. She reports that the clearest signs are found at The Hoher Meißner, a mountain range in Hesse, Central Germany, where we find a beech tree forest.[21]

Her special tree is the Elder tree (*Sambucus nigra*), Holunder in German. The first syllable *hol* has been linked by etymologists to its equivalents, the Swedish Hylle and Danish Hyld. In Germany the Holunder is also known as Holder, Hollerbaum and similar variants.[22]Every elder tree is said to be a portal to Holle's realm. The lime tree is also consecrated to her, in her brighter life-enhancing manifestation (fertility, marriage and domestic peace).[23]

The legend has it that Frau Holle turned lazy and argumentative girls into cats and locked them up in the Kitzkammer. However, the word Kitz comes from Kiez (not Katze – cat), meaning *screech owl!* (The name of demonised goddess Lilith also means screech owl).[24]

In Northern Hesse *Hollen* are dwarves or imps, and the servants of Frau Holle.[25]

Young wives would bathe in ponds in caves associated with Mother Holle and usually get pregnant within a year. However, this special bath could only be taken on Christmas Day or May Eve (Walpurgisnight). The herb *Friggjargras* (which is the Icelandic name for the Orchis maculate) was used in love magic as an aphrodisiac, its name sometimes translated into "lovemaking grass".[26]

Juniper is also said to have a connection to both Frau Holle and Frigg. Juniper smoke chases off bad spirits and the berries were viewed as a panacea.[27]

Lady's Bedstraw (Galium verum, also known as cleavers), said to be connected to Frau Holle, is used for cancer, hysteria, sexual desire, spasms, and many other conditions. It is sometimes applied directly to the skin for scaly, itchy skin (psoriasis), poorly healing wounds, and to stop bleeding.[28] Cleavers (*Galium aparine*) is used as food for geese and chickens and is also known as 'Goosegrass' and 'Gosling Weed'.[29] I find it interesting that GardenStone associates this with Frau Holle due to the connection to Mother Goose.[30]

GardenStone tells an interesting story about Odin meeting three women in a forest while riding Sleipnir. He stays the night in their cave and the eldest woman, a great sorceress, admits she lured him in, as she wants to conceive a child with him. The other two women are Thorgerd and Irpa, her daughters. Odin makes Huld the Queen of the Northern Realm and she gives him his two ravens: Huginn and Muninn. Here again we find a connection between an ancient goddess and ravens (think back to Baduhenna and The Morrigan).[31]

In Denmark people believe that the Hyldemoer lives under the elder tree and that every elder tree is a gateway (just like rune Haegl is a gate and it may well be Holle's or Hel's gate!) In ancient times people believed that sleeping under an elder tree for one night was sufficient to cure any disease. A married woman wishing for a child needs to kiss an elder bush!

Frau Holle presided over The Twelve Nights period. Each of the Twelve Nights was linked to one of the twelve months of the coming year. This is the traditional time for Omen Walks: going for a walk and writing down all messages, all signs from the spirit world, as a month-by-month prediction for the year to come.[32]

GardenStone claims that Frau Holle is one named member of a larger collective of white women (Witte Wieven, Chapter 7) and that those Hollen gather at New Moon to dance around a birch tree.[33]

The Hoher Meißner is a mountain massif with a height of

753.6 m and is located in the Meißner-Kaufunger Wald nature park in Hesse, Germany.

Frau Holda is a Goddess of the Underworld, death & regeneration. Small stiff white Goddess figurines with small breast & exaggerated pubic triangles, were placed alongside the dead in order for her accompany the person on their journey of renewal.

Both Holda and Hel were associated with the Elder tree, Hollebier and Holantar in German, whose spirit (also seen as a dignified old woman) is said to guard the road to the Underworld ... be it quiet Helheim or Holda's magical realm.[34]

Perchta

Some scholars equate Vrouw Holle with the Germanic goddess Perchta but other people (including myself) insist that they are two distinct goddesses, just as Freyja and Frigg are perceived as two distinct goddesses in our time. She hails from the Alpine regions of southern Germany and Austria and is also known as Berchta, Bertha or the *Spinnstubenfrau* or Spinning Room Lady. She is strongly associated with the Winter Ember Days falling on the Wednesday, Friday and Saturday after the Dec 13th Feast of St Lucy.[35]

Perchta (also Berchta, Berchte, Pehrta and Berta and a myriad of related local names) personifies the land and acts as a patroness of mothers. North of Bavaria, her counterpart is Holda (Hulde, Holle). Both are ambiguous beings.

Ridenour reports that Martin Luther seemed to know her as a weird "fraw Holda" characterized by a long snout, rags and "straw armor". Until today Alpine folklore depicts her as a frightening monster: eating, tearing asunder or disemboweling those who displease her.[36]

Austrian mythologist Lotte Motz says that Perchta was said to wipe unspun flax (left on the distaff) with her excrement and Grimm mentions her burning the hands of lazy spinners.[37]

Perchta is depicted as an old crone with a long and beak-like iron nose, dressed in rags. Her hands, teeth and warts are sometimes also described as made of iron. She carries a cane and hides a knife under her skirt. She is said to resemble Frigg (but not in outward appearance!) as both are associated with spinning and housekeeping. Women needed to make sure all their flax was spun by Twelfth Night, or else she would wreck your house. People would leave out a bowl of porridge for her, just as they did for Vrouw Holle. She too is associated with The Wild Hunt. The last three Thursdays before Christmas are known as Berchtl Nights (or Knocking Nights).[38] Again, we find an 'army' of dead children riding out.[39]

Just as we find Perchta as a witch, wearing a red cloak, flying around on her broomstick and dropping presents into the shoes of children. Today this job is performed by St. Nicholas and Dutch children still engage in "schoenen zetten" (setting out their shoes to receive treats and small gifts).

In many villages of the Franconian Jura, January 6th was called Berchta's Eve. Tradition required them to set out a table with food and drink (this is sometimes called a Dumb Supper in English). Lady Berchta came calling with her troop of children. They would all eat and drink – and then bless the house, family and cattle. She would shimmer in the moonlight. The children would sing their songs and play musical instruments (the huldreslaat).

Perchta is closely link to the contemporary phenomenon of *Perchten*, actually it is the plural of Perchta! This is the name of both her entourage and the animal masks worn in parades and festival, in the alpine regions of Austria and Germany.

The Perchten are divided into two species: *Schönperchten* (schön means 'good' or 'beautiful') and *Schiachperchten* (darker or creepier perchten). The contemporary perchten are Schiachperchten. The modern Percht is largely indistinguishable from the Krampus, wearing the same furs, horned mask and bells. It often carries a switch or horsetail whip, using to simultaneously 'bring luck' and 'drive out evil'.

They are associated with Epiphany and their name is understood to be a corruption of the Old High German term for Epiphany: Giberahta naht = the night of shining forth or manifestation (the Christ child). Both Perchta and Holda are sometimes associated with the Ember Days, which are the four days set aside for fasting by the Church.[40]

Perchta is described as having large feet or one large foot: e.g. *Behrte mit dem Fuoze* or *Behrta cum magno pede*. This is the spinner's foot on the treadle. One mismatched foot is an archetypal signifier of a supernatural being, comparable to the cloven hoofs of the Devil.[41]

The argument has been made that in Adenes le Roi's 13th century poem Berte aux grands pies, a French fairy figure evolved from Perchta: Queen Pedauca (from pied d'oie or goosefoot). Like Perchta she is associated with spinning and depicted as a storyteller, relating her to the English Mother Goose.[41]

Specific foods were prepared on the nights of her visits. Families at their fill of this and left out uneaten food for Perchta & her company. Saved portions of this ritual meal would either be left on a specially prepared *Perchtentish* (Perchten table) or fed to the farm animals to bless them with good health and fertility. For convenience of the retinue, the offering might be left outside under a tree, or in the branches, or on a rooftop where night-flying spirits might most easily receive it.

Many scholars equate Holle and Perchta and refer to them/ her as Hold-Perchta, one single ancient entity, where Perchta is a local name for Holda. Please note that Christian missionaries had already arrived in the Alps around the second century (much earlier than further north). Perchta and the first mention of Perchta appear in written sources occurs around the year 1200.[41]

Berchta or Perchta is sometimes called the Queen of the Ghost Children. In one local legend she meets a ferryman and tells him he needs to take three loads of passengers across the river. Only then does a large group of children move into view. The elder children carried parts of a shiny plough while the younger ones were riding small goats. He realised it was Berchta and her *ghost children*.[42]

The plough links the dead to fertility and we need to remember that the Big Dipper (asterism Ursa Major) is called The Plough in Ireland and the UK.

Another interesting snippet is that the female side of the family is called the distaff side while the male side of the family is called the spear side. The spear was considered a man's tool in the same way the distaff belonged to women. Today this way of describing genealogy has become rare and antiquated.[43]

The Middle Low German word *dise* means 'a bunch of flax on a distaff'. (Remember that Völva means staff-bearer and that ancient pictures show her staff was a distaff, not a regular stick!) The similarity to the word dis or Disir is strong, but I cannot find a straight etymological connection. The word Disir refers to deified and protective female ancestors. Freyja was the Vanadis – the great goddess of the Vanir.

St. Distaff's Day (1640s) was Jan. 7, when women took up spinning again after the lull over the Twelvetide Period. The distaff is essentially a long forked stick that holds the flax for spinning. *Dis* is a bunch of flax and in Middle Low German staef is stick or staff.[44]

*The basic meaning of the word dís is 'goddess'. [...] It is now usually derived from the Indo-European root * dhēi-, "to suck, suckle" and a form dhīsana. Scholars have associated the dísir with the West Germanic Idisi, seeing the initial i- as having been lost early in Old or Proto-Norse.*[45]

Perchten – The Alpine Festival

The ancient pre-Christian festival is still celebrated in the Alpine regions and connected to the 'driving out of devils' or 'bad souls' (more likely dead souls) The costumes are stunning (run a search and look at some photographs), made from corn leaves combined with masks and horned head dresses. Some costumes weigh a hefty 30 kg (that is heavier than the personal luggage limit of most airlines!)[46]

While Perchta first appears in 12th century sources, the word Perchten first occurs centuries later. In 1468 there is a reference to her retinue viewed as souls of deceased people, but the members are not called Perchten. We hear about both the spectral night-travellers and masqueraders impersonating them.

People who engage in the contemporary Perchten festivals prefer claiming a heritage stretching back to the Deep Ancestors – but Ridenour challenges that in his Krampus book. He says that before the 19th century there were only Perchten, not schon and schiach, though likely they were all Schiach [ugly and frightening]![47] The Bavarian word *Krampn* means lifeless or shriveled and so clearly has death and decay connotation. In this festival a surprising pairing occurs: St Nicholas and Perchta!

Ridenour also reports that in the small town of Rauris, 30 miles west of Gastein, we find birdlike Schnabelperchten inspecting homes etc., while creating messes along the way.[48]

Males cross-dress as old women: grandmotherly kerchiefs, parched skirts, sweater and archaic straw slippers sometimes called "witches slippers". Unlike the bell-ringing Perchten they move about with eerie stealth, slipping into homes in groups of four or five, softly clucking "ga-ga-ga" in droning chorus. Their elongated beaks, inspired by Perchta's prominent nose, are made of old linen and sticks. They are intricately rigged to clap with each chirped syllable. The Schnabelperchten carry brooms for sweeping and large scissors hinting at P's tendency to cut open bellies.[48]

Just like children trick-or-treating at Halloween, costumed Perchten also expect food in exchange for "bringing good luck" and they use a mix of threats and begging.

Kinder ode Speck
Derweil gehe Ich night weg
(Children or bacon, Or I won't go away!)

Feeding Perchta greasy foods could save you from her iron grip as she needed to remove her iron gloves in order to eat such things! The Perchtenmilch was linked to the earliest trials of witch persecution.[49] This tradition, of feeding (what Chinese Buddhism calls) *hungry ghosts*,[50] lives on, in our time, in the form of Dumb Suppers: laying a table for the dead and setting out food for them. The word 'dumb' refers to silent (not 'stupid').[51]

The Heimchen

There was a belief in medieval times that faeries were the reborn souls of dead and unbaptized infants. This brings us back to the Heimchen, Holle's child companions. Sad music is heard when they appear: the *huldreslaat*, said to be played by the Huldrefolk (who sometimes take on human apprentices). Another word, used by GardenStone is *Wichtlein* (a kind of imp).

These invisible deceased infants visit houses to drink a bowl of Perchtenmilch (porridge made from cow's milk) in the dead of night. The bowl was said to be emptied and mysteriously refilled (meaning that the Heimchen only absorb the spiritual nourishment, not its physical counterpart). How the bowl was found the next day would lend itself to interpretations for the year to come (as an oracle).[52]

The word *heimchen* translates as cricket and it is also used to describe a shy or retiring individual, especially a young female. As a Dutch speaker I will point out that the German word 'heimchen' can also be a diminutive of the word home. In English we speak of 'homely' individuals... (simple, unpretentious, possibly unattractive).

Grimm says about the Heimchen: "As the Christian god has not made them His, they fall to the Old Heathen One".[52]

Holda also takes care of the unbaptized dead, where a peasant assists a Heimchen and calls the child a *ragamuffin*. This means that the child has been unintentionally christened and given a kind of name. The accidental 'baptism' frees his soul from nocturnal wandering (please note spirit workers!)[53]

Conclusion

Frau Holle deserves to return to our collective consciousness and take her rightful place as one of the most ancient deities of Old Europe who performs crucial tasks. With the passing of centuries the feasting of the Venusberg and drinking in wine cellars was slowly transformed to the more 'Satanic' revels of the modern witches' Sabbath (in other words: the filter of demonic perception gathered strength).

In Nordic literature, there is a giantess named Hulda in Sturlunga's Saga who may be related to Holda (or may be Holda). In the Ynglinga saga, the Völva and Seithkona named Hulla may be related to Holda. She also may be related to a woman named Hulda who was said to have had an affair with Odin, bearing the goddesses Thorgerdhr and Irpa who appear in various Germanic sagas. They may have been local land-goddesses in Germany, giantesses who had cults in their own right.[54]

Ridenour notes that even the saints once twisted themselves into sinister forms during the December month. On St Lucy Day (December 13th, still celebrated in Scandinavia) the shrouded Lutz or Lutzelfrau once threatened children with evisceration or drowning. On Thomas Day, bloody Thomas stalked the forest with a gore-drenched hammer...[55]

Dark Lucy reminds us of Baba Yaga. She also appears in Scandinavia, particularly Sweden, where St Lucy's wicked counterpart, the Lussi, was well known for haunting Lussinatta - on this night she flies thru the skies like Holda or the Wild Hunter with her ghostly retinue the Lussen, Lussiner or Lusseguber.[55]

The terms army and hunt are misleading as the prey is rarely specified. It is more of a stampede or figures chasing each other.

My own interpretation is that the end of year (Northern Hemisphere) is a time of encroaching darkness and dismemberment. It is easier to form a relationship with these forces if they take a humanoid-shape. Winter used to be the most dangerous time of year in Northern Europe. Poor people literally died from exposure and starvation. This tragic phenomenon lives on today in form of homeless people perishing on our streets.

Huldreslaat – eerie otherworldly music

Midnight is the hour when the Death Folk move around and the bony figure of Death leads with his violin all who will die within the year...[56]

However, we should not miss the references to resurrection and rebirth. The Night People have many names: Nachtvolk (Night Folk), Totenvolk (Dead Folk) or Totenschar (Throng of the Dead) but they are reported to bestow a supernatural musical ability! They also restore living creatures from bones...

Sometimes there is an ethereal music or sounds of drums and pipes, a strange hum like the buzzing of bees, a song sounding like a Psalm or the rattling of bones, many voices in prayer... Crescendos and crashes. Those sounds could predict the future: beautiful music signifies a good year to come. However, a discordant noise or cacophony predicts sickness or war.[56] *(Did anyone hear any eerie discordant music before Covid-19 arrived?)*

On New Year's Eve the backdoor is opened – through which good luck arrives! A clean home is important, as dirt and disorder might attract malevolent spirits. To finish on a positive note:

> *Women & children would not go out unescorted after sunset for fear of the Wild Hunter etc. BUT those who did might see wondrous sights: a midnight on Xmas Eve some brooks turned to wine, bees buzzed and swarmed in the frigid air & standing under an apple tree one might look up & see the heavens open. Animals spoke in their stalls and stables. Domestic animals might also use the gift of speech to talk to the Hausgeist or Spirit of the House.*[57]

Old folklore about the Heimchen sees them manifested as will-o'-the-wisps, the ghost lights, corpse candles or *ignus fatuus* appearing, particularly over swamps, and said to lure from known footpaths unwary travelers mistaking them for village lights or helpful beings. This leads us to our next chapter: Corpse Roads.

Activity #12 Omen Walk (and some questions)

Scandinavia knows the tradition of Årsgång (literally The Year's Walk) or Omen Walk. Follow the footnote, read the article and perform this practice.[58]

Please note that you can do this any time, not only on Christmas Day or New Year's Day.

Next (attempt to) formulate answers to the following questions:

- Whom do I demonize (meaning: project my own negative thoughts onto, blame for things I engage in, or am capable of, myself)?

- Have I ever heard the Huldreslaat or otherworldly music? If so, when and under which circumstances?
- What do I believe happens to the souls of dead babies and children?[59]
- Could the following passage inspire me?

In Lower Bavaria the fast after midnight mass was broken with sausages, with a portion set aside for the departed. If on Xmas morning the food appeared untouched, it was donated to a needy person to pray for the dead & offer sustenance in another form.[60]

Chapter 13

Dodenwegen - Corpse Roads

Now it is the time of night
That all the graves are gaping wide
Every one lets forth his sprite
In the church-way paths to glide
-Words spoken by Puck in Shakespeare's Midsummer
Night's Dream[1]

My legs preserved a ghost sense of stride, a muscle memory
of repeated action, and twitched forwards even as I rested.
-Robert Mcfarlane in The Old Ways – A Journey on Foot[2]

Corpse Roads today

In contemporary Dutch the term *Dodenwegen* (Death Roads or
Corpse Roads) has taken on a new meaning. In the extremely
crowded country that is the Netherlands, it refers to roads that
clock up many fatal accidents.[3]

The media will use this phrase when serious accidents
repeatedly happen on the same roads. A related concept
is *'polderblindheid'*: a form of reduced alertness (hypnotic
blindness) brought on by extremely straight roads and a lack of
visual stimulants. The driver switches to autopilot while his or
her mind roams elsewhere.

A polder is a low-lying tract of land (below sea level),
protected from the sea by means of embankments called dijken
(dikes). Today many of these polders are farmland and fields
with extremely straight roads running through them. Therefore
polder-blindness refers to the almost hypnotic trance state
brought on by driving in a very straight line through a landscape
with almost no visual stimulants. (The notable exception is of

course when the tulips fields are in full bloom! My mother lives in the *polder* and for many years she had the tulips fields and windmills right behind her house!)

'Dodenwegen' or Corpse Roads historically speaking

In Brittany there is a folk belief that wherever a Yew tree grows in a churchyard, one root of this tree will grow through the mouth of a corpse. Morbid as it sounds, this was probably intentional: the Yew tree took the deceased under its wings (as it were) and guided it to the next step in mysteries of Life and Death. Death is a rebirth into the world of spirit.[4]

Corpse Roads are also known as coffin roads, church-ways and funeral paths. They all lead from a remote village to the lych gate of a parish church many miles away. The word lych is derived from *lich*, meaning corpse (lik in Old Norse, lijk in Dutch).[5]

Other British terms for such a road are: bier road, burial road, coffin line, corpse way, funeral road, lych way, lyke way or procession way.[6]

If the dead person fails to embark on this journey, he or she becomes 'the living dead' or a vampire, bothering and haunting the living. This outcome was much feared by pagan peoples and it explains why many special precautions were taken, in taking someone to their final resting place. (In plain English: people tried to prevent hauntings!)

The Wild Hunt was also said to follow these corpse roads. Symbolically speaking it is the road travelled by a human soul to the otherworld realm of the Norse Goddess Hel.

Corpse roads were created in medieval times as the general population increased and villages sprung up farther and farther afield. This means that an expansion of church building occurred as well. Canon law of the period stated that a parishioner must be buried on the grounds of the Mother Church, no matter how far away from the village this way, or how dangerous it was to travel the path. Therefore, corpse roads connected outlying villages and locations to their mother church, at the heart of the parish, that held burial rights.[6]

We find these paths in the Netherlands, the United Kingdom and the US. For obvious reasons many of these paths have a special significance and they are associated with folklore and superstition, such as tales of ghosts and spectral funeral processions.

Eight men would take turns carrying the body along a corpse road. Four men, one at corner, would carry the deceased until they came to a coffin stone. Those stone were deliberately placed along the path at set intervals. They were designated as place where the bier could be 'parked' for a rest and hand-over. At this point the other four men would take over and continue the journey, while the others got some rest.

Corpse roads were usually straight because they followed the most direct route from the village to the burial grounds. Depending on the location, they could vary in length from a few miles to close on ten miles. (Please note that ten miles is just over sixteen kilometres!)

It was believed that any field used as a coffin road would fail to produce good crops. Those paths were also associated with spirits, wraiths and ghost stories. Over time many of those 'new' churches were also granted burial rights and the corpse roads fell out of use.[6]

Lijkwegen in the Netherlands

In the Netherlands some of these corpse roads (*lijkwegen*) can still be walked. They still appear on certain maps and in old regional records.

But elsewhere, in [the province of] Gelderland for instance, we still find the corpse roads marked, that every funeral procession from

*every farm followed to reach the churchyard. As it was important
to be able to bury the dead in winter as well, those paths were
given the best maintenance and care possible. Thus they naturally
became the regular traffic paths as well, the same as everywhere in
the country, these were also called the "church paths (1875).*[7]

Dutch folklore speaks of a 'helmdrager': a person born with the
caul over their head. They are often, but not always, the seventh
son of a seventh son. They often find themselves driven from their
beds and hurrying to the corpse road, in order to *see* (seeing in
the sense of foresight, receiving advance knowledge) any deaths
about to occur in the neighbourhood. Those *helmdragers* (helmet
wearers) were never a welcome presence in the community
because everyone feared something bad was bound to happen,
the moment a *helmdrager* appeared.[8]

Folklore related to Corpse Roads

The essence of all ancient spirit-lore related to corpse roads is
that spirits move through any physical landscape following
specific paths or routes. They travel, as the crow flies, meaning in
straight lines, wherever possible. This is also why corpse roads
are so straight that they sometimes cut right through hedges,
walls and even private dwellings!

This means that the opposite thing: non-linear, curved or
loopy shapes hinder the movement of spirits. This explains (at
least in part) why traditionally labyrinths have been built to
capture spirits. It is said that in Scandinavia fisherman would
build stone labyrinths to catch and delay trolls and other ill-
meaning spirits, so they could get on their way with good winds
and decent weather conditions. We find many such labyrinths
on the coast of Sweden.[9]

In a similar fashion ghosts are said to fly close to the ground,
setting a direct course. For that reason, a straight line or path
connecting two places was often kept free of walls, fences and

buildings, to give those 'flying phantoms' plenty of space. Corpse roads run in a straight line over mountains and valleys, through marshes and towns and sometimes even through houses! Corpse roads were left unploughed as it was considered very bad luck if for, whatever reason, it became necessary to take a different route.

Doling Lights and Corpse Candles

A corpse candle or corpse light is a flame or ball of light, often blue, that is observed travelling just above the ground from a cemetery to the home of dying person, and back again.[10]

Corpse fire is a similar phenomenon. It refers to lights appearing in graveyards as an omen of death or impending tragedy. They marked out the route of an imminent funeral, from a victim's house to the churchyard. It would vanish into the ground at the site of the burial. This was said often said to occur the night before a death.

The scientific explanation for *'dwaallichten'* (literally wandering lights) is that gas generated by marshes slowly ignites, due to a fermenting of organic material small blue flickering flames appear.[11]

Dwaallichtjes (*small* wandering lights –the Dutch language overdoses on diminutives) could also be caused by fireflies. Barn owls are literally called 'church owls' (*kerkuilen*) in Dutch and their plumage is so light that it can reflect light from other sources (for instance moon light) and produce light effects which resemble dwaallichten. This is called bioluminescence.

In Dutch folklore we find many spiritual explanations. Some say that these wandering lights are the souls of stillborn or unbaptised children. They are said to approach passers-by in the hope of leading them to a well or pond, in the hope of being baptised so they can go to the Christian Heaven.[12] They were also perceived as lights created by The Devil to lead people astray and into sin.

Vuurmannen – Men (Human figures) of Fire

Yet another explanation is that they are souls of dead people returning to keep a promise or tend to unfinished business, the souls of 'sinners' or thieves (again, people banned from entering Christian Heaven). These are sometimes called *vuurmannen*, also *vuurgeesten* (fire ghosts).[13]

One very serious crime in the Netherlands was the moving of boundary markers or pillars that demarcated the borders between properties. Farmers sometimes did this to grab more land and a larger share of the harvest. It was said that people who did this would not find peace after death. They would curse themselves by doing so and instead of going to Heaven, they would end up hanging around the scene of their crime where they appeared to others as balls or figures of fire, often carrying the boundary stone (or wooden pillar) on their backs.

The good news was that salvation was within reach: when you meet such a Figure of Fire and it asks: 'Where do I put this boundary marker?', you only need to reply: 'Put it right back where you took it!' Once the fire ghost does this, it is released from its existence as a lost soul wandering the world.

The same fate befell murderers, which indicates just how grave a crime messing with boundary markers is! Murderers were said to return to the scene of their crime(s) after death.[14]

There are many local variations. I have provided a summary of the most common themes. For those of you who speak Dutch there is a wonderful resource called the Verhalen Bank[15] with a search function. You can type in some key words and the most relevant stories will appear. You can also add your own stories to this ever-expanding national archive. For instance, for more stories about these ghostly Figures of Fire, type in *Vuurmannen* and the system will bring up stories from different Dutch provinces. (Also try *Lijkwegen*!)

Folk wisdom teaches us that it is not appropriate to point at or whistle at dwaallighten. The best thing is getting home as soon as possible but you may find a blood stain or scorch mark on your door.

Spirit Children

Up to and including the 19th century stillborn children (or children who died soon after birth) often did not receive a funeral with its attendant grief rituals. The parents often did not know where and how their children were buried or cremated. Here we need to remember how, in that period, most families did not have access to medical care as we know it, or the instruction about hygiene, health and safety that all Western parents now receive as a matter of course.

In the Dutch province of Noord-Brabant many monuments have been erected in recent years to honour those children. The death of a baby or child is enough of a tragedy. However, the Roman Catholic doctrine that the souls of unbaptised children cannot enter Heaven" must have caused unspeakable additional agony for bereaved parents. The Church would not grant those children a grave of their own. Their remains were often stuffed out of sight in remote corners of churchyards, in unhallowed ground.

There were brutal sayings about this, that we also find in other countries, such as: 'One mouth less to feed is good news!' The death of babies and children was a taboo subject at the best of times and this got even worse when a child died before baptism.[16]

Dwaallightjes wandering lights) were perceived as the souls of such children. In Brabant they were sometimes called '*stallichtjes*' (farm stable lights), '*stalkaarsjes*' (farm stable candles), in local dialect: '*stalkerskes*' (not to be confused with the English word stalker), lights bobbing and flickering over farmer's fields. People lived in fear of those. They said that dark magic was in their air whenever there were sightings of these otherworld lights.

It was also said that such lights could appear in large numbers (up to a thousand) and beg for baptism. They could pull living people to bodies of water.

(Speaking as a spiritual teacher: many cultures teach that 'the dead pull on the living' and that this poses a real risk. This is one reason why elaborate death rituals are performed and in heathen times graveyards were situated well away from villages – to reduce this risk and tend to maintaining the balance between worlds).

The Roman Catholic Church responded by writing some fairy tales of its own to console heartbroken parents:

The fairytale of Donskopje (Little Downy Head)
Donskopje is also known as 'the child smiling in his sleep'.

Donskopje lived in Heaven with The Holy Mother of God and loved it there. However, one day it was his/her turn to be taken to Earth by the Angel of Life. Donskopje was not keen, he was happy where he was. After some negotiation it was agreed that Donskopje was allowed to return to Heaven if the homesickness got out of control. Donskopje was delivered to a loving father and mother on earth. He often smiles in his sleep. The parents think that Donskopje is dreaming but no one knowns that Donskopje dreams that he is back in Paradise, seated in the lap of the Holy Mother...[17]

These types of Roman Catholic fairy tales were designed to turn the situation on its head, as it were: 'Your child is better off with the Divine Mother'.

In the countryside in many European countries (especially in Gaelic, Slavic and Germanic folklore) we find the phenomenon of *will-o'-the-wisps.* They are mischievous spirits of the dead (or possibly other otherworld beings) that attempt to lead travellers astray. Sometimes they are believed to be the souls of unbaptised children, journeying between Heaven and Hell.

Other names for this, in English, are Jack O' Lantern, or Joan of the Wad, Jenny Burn-tail, Kitty wi' the Whisp, or Spunkie.[18]

Otherworld geography

In a Midsummer Night's Dream, Shakespeare suggests through the words of Puck (quoted at the top of this chapter), that corpse lines do not only run through the physical countryside, but also through both the spirit world (or astral world) and even the minds of human beings. You could call this *otherworld geography*.

The physical corpse roads came to be perceived as highways for the spirits. I spoke earlier of winding paths confusing spirits and Scandinavian fishermen trapping trolls in labyrinths. One reason for conveying corpses along dedicated pathways was to prevent their souls from returning to haunt the living. The feet of the corpse, for instance, were kept pointing away from the family home.

Similar measure taken involved ensuring the route taken involved bridges or stepping stones across running water (which the spirits could not cross) but also stiles and other liminal barriers. Those were designed to actively hinder the free passage of the spirits. In mediaeval Europe the belief in, so called, revenants (ghosts, in Dutch: *spoken*) was widespread.

For this reason corpse roads were edgy, liminal and possibly dangerous places. It is even possibly that this way of thinking informed the lay-out of Neolithic stone structures (for more about that see the Hunebedden Chapter). There are often 'spirit avenues' connecting structures we know were used as funerary sites. Using large stones to block openings to passage graves or burial chambers may just be another example of this.

Ley Lines

Some people make a direct connection between corpse roads and ley lines and this takes us to the field of geomancy.[19]

Ley lines are invisible lines drawn between landmarks, or

points of significance, in the landscape. ... This concept was put forward by the English antiquarian Alfred Watkins in the 1920s, in his book The Old Straight Track. He argued that straight lines could be drawn between various historic structures and that these represented trade routes created by ancient British societies. Although he gained a small following, Watkins' ideas were never accepted by the British archaeological establishment. Until today some people believe in such lines while many others don't. Some people actively working with this concept in the UK today are Chris Street and husband and wife team Gary Biltcliffe and Caroline Hoare. For example, they run a group called Spine of Albion[20] and Chris Street created the Earthstars Network.[21]

A Dutch journalist called Hans Jilesen uit Veghel made the discovery that The Inquisition deliberately did away with both corpse roads and the ley lines.[22]

He discovered that corpse roads were also called 'lichtwegen' (roads of light) once upon a time. They did not only lead from villages and remote rural location to churches. The phenomenon extended beyond that: all churches and other holy sites (heiligdommen in Dutch) are connected and positioned on a grid of intersecting straight lines.

Where these lines cross, we find remains of grave mounds, hunebedden and stone circles. Of interest for us is that Jilesen claims a more ancient take on the material we are exploring: those lines were said to create a grid or web of light that caught the lost souls, so they were scooped up and transported to The Light. These crossroads or intersections were places of power (krachtplaatsen in Dutch), even 'soul catchers'[22]

I cannot help but wonder how the arrival of Christianity, the fear of 'all things dark and heathen' and the subsequent layer of witch hunts and persecution affected the lost souls and 'spirit highways' (or "spirit flyways").⁻

Number 13 – Deadly and Divine

People working with numerology and the magic of numbers consider number thirteen Divine (or sacred) for the following reasons:[23]

- The Bible assigns to number 13 the meaning of rebellion against established authority, also making it the number of the moral outrage or corruption, causing Satan to rebel against God.
- Occultists make number 6 the number of man (think of Rune MADR or Mannaz) and number 7 the number of divine perfection. A human being is said to climb Jacob's ladder towards perfection (or enlightenment). Man plus enlightenment equals 6 + 7 = 13.
- On the road to enlightenment a person encounters many tests and challenges (initiations) therefore 13 is also the number of Death (and by extension rebirth as a fully realized being!)

Activity #13 Find a Corpse Road

Do some research: can you locate a Corpse Road (or lych gate) near you?

If not, look into ley lines and any work done by local geomancers or dowsers.

Consider training in Psychopomp work: skilled groups can re-activate ancient grids of light and portals!

Become the keeper/guardian (NL *hoeder*) of a piece of land, public land if need be (remove garbage, communicate with nature spirits etc.)

Dutch author and teacher Linda Wormhoudt makes the valid point that people in charge of woodland (*boswachters* in Dutch) or nature parks do not appreciate ribbons tied to trees or offerings left by ponds. This is perceived as pollution and removed as rubbish. Unless you are on your own land, make offerings that leave no trace: prayers, songs, pour out some water from a different location or make an arrangement of Autumn leaves that wind will soon disturb. Leave no trace and remember that if everyone takes a pebble home from the same beach – there soon won't be any pebble beaches...

Become aware of spirit children who linger in certain locations. Some have been there for centuries. Once upon a time it was not uncommon for unwanted (or disabled) babies to be left outside to die from exposure. Call on Vrouw Holle! Please involve someone with expert skills, if you sense something but the task is beyond you.

Chapter 14

The Landscapes of my Soul

This chapter provides some guidance for others where to go, if they plan to make a sacred journey to the Netherlands. (Please note that I have not included the wind mills, tulip fields and cheese markets you will find on any website aimed at tourists!) I am grateful to Dutch authors who have published their own favourite destinations and sacred journeys, all have been referenced. This list is only a starting point, it offers a limited selection of suggestions to get you started.

The province of Noord Holland

Den Helder

Our family moved around but I mainly grew up in the naval city of Den Helder (the far northern tip of the province Noord Holland). I loved living by the sea. I remember walking on the beach in all weather conditions with a close friend, discussing 'whether we could ever live in a place far from the sea'. It was my first experience of knowing that the landscape around me also shapes the landscape of my inner world, the landscape of my soul. In Den Helder you can take a ferry to the island of Texel, a popular summer destination.

Amsterdam

I lived in Amsterdam for five years but I think everyone arrives at their own version of Amsterdam, depending on interests and perception! It is a fairly small city so you can get around on foot or by bike. I recommend walks by the canals and talking to locals. Most Dutch people speak fairly fluent English.

My husband and I recently flew to Amsterdam and spent two nights in a youth hostel on a barge, just minutes from the Central Station. I did like sleeping right on the water of the

Amstel and had some interesting dreams rising from the black water, one dark February night.

Huis of Hilde

The Huis of Hilde, situated in Castricum, is a museum dedicated to the archaeological finds made in the province of Noord Holland. It opened in 2015 and the collection maps local discoveries. It was named for one model, on display in the museum, made as a facial reconstruction of a skeleton from the 4th century. The people who dug her up affectionately called her Hilde and this centre is named after her![1]

I enjoyed visiting this centre. The exhibition is laid out in an inviting way with many visual and interactive displays. The descriptions are in Dutch, I do not recall seeing many, or indeed *any,* translations into English.

Marken

A traditional village located on a peninsula in the Markermeer, in the province of Noord Holland. It used to be an island. It is a tourist attraction for its wooden houses and the inhabitants wearing traditional clothing (*klederdracht*) on special occasions, such as the Queen's Birthday (*Koninginnedag*, though Holland has had a king for years now, the festivities are still set for his grandmother's birthday). These clothes (but also bedding and other textiles used in the home) feature embroidery. Some textiles feature distinct small tassels.

The entire population of Marken wore *klederdracht* until about 1930. This custom gradually faded out over the second half of the 20th century. Today this custom is reserved for special occasions and feast days.

Marken used to belong to the mainland but a heavy storm separated it. Initially it was inhabited by Frisian monks who founded a monastery and chapel there. In 1957 a dike was constructed to connect this island back to the mainland. Today tourism has replaced the fishing industry of an earlier era.[2]

Heiloo
Visit the Runxput (Runx Well), the Chapel of Our Dear Lady in
Need (Onze Lieve Vrouwe ter Nood) and the Witte Kerk (White
Church). Try to connect to the fact that the earliest evidence
of human settlement was found here. Even today people go on
pilgrimages here.[3]

Province Zeeland: Walcheren and the Temple of Nehalennia

As the Netherlands (and Netherlanders) are profoundly
shaped by the sea, in their struggle to claim land from the sea,
Zeeland is a perfect place to start your sacred journey. Visit
the (modern) temple of Nehalennia In the year 1996 a number
of people came together to design this historical landmark.
It is situated in the yacht harbour at Colijnsplaat. The official
opening ceremony was in 2005. The temple is maintained by a
foundation called Stichting Nehalennia te Colijnsplaat.[4]

Province Friesland: Museum and Mummies

Het Fries Museum in Leeuwarden
This museum, dedicated to the history of Friesland[5], features
treasures from the terpen (dwelling mounds).

The Mummies of Wiuwert
Dutch author and photographer Henk Ganzeboom points us to
a village in central Friesland called Wiuwert. The church there
displays mummies discovered when a crypt was built in the 13th
century. Eleven mummies were originally displayed, of which
four remain today (and have not yet turned to dust).[6]

Province Drenthe: Hunebedden

To see a glimpse of the Stone Age, visit the Easter province of Drenthe (near the German border). Spread out over an area about 30 square kilometers we find 54 Hunebedden and *they are more ancient even than the pyramids in Egypt!* They were built from huge granite boulders, some of them weighing more than 25,000 kg! The big rocks (not a natural feature of the Dutch landscape) were delivered by Scandinavian glaciers in one of the Ice Ages. And, same as with the pyramids, we do not know exactly how the people of that time constructed and lifted these boulders. It remains a tantalising mystery![7] The most famous Hunebed is the one in Loon.

There is an on-line map.[8]

In Borger there is a Hunebed Information Centre you can visit.[9]

Province Overijssel

The Tankenberg, in the forest near Oldenzaal, is said to have been the sanctuary of goddess Tanfana. This 'mountain' (*berg* means mountain) is 84 meters high, which makes it the highest hill in the Netherlands. An interesting place to sit out and request an audience with Tanfana.[10]

Province Gelderland: Fever Tree in Overasselt

In the woodland near Overasselt, just south of Nijmegen, you can visit a *koortsboom* or fever tree, situated right next to the ruin of the medieval St. Walrick's Chapel.[11]

De Veluwe

The Netherlands does not have many large truly wild spaces but the national treasure is our national park De Veluwe: a forested ridge of hills (1100 km^2 in total) in the province of Gelderland. It features a variety of landscapes: woodland, heath, some small lakes and Europe's largest sand drifts. The Veluwe was formed by the Saalian glacial during the Pleistocene epoch, some 200,000 years ago. It is populated by deer and wild boar.[12] Wolves have recently made a come-back in the Netherlands!

Ancestral Blood

The most interesting journey to make is of course your own unique ancestral journey. If you have Dutch ancestors or connections, do some research to find where they lived and visit those locations. Also research the meaning of their names (first names and surnames both), as that may give you material to work with. Alternatively get lost and end up exactly where you need to be: be spirit-led and be surprised!

Chapter 15

A tentative reconstruction of a spirituality indigenous to The Low Countries

Een waarheid als een koe!
A truth the size of a cow!
(Dutch proverb)

If I wrote fiction, I would claim that Holland is the country of, and named for, Mother Holle, but no, Holland is derived from Holt Land, which means *Land of Many Trees*, something to remember in our time of deforestation and overpopulation.

Writing this book has been a labour of love, which has healed my relationship with my country of birth. It has helped me separate off personal and ancestral issues (my experience of growing up in a deeply traumatised family in the Netherlands) from the land, its spirits and its rich traditions. I can truly say that I am proud to be Dutch and to have a Dutch passport in our post-Brexit world, forever changed by Covid-19.

The question that drove my research for this book was: *is there enough material for a (tentative) reconstruction of a native spirituality rooted in ancient and ancestral material, unique to the people of (and informed by the land and waters of) the Netherlands?*

Once I had asked myself this question, it could not be un-asked, I could not return to the mindset I had before (of a strong focus on the Old Scandinavian spirituality I married into and teach globally). Initially I was sceptical. I have always perceived Scandinavia as far richer in folk traditions, a place where the old ways are so much closer to the surface of everyday modern life.

The discipline and one-year commitment of writing this book has blown me away: I am astounded at how much material lives on, in some way, or remains available to us, in other ways. Add to that a strong belief in personal revelation. An animist or profoundly non-anthropocentric mindset allows the land itself, bodies of water, trees and animals (and so forth) to be our daily teachers. Land, water, our own body, our ancestral field – all hold memories!

Nothing is ever completely lost to us. It leaves energetic fingerprints and continues to exist in other worlds.

Questions asked and answers found

It is perfectly possible to develop a personal spirituality deeply rooted in ancestral material from the Low Countries. I disagree with the assumption that spiritual Dutch people are 'practically forced to' resort to either studying core shamanism or adopting a spirituality from far-flung places (Native American, Peruvian, Buddhist.... Etc.) There is great value in all world traditions, but please know that there is plenty of material for *going native*! It would take more than a human lifetime to explore all the material our ancestors and the land have left us!

I have made a daily habit of chanting the Frisian rune row, standing in my ancestor gallery (where the pictures and names of our family's ancestors are mounted).

What about the Old Gods of the Netherlands? Are Odin and Wodan even the same god?

The field called comparative religion explains how we find apostasies of gods and goddesses. For instance, in Scandinavia the ancient proto-goddess Nerthus split into two goddesses: Frigg and Freyja, during the time of the Aesir. Tyr (Tiw, Ziu) was probably the leading god before Odin took over that office. Gods are always evolving in partnership with human beings. Therefore, I would say that *Odin and Wodan are not exactly the same god.* The Norse Odin takes on a different cloak of characteristics further south (in the Germanic territories) as Wuotan, Woden or

Wodan. For a Dutch person working with Odin is a great start, but sooner or later you will come face to face with Wodan.

Another thing to bear in mind is that the territories called The Low Countries today were occupied by other tribes and forces for extended periods. The well-defined borders we have today were not in operation for all of history. Instead, the borders were always shifting. There was a continuous process of expansion and contraction. (To understand this phenomenon, I recommend you read up on the history of Fryslân, the land that became the Dutch province of Friesland today).

The Roman occupation left a lasting legacy. Roman names were imposed on the Norse gods: Tyr – Mars, Odin – Mercury, Njord – Neptune, Frigg and Freyja – Ceres, Thor – Hercules etc.) We need to unpick this as *they really are separate gods from different pantheons and regions!* We need to make a focussed effort to stay clear of glib simplifications. In the Romantic period it was fashionable to make such cross-identifications, but today this has been discredited and scholars now scrutinise the differences. We also need to resist the temptation to limit our information gathering to popular mythology books and on-line sites such as Wikipedia. (Wikipedia is great starting point but then proceed to sites such as academia.edu, where experts share research papers and PhD dissertations).[1]

Sinterklaas – the Great Psychopomp

For children St Nicholas will always be Sinterklaas (I sincerely hope that Sinterklaas will not be usurped by his cousin Santa Claus!) However, spiritually-minded adults would do well to educate themselves about the Saint as a psychopomp (soul conductor) and by extension his, and our, relationship to the dead. Dutch people skilled in shamanic work would do well to actively call on this Saint when they do psychopomp work!

Just as individuals need to perform ancestral healing work to unravel imprints active in their family line, countries and nations need to do ancestral healing work too. This means unravelling and healing collective trauma, conflicts with other nations, the way collective shadows are projected onto other nations or groups and so forth. The issue of counter-cultural appropriation too needs skilful examination and unravelling; just as the issue of cross-fertilisation deserves celebration.

Having lived away from the Netherlands for 30 years I can see how my country of birth too readily and too easily absorbs the language and culture of neighbouring countries. This makes us a nation of natural born linguists but things go too far when we de-value our own heritage and lose touch with ancestral wisdom teachings.

We urgently need to bring back the tradition of honouring, feeding and consulting our ancestors, Those Who Came Before Us. There is a treasure trove *right here on our doorstep!*

Mastering the ancient art of psychopomp work again

Earlier we encountered an extraordinary account by the Byzantine historian Procopius of Caesarea, who wrote a famous passage in the Gothic Wars, around 552–553 CE. He describes an island called Brittia, where the inhabitants of certain fishing villages, located on the ocean's shore right opposite Brittia, perform a sacred service. The destination of souls of the dead is the island of Brittia and the inhabitants of coastal villages face the task of ferrying them across. This is the work of the psychopomp or soul conductor: taking souls to the right destination in the Afterlife.

The men who know that they must go and do this work during the night, relieving those who did it before them, as soon as darkness falls withdraw to their houses and go to sleep, waiting for someone who will come and call them for that task. Later in the night: knocks on the door. They jump out of bed and go to the edge of the sea.

On the shore they find special empty boats. When they climb into them, the boats sink almost to the surface of the water (as if heavily laden). They begin to row and after about one hour they arrive in Brittia (normally the voyage lasts a night and a day). After disembarking their passengers they depart with light ships. They have not seen anyone, save for a voice that informs the boatmen of the social rank of the passengers, the names of their fathers, and in the case of the women, the name of their husband.[2]

This is an extraordinary passage: did common people (not trained 'shamans') commonly perform psychopomp work in an era long before the (so called) Enlightenment? Does that mean that we all carry the soul conductor archetype within our psyche and that there are more psychopomps in our ancestral lineage than we realise?

I hope that groups of Dutch/Flemish/British people will actively start working with this template or blueprint. It befits people living on land reclaimed from water to ferry souls across water to the Land of the Dead, the Land of the Ancestors.

Portals in the landscape

We have explored how portals in the landscape have shut (through abuse of land) or been closed deliberately (wise ancestors and elders deliberately closed portals as the cultural mood changed, accessing otherworlds became a dangerous occupation and the keepers/guardians of portals and sacred sites no longer had well-trained apprentices and successors).

Some people are actively working to open and map both portals and energetic meridians again (please check out the work of Linda Wormhoudt [3] and her associates). I hope that more people will focus on re-membering (putting back together) the limbs of ancestral wisdom.

From the writing of clergy and Church Fathers we know that water spirits and other nature spirits respected by Heathens were *driven out*. In 1295 Archbishop Burchard of Worms performed a blessing ceremony near Maagdenburg to expel 'evil' (demonic) water spirits.[4] Water spirits are neither evil or demonic, *they just are*. They are closely tied to the quality and vitality of any body of water and they have every right to exist, just as human beings do. (We need to drop our human-centered arrogance!)

There are also air spirits, forest spirits, earth spirits (see chapter 10), ship spirits and so forth. Our mandate is to live in harmony with these 'Others', not to displace and eliminate them along with many animal species. This loss is the hidden face of the global extinction caused by humanity and its addiction to expansion and me-me-ME, more-more-MORE, as explained in Chapter 10 of my third book, Medicine of the Imagination.[5]

Please educate yourself about the workings of Wetiko[5]. In English the word evil is *the word live spelled backwards...* Instead of adopting ever more foreign words I hope that Dutch people will coin their own Dutch words, the way Icelandic and Flemish-speaking people do. This is one feature that distinguishes Flemish from Dutch. Dutch needs a word for Wetiko!

Where this process failed (as the Heathens were not going to give up their ancestral ways without a battle) such spirits were often turned into saints ('enforced shapeshifting'). Rather than staying well clear of this material (still feeling the trauma and devastation inflicted by the Church in our ancestral field) we need to *get over ourselves* and make a fearless inventory of these issues. This requires painstaking research of what or who 'came before', what the earlier manifestations of many saints are. I thank Dutch authors such as Abe de Verteller and Linda Wormhoudt for their commitment to doing this work and writing about it (in Dutch). I deliberately wrote this book in English to reach a wider, global, audience with Northern European ancestry, and make the material accessible people who do not speak Dutch.

Pointers for getting started

There is no need to travel to Peru or Ecuador to work with shamans. They will teach you a spirituality closely linked to their mountains and cosmology that will not necessarily translate well to the Low Countries. Covid-19 brought us Lockdown and a major teaching about *staying local*. The largest mountain in the Netherlands is a very small hill.

The Yearly Cycle

Many contemporary pagans use the concept of the Wheel of the Year as an annual cycle of festivals and key events (solstices, equinoxes and their midpoints). This is not a Dutch concept but I remind the reader that in pre-Christian times there would have been a farming almanac. Before the days of agriculture even hunter gatherers would have had an awareness of variations in daylight, seasons, the breeding of cattle and migration paths of wild animals, and so forth.

Resist the temptation to adopt an existing Wheel of Year wholesale (unless one resonates with you 100%). Instead research old calendars in your area and write your own almanac: what are the key events in *your* year?[6]

Calendars essentially track the rotations of the luminaries: Sun and Moon. Some ancient cultures had solar calendars while others followed lunar calendars. Depending where you are in the world (especially depending on what hemisphere you are in, how far North you are or how far South you are) some seasonal events will follow a very local timing. (E.g. the Celtic Wheel of the Year cannot be applied straight to Scandinavia, which traditionally still is under snow and ice while Spring is already welcomed in Wales or Ireland).

- What are the seasonal cycles in your location? What is the climate? When do you observe turning points in nature?
- What do you pay attention to? (The flowering of plants acts

as a clock for some, birdsong does for others, and again others follow the weather and temperatures religiously).

- Formulate your own names for all thirteen full moons of the year!

Personal

Further down you will find suggestions for personal practices and observances based on practices indigenous to the Low Countries.

Please evaluate other cycles in your life. What are your existing spiritual practices? Has reading this book perhaps opened your mind to adding or changing some? Here are some questions to help the process along:

- If you have Dutch family members, make a point of visiting them and asking them about their traditions and family memories. Make a memory box (or computer file) to preserve any information you find (use video, voice recordings, make a digital copy of old publications or family photographs, photograph family heirlooms, visit and photograph locations or even homes where it is known family members used to live...)
- Do you have an altar or another focal point for your spiritual practices? If not, consider making one. If you live with young children or adventurous pets, make a small altar in a shoe box you can close and keep out of harm's way, e.g. on top of a wardrobe.
- What form does The Divine or Ineffable take for you? For some this is in the landscape, for others it is their own innate divinity and for yet again others this takes the form of 'external' deities.
- 'Befriend an obscure deity'. Writing this book flushed out many almost forgotten deities, spirits and matronae.
- Do you have a prayer practice? Do you feel you would

benefit from having one? Ask people you trust and admire to share some of their favourite prayers with you.[7]

- Remember that the best prayer is one spoken with an open heart and sincere intentions to connect to powers greater than yourself! Also remember that there is no free lunch in the Germanic/Norse cosmology: every gift requires a return gift. There is no concept of 'always being on the receiving end'. *If you wish to receive, start by giving...* If you wish to attract the protection of powerful forces, start paying attention to them.
- Build a relationship with one tree. It does not need to be a tree other people consider sacred but this tree will soon be *sacred to you*. Ask it for Tree Teachings and speak up for that tree species in turn. Donate to an organisation who guards or plants those trees.
- Remember that in the Norse/Germanic cosmology trees are seen as the ancestors of human beings. Give Ask and Embla some thought (or even a prayer). Speak up against logging and the destruction of habitats for flora and fauna. Plant trees if and where you are able to. Support sustainable energy sources and farming.
- Give voice to other beings who cannot speak for themselves: animals, children, land... Align yourself with both Tyr (the spiritual warrior) and Forseti (god of justice and reconciliation), be a force for justice in our world
- Form an active relationship with the weather spirits, value their contributions and teachings, perhaps even study some so called *weather shamanism*, it can be practiced anywhere.
- Are there any fixed spiritual points in your week? Would your life benefit from having some times set aside for spiritual work? (For a cue: look at the names of the days of the week)
- Form a more active relationship with the spirits of land and home. Leave out offerings and ask for their help and

blessings, for their assistance in finding lost things or lost animals... etc.

- Visit sacred sites in the Netherlands (or your own location). Visit a Hunebed, do active dreaming: can you catch a glimpse of the *Witte Wieven*?

Examples of things you may wish to give a dedicated slot in your schedule

- Connect to the days of the week and the beings they are named for: honour Tyr on Tuesdays, Odin on Wednesdays, Thor on Thursdays, Freyja and Frigg on Fridays (and so forth). On Saturdays I don't honour Saturn, I connect to the Norns instead – both are said to rule the realms of death and necessity.
- Ceremonies: can be performed with others or alone, to mark a special occasion, express gratitude, mark the seasons etc.
- Connecting to our Ultimate Mother: The Earth. In Dutch she is called *De Aarde* or *Moeder Aarde!* Even just lying on the earth for a few minutes a day, on your back or front (in a garden, park etc.) helps greatly with grounding.
- Honouring and feeding your ancestors, telling them the family news, asking them for support (if that makes you feel nervous, insert the word *compassionate* before invoking ancestors!)
- Consider honouring the Matronae, the Great Mothers again. Did any resonate with you especially (because of focus or location)? Make them a small altar, speak prayers to them, request their guidance and assistance.
- If there is a particular deity you have a connection to, set a time in your day or week for connecting and honouring. *(One spiritual teaching says that what we honour, honours us back)*

- Spiritual outreach work: if you feel your spiritual practices improve (or have improved) your life beyond measure, consider mentoring another person just taking their baby steps and in need of support.
- Psychopomp work: helping dead people cross over and find their way in the Afterlife. If this work resonates, do training with a competent teacher and please stay safe at all times. Start working with St Nicholas in his manifestation of the Great Soul Conductor who comes to collect the dead.
- If you are a skilled soul conductor, consider connecting to kindred spirits and reviving the Wild Hunt ceremony as an indigenous Winter Ceremony (make sure to clock up the required training and competence first!)
- Make *sitting out* a regular practice.
- Walk some *doodswegen* (corpse roads) as a form of walking meditation.
- Eat some typically Dutch food and share some with your ancestors (e.g. Gouda kaas or *stroopwafels* are available in many well-stocked supermarkets abroad).

Group practices and Ceremonies (for experienced practitioners!)

- Ceremonies honouring the seasons and festivals.
- Group Psychopomp ceremonies calling on St Nicholas and Vrouw Holle (who both have a connection to water: ferrying across souls).
- Wild Hunt Ceremony.
- Ceremonies for Ancestral Honouring and Healing family lines.
- Ceremonies to heal land and conflicts between nations.
- Reviving the celebration of old festivals.

Suggestions for indigenous devotional practices

Bodies of Water

Wormhoudt reminds us that water can copy information and retain it. Water is said to remember the creatures which once lived in oceans. Glaciers may literally carry aeons of memories. Reading water means reading the cosmos! I have personally received this guidance while visiting Greenland: as the ice pack melts, memories are released into our oceans. People start remembering previous lifetimes and understanding how karma and unfinished business work (they are forces in service to personal, global and cosmic balancing; also forces of a 'second chance' at something).

Visit features in the landscape: woodlands, dunes, islands, bodies of water (sea, rivers, canals, lakes) and sit out. Open yourself to a dialogue with the spirits of place. If possible do work inviting water spirits to return (there are many lost spirits at large on the land) but clock up some specialist training first and stay safe. Work with an experienced geomancer if spiritual work with land calls you. Check out the work of Marko Pogačnik, a leading light in the world of geomancy. Read books by Linda Wormhoudt and Abe de Vertekker (if you speak Dutch).

Wormhoudt points out that the Dutch language lacks songs for local water spirits. Invitation for singers and musicians. Using your own voice can be the greatest gift and vibrational medicine for the land![8]

Give thought to *appropriate* offerings! Ordering white sage from the US or Palo Santo from South America is not the way to go (carbon footprint, cultural appropriation). The message of our time is *staying local*: Germanic peoples used mugwort *(bijvoet)* for purification and smudging (cleansing with smoke). My students in Sweden have revived this tradition joyfully and successfully!

If you have no offerings on you, use yourself: sing or chant spontaneously, leave one of your hairs, recite a poem, offer deep listening and environmental activism, remove some litter...

White pebbles *(kiezelstenen)* were offered to bodies of water and at sacred sites[8]. I remember filling my pockets with pebbles during my childhood in the Netherlands! Adopt the mindset of a child: how does a child work their magic with pebbles, twigs and pine cones?

From historical sources we know that Germanic tribes honoured *paalgoden* (pole gods). Paalgoden are wooden pillars with the carved head of a deity mounted on top. It is believed that they were used in fertility rituals. Some contemporary heathens and craftspeople have started carving and erecting such pole gods (or god poles) again.[9]

In many areas in North Western Europe, which used to be bogs or swamps, basic wooden statues of local deities have been found, carved from large tree branches. Sometimes they were anchored with a pile of stones and often they come in pairs. Scholars think that they were used in fertility rituals. Offerings were found near them: e.g. flax and white pebbles. Examples of such locations are Braak and Oberdoria in Germany and Assendelft in the Netherlands.[9]

Sanctuaries dedicated to local goddesses were often situated on an island in bog land or wetland, lake or sea. There is some evidence that the Waddenzee island of Ameland once was such a Sacred Island. The existence of an old abbey right next to a sacred well points in that direction.[10]

Traces of poles have been found as well, indicating a large rectangular building (13 m long and 5.2 m wide) stood there in the Iron Age. Dutch researchers think that Rosmerta was probably a goddess of abundance and fertility honoured there, with her attributes of the horn-of-plenty and a money pouch. There is also evidence for a similar local goddess in Lotharingen and the Rhineland.

The older custom of making offerings to rivers and river

deities continued right through the Roman period in the Low Lands. People often dissolved sugar in well water to make a healing potion and special round medicine cookies were baked from well water too.[11]

In many rivers large numbers of swords have been found, e.g. in Alphen aan de Rijn. All swords had been disabled, following the principle what is broken in this world becomes whole again in the other world.[10]

We observe a move where initially larger areas or bodies of water were perceived as sacred but over time these split into small 'cult' areas with shrines. (In this context the world cult just means a place where veneration occurred. It does not carry the connotation of contemporary religious cults). Those places became associated with specific deities desiring specific offerings (swords, sickles, kettles or cauldrons...)[10] Other popular offerings in the Netherlands were statues, coins, animal bones, iron nails and other iron objects.

Sitting Out

The Netherlands still has about 5000 grave mounds dating from the Bell Beaker Culture[12] in the late Neolithic (about 2500 – 2000 BCE). If you speak Dutch please google *hurkgraf*!

Germanic and Norse peoples had a tradition of sitting out on grave mounds. Take up this practice. Make notes of any visions and guidance you receive. Share your notes with others, or get together and do this collectively (I do this work with my students in Scandinavia).

I had an interesting dialogue with fellow authors Caitlin Matthews and Nigel Pennick about this. Caitlin wondered whether the Dutch language has a word for *sitting out*. Nigel Pennick says that, after the period of the witch trials, people continued to practice the old customs but shrouded this in veils of protection and secrecy (to put, for example, church officials and law enforcement off the scent). Phrases such as 'the nameless art' were coined for this reason.

To my best knowledge the Dutch language does *not* have a specific term for this, but people still use this practice. One of my Dutch students[13] researched church records and found disapproving references to people sitting out on grave mounds or graves. So... here is another item ripe for re-discovery. It offers a viable alternative to the non-indigenous concept of *vision quests.*

Healing work

Certain days were favourable for healing, especially the feast days of certain saints (and we now know how ancient deities live on in our awareness, with the figure of a saint superimposed). Bearing that in mind, please do your own research: which causes and saints (older deities) resonate with you? This can guide you in identifying days of the year special to you personally and suitable for powerful work! Do you share a name with a saint? This might be a special day for you!

Amsterdam

Archaeological research shows that people lived in the area of what is greater Amsterdam today long before the city existed (meaning near the Amstel and IJ rivers). Items from the Neolithic period have been found especially where *Het Damrak* and *Het Rokin* are situated today (very near the Central Station please consult a city map!) The history of Amsterdam as we know it, starts around the year 1000.[14]

Most people visiting the Netherlands pass through Amsterdam and Amsterdam Schiphol Airport. Budget some time in your schedule to find a quiet place in Amsterdam and connect to this older history.

Go off the beaten track and take the ferry to Amsterdam Noord, location of the former executions by hanging. People were executed on De Dam (where today you will see clowns, balloon artists, musicians and swarms of feral pigeons), their bodies put on display at the Galgenveld. Eventually the rope holding them rotted away and their bodies dropped in a pit (mass grave).[14] The area was then called Volewijck, which became Vogelwijk (Bird Quarter) today.

Here we also find the theme again of ferrying the dead across a river or the sea: the corpses of executed people were ferried across Het IJ in small rowing boats. That is how Amsterdam Noord became a physical manifestation of the Land of the Dead.

There is a twist because aspiring Amsterdam parents rowed across the same river to collect the souls of babies. Legend had it that, in this same dismal place, babies grew in baskets and wraps in the Kinderboom (Tree of Children). The souls of those babies yelled at prospective parents and midwives: *Pick me! Pick me! I will be good every day of my life!* [14]

Obviously, this indigenous story rather challenges the fond notion of newborn babies arriving as a blank slate (tabula rasa) but for a healer working with clients on fertility issues, it is useful information.

Dutch author Fanny van der Horst recommends adding three drops of well water to a bottle with 30 cc tap water to create a remedy (please note: not a homeopathic dilution) which is safe to use internally. After all our own bodies are (on average) 57 – 60% water![15]

Old Festivals

Research old festivals of the pre-Christian period and find your own way of celebrating those. It does not matter if we don't mark those occasions in the exact way our ancestors did. We do not need a full and binding description. All we need is an open heart and sincere willingness to connect to the ways of our Ancestors. They will guide our hands and speak through our actions! There is no right and no wrong, connection gives rise to both reconstruction and revival.

Start celebrating Modranecht! Honour the night of our ancestral mothers! Embark on an ancestral discovery project: make a family tree, write down the names of your ancestors, ask older family members to tell you stories about those who have passed to spirit. Write down your own story and message for the family descendants. Lodge this with your Will, where it will be found.

Revisit Chapter 6 and select the name of a few *Matronae* who resonate with you (for whatever reason). Tune in, be willing to start a dialogue across the centuries, keep a journal of what you learn and discover, hook up with other people who share this interest! Example: Afliae, the Powerful and Creative Mothers. If you live near a river, connect with the Mother or Rivers. If your surname has a tree in it (as mine does: Elm Tree) connect with the Mother of that tree species.

Connect with Vrouw (Mother) Holle. Be brave and ask whether she will take you on as her apprentice. Guided by her, make a contribution to changing the way that people in modern Dutch society handle grief and discuss miscarriages, abortions and the emotive topic of dead children.

Become aware of spirit children who linger in certain locations. Some have been there for centuries. Once upon a time it was not uncommon for unwanted (or disabled) babies to be left outside to die from exposure. Call on Vrouw Holle! Involve someone with expert skills, if the task is beyond you.

Connect with the Norse or Germanic gods in their Low Lands manifestations, journal on Wodan or Wuotan being different from Odin (or not). Do the same work for Freyja and Frija or Vrouw Freke. Seek an audience with Rosmerta!

The *Annales Drenthiae*, dating from 1660, states that foremost in these lands (the Low Lands) are venerated: Lahra, Welda, Freja and Wodan.[16] I have not been able to find further information about Lahra but I encourage you to embark on your own investigations (old records or personal revelation!)

Connect with *Welda* (German: Weleda), her name may be a Latin rendering of the Celtic title *veleta* (prophetess) or it might be derived from the Germanic word waldon, which means 'to have power'. She was both a political leader and a prophetess or Vǫlva (conduit of Divine will) but Tacitus also called her a goddess in her own right! She dwelled in a tower and carefully selected relatives passed messages between the divine realm and human seekers.[17]

High Seat work and seeking an audience with the (Norse) Vǫlva has gained popularity in recent decades, but Dutch/Flemish/Northern Germanic people may want to reconstruct ways of working with Welda-Weleda instead, using a 'tower' structure rather than a raised seat. Journal on this and write blogs or articles. Share your discoveries with others!

Männerbund and Rites of Passage

People who have read my previous books or listened to my presentations at (on-line) conferences and interviews will know that Rites of Passage are a big theme in my work, even a red thread connecting all my projects.

Germanic Tribes had rites of passage for their young men while girls learned about death and birth from their (grand) mothers. The term Männerbund refers to a bond, a binding together of young men, boys of a similar age on the threshold of adult life. These young men were young warriors bound together by an oath and they went raiding together (they did on a smaller scale what the Vikings did on a larger scale). They especially raided cattle as a way of creating some starter wealth for themselves. Our culture frowns upon this and I certainly don't recommend we bring back this tradition but many young people run now *start-ups* in a very different way!

The point is though, that other than school exams, sporting activities (which only athletic children gravitate towards) and military service (no longer mandatory in the Low Countries) young people are not initiated or tested by their elders. They actually need to test their strength against others and discover their own limits, they need to survive ordeals to become fully-fledged members of their tribe or society. If this stage is not completed, we end up with a large number of 'Peter and Petra Pans who do not grow up', they become eternal students, commitment-phobes, ladettes or mothers' boys…. So, I would like to make my case for Elders being honoured as Wisdom Keepers (again) and them initiating young people. This involves holding a safe container for these experiences and close supervision, (so teenagers do not end up self-initiating through drug overdoses, car crashes, unsafe sex etc.) It is kinder, that is the great paradox.

My year
Some people might wonder what 'my year' looks like as a Dutch woman with a Scandinavian family, dividing her time between London UK and Sweden. I will follow the modern convention of starting the new year on January 1st.

January:
1st New Year's Day

5th *Epiphany (Trettondedag Jul in Swedish)*, connect with Perchta/Befania, do a ceremony to unwind (karmic) entanglements and clear 'the human spindle that is me'.

13th *Tjugondagen Knut*, also the day that the Crone Goddess re-ties the cosmic knot securely.[18]

February
Dísablót: offering ceremony to honour the female ancestors. Not everyone agrees on the timing (which can be flexible and personal) but for me this happens early February (meaning it more or less coincides with the Celtic Imbolc).

14th, Valentine's day. My Swedish mother-in-law insists on calling this *Alla Hjärtans Dag* or the Day of All Hearts (to make it inclusive of everyone we love). In our house we do not get away with a failure to observe this – she'd take it personally!

March

The *Vernal Equinox* is also my birthday. I focus on the themes of balancing and extending tender care to new beginnings.

April

Easter Our family celebrates Easter but I give this a Nordic twist by making Easter Witches and Påskris (literally Easter twigs, branches of trees decorated with feathers).

22nd, a new pagan invention is Yggdrasil Day.[19]

30th *Valborgsmässoafton or Walpurgisnight* (which I privately call the Night of Witches). It was believed that on this night witches met at the Hexentanzplatz (a particular location for a Witches' Dance) and then flew as one to Mount Brocken, the highest peak in the Harz Mountains in Germany.[20]

In the Netherlands April 30th is Koninginnedag or the Queen's Birthday and a public holiday. The Dutch King (and his mother before him) preserved the tradition of celebrating his grandmother Queen Juliana's birthday. They did not change the date to their own birthdays.

May

5th is Bevrijdingsdag (Liberation Day) in the Netherlands, celebrating the end of German occupation during World War II. I always put some attention and gratitude on this event and extend it to powering visions of world peace and freedom from occupation to other nations and tribes.

June

Midsummer Eve (our family tries to celebrate this in Sweden when possible. We dance around a Maypole and pick seven kinds of flowers to put under our pillow at night (to dream of our beloved).

July
We drive from our house in London to our house in Sweden with a stopover in the Netherlands.

August
I welcome the Mushroom Season with great gusto and forage for chantarelles in the forest. I actively welcome Autumn, my favourite season.

September
Autumn Equinox, I do ceremonial work on the themes of balancing and embracing darkness as a cloak. I welcome back Darkness (after the midnight sun of the Scandinavian summer) as a much-loved cloak. I also connect with Greek goddess Persephone, who makes her descent to the Underworld at this time.[21]

October
Around Halloween/All Saints I perform the Álfablót or offering ceremony for the male ancestors. I also call out the names of all the 'recently deceased' known to me.

November
11th, St Maarten (Feast Day of St Martin) Dutch children knock on doors and ask for treats. Growing up in London our own three children went trick-or-treating at Halloween instead.

As the winter storms (and first snow) arrive I do Wild Hunt ceremonies (both with students and I sometimes ride with the Hunt on my own).

December
5th, Sinterklaas: our family celebrates Sinterklaas.

13th, we celebrate the Swedish festival of Sankta Lucia (St Lucy), preparing for the return of light and lengthening days.

21st, Winter Solstice

22nd, Modranecht

24- 26th Christmas

In the period of the Twelve Nights (between Christmas and Epiphany) I embark on daily Omen Walks to see glimpses of things taking shape in the year to come. This practice is called Årsgång and it stretches up to Epiphany (Perchta's Festival). For more inspiration you can research Dutch *thema-dagen*, days for honouring specific causes or themes.[22]

Swedish people observe Name Days as well, a day of year associated with their given name. The custom originated with saints on the Church calendar (another possible source of inspiration). My husband celebrates two 'Name Days' in addition to his birthday but unfortunately my name does not appear on the Swedish calendar! However, I just ran a search and the official Imelda Day is May 13th.[23]

While writing this book I was struck by the contrast of "feasting and fasting", both had allocated days on the calendar (and still do for many people, e.g. Christmas and Lent or Muslims observing Ramadan). The general level of over-eating in Western culture shows that today feasting can be a daily act, not always balanced by fasting. Consider connecting to the Lady of the Fast and rediscover the benefits of fasting married to prayer, soul-searching, shadow work and community service. Spiritually speaking, a day of fasting can also be dedicated to a cause.

Last but not least: PLEASE tell children about the spiritual beliefs of their ancestors. They are free to reject those – but at least they will know about them...

Always remember that there is still healing and balancing to be done for outcasts, family members with disabilities and mental health problems who were shut away in asylums, (spiritual) ancestors who died in the witch hunts etc. Say prayers and do apology work. Consider training in ancestral healing work.

Another discovery always awaits! This book is detailed but not exhaustive. I have not set out to write an encyclopaedia. I hope other people will add and share their own discoveries.

Appendix

The Frisian Rune Row

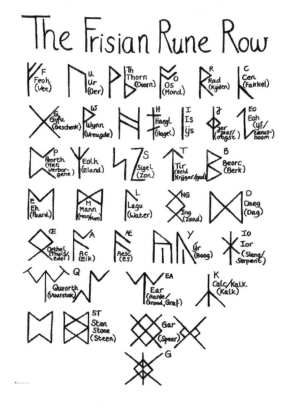

Germanic peoples used the runes from the third century onward. In Scandinavia, especially Sweden, we find many large standing stones with runic inscriptions. In Frisia, the runes were commonly carved in small objects such as combs and amulets. In Scandinavia, the runes of the Elder Futhark (twenty-four characters) gave way to the Younger Futhark (sixteen characters) around the ninth century.

Frisians used the Frisian rune row, which is identical to the Anglo-Saxon rune row minus one mysterious letter (Gar, the spear). It can be surprisingly hard to define such rune rows because some runes appear only in one or two rare inscriptions. Of the 31 runes listed, five have major variants and their meanings have shifted over time, as everyday reality changed.[1]

Most of the information we have today, regarding the order of the Anglo-Saxon and Frisian rune rows, is derived from the Thames River Knife (also known as the Thames scramasax). Another source is the Vienna Codex, an early 9th century manuscript which provides a complete version of the Anglo-Saxon rune row.[1]

My next book will be about rune magicians and advanced rune studies. For the purposes of this book, I will provide an overview of the Frisian runes and their meanings, deliberately set in a very local (Dutch) context. For the pronunciation, please check out a video I posted on YouTube.[2]

Feoh: Cattle, mobile wealth, property, money

Cattle was not only a main source of food it was also a marker of social standing. Cattle were used as a form of payment or exchange and probably in dowries as well. Human beings and cattle lived under one roof in so called *woonstalhuizen*, buildings divided into a home and separate stable segment (with a separate entrance).

Wealth was measured by the amount of a cattle a person owned. The Frisians were taxed by the Romans in cowhides.[3]

Ur: wild oxen, primordial power, untamed force or power (Dutch 'Oer')

The Frisians payed tax to the Romans in the form of cattlehides until a new commander (Olennius) demanded aurochs hides instead and resorted to extortion. This ultimately resulted in an uprising and a Battle in Baduhennawald.[4] The aurochs is a feral, un-domesticated, animal and this rune represents its untimed and unbridled power.

Thorn: Donar's rune, imminent danger, giants

In the Elder Futhark this rune is called Thurs. It refers to both the god Thor (Donar) and the giants he is forever fighting (the thursar). Thorn is another meaning. It can refer to the hawthorn staff the Winter Goddess bangs on the ground to announce winter. Dutch people may think of the fairytale *Doornroosje* (Sleeping Beauty or Briar Rose).

People carried white pebbles in their pockets as protection against lightning (associated with Donar). They were also cast in wells and ponds for good health and for healing of humans and animals.[5] Stone age tools, such as small axes or shards, were thought to represent Donar/Thor's lightning.

Os: (river) mouth, (mouthpiece for a) god

Os is derived from *ansuz*, a proto-Germanic name for the principal deity (generally perceived as the rune of Wodan/Odin). It is connected to the Gothic word *ansis* or the Norse word *Aesir* (the name of dominant tribe of gods).

The Frisian word *eisenweg* means road of the gods. The Pomphul Well at Hoog Soeren was said to have been dedicated to Wodan, said to be haunted by a White or Wise Lady (*witte juffer*).[6] During Roman occupation the Germanic gods were given Romanized names such as Magusanus, Hurstrga, Seneucaega etc.[7]

In some (former) swamplands in North Western Europe, Oberdoria in Germany and Assendelft in the Netherlands, rudimentary statues of deities, carved from tree branches, have been found. Sometimes they were fixed in place with stones and appeared in pairs. They have been linked to fertility cults and rites. Offerings were discovered with them, e.g. white pebbles and flax.[5]

Rad: riding, 'all things that spin' or come full circle (planets, star constellations), wagons of the gods

Rad means wheel, it still does so in contemporary German!

This rune refers to all things that rotate and spin, also to cycles, movement and things coming full circle. This rune looks like our letter R. Some say it represents the rudimentary of Ursa Major, star constellation Big She Bear rotating around the pole star like the hands of a clock.

Cen: (pinewood) torch, ulcer/sore, (forge/rune of the blacksmith)

'The smith is the elder brother of the shaman', Siberian proverb (Kolyma District).[8]

I was taught the core meanings torch and ulcer but working with this rune intensely for years added the meaning forge. The blacksmith is an archetypal figure who works his magic and forges new creations. The spirits are often said to be repelled by iron yet nails were thrown into wells as offerings[9]. Metal is said to ward of negative forces.

At the temple dedicated to goddess Rura (at the Maas river mouth) many swords and other weapons were offered to a river deity, in the Early Iron Age. The most ancient archaeological soil evidence of campfires in the Netherlands was found near Keersopbeek and dated as 32,000 years old.[10]

Gyfu: gift, act of giving, generosity, exchange, sacred marriage

This rune looks like a cross: X. Crosses appear in petroglyphs all over Scandinavia and are also common mason's marks. The Slavic countries also have a rich tradition of pagan symbols, many of which are variations on crosses.

Many rituals appear to have been performed at night and probably near wells or water. It is also likely that people had sex near bodies of water during fertility festivals (a Dutch equivalent of Celtic Beltane).[11]

The excavation of a terp near Wijnaldum produced a fibula (brooch for fastening a cloak) and golden lyre-shaped hanger with runes engraved on it, from about 600 BCE. It probably symbolises female fertility. On the back runes spell out "HIWI", from the Germanic "HIWA" (spouse/wife), root of the contemporary words huwen (getting married) and huwelijk (marriage) in Dutch.[12]

While the Roman Empire operated money (coins) the Frisian people operated a gift economy, they exchanged goods and services.

Wynn: joy, harmony (think of a winning streak)

Said to be the rune of Norse goddess Frigg. The rune means joy and is etymologically related to our contemporary verb *to win*.

Academic research shows that the West Germans were not familiar with Freyja but they venerated Frigg as the goddess of home and hearth. Her name is connected to an old German word for love and also the contemporary Dutch verb for making love: *vrijen*.[13]

Haegl: hail, sudden cataclysmic event

The word *hagel* still means hail in contemporary Dutch. This rune refers to a sudden and cataclysmic event. The Covid-19 pandemic is a global Haegl event!

Haegl has a crystalline structure and so does salt. In Frisia salt was harvested in the fens through solar evaporation. The salt was used in food preservation as well as preparation, i.e. in *vis pekelen*, salting fish. Salt was a longtime export product of the Netherlands.[14]

Nyd: need, necessity, restriction/constraint (discipline)

This is a severe rune, indicating restriction or obligations. To me this is the rune of the Norns, said to weave fate (but the Eddas strongly indicate they work with water!) Also, a need for positive constraint or restriction in the form of self-discipline.

In Frisia women had a separate building (dug about half

a meter into the ground) where they did their spinning and weaving: *hutkommen* or *kuilhutten,* also known as *weefhutten* (weaving huts). Those buildings were seen as sacred and inviolate, breaking into one carried a death sentence![15]

Is: ice, clarity, transparency, (cooling-off period)

Some 2.5 million years ago the Ice Age started: periods of an extremely cold climate, when a thick ice cap covered north-western Europe, alternated with shorter periods of warm climate. At least 23 spells of a very cold climate have been recorded. The northern Netherlands have been sculpted by moving land ice and vast amounts of melt water.[16]

Sidenote: amber (*barnsteen*) is fossilised pine resin from the amber pine. It was commonly found on beaches in the low lands, described by classical authors as 'products of a frozen sea'. The Greeks called amber electron; our word electricity is derived from this (because of its static electricity).[17]

Ger: Harvest, Fruitful Year, Abundance

Elder Futhark: *Jara* or *Jera,* forerunner of our English word *year.* Completion of a cycle, harvest. Death feeds Life.

Dodenakker (Death's Acre) was a 19th century expression for a graveyard. Christianity perceived a dead person as a seed of grain resting in the Earth until the day of the Resurrection. This concept was appropriated from a far more ancient time when people practiced fertility rituals. Snippets of this survive in reports of witch trials.[18]

Dutch author Michiel de Nijs links star constellation Canis Major to harvest time. He suggests that offerings were not just thrown in a body of water but that they were arranged in a pattern which had meaning.[19]

Eoh: cosmic tree, axis mundi, yew

The Yew is linked to the runes Eoh (Elder Futhark) and Yr (Anglo-

Frisian Rune Row). Oak trees, springs and wooded groves were magical places. Dowsers find that ley lines often cross where sacred trees stand.

Peorth/Perth: rock, dice cup, (tomb/womb – mysteries of death and rebirth)

Do the gods have a hand in the rolling of dice? Stone graves and stone monuments are often found near wells and water and healing stones (or pebbles) often have a connection to water. All over Europe hag stones (stones with a hole in them) are viewed as magical objects. People often carry them on their person.[20] In the Germanic territories white pebbles (*kiezelstenen*) were a popular offering to bodies of water. In the Christian era many edicts were issued forbidding 'the veneration of stones and rocks'. In Ireland and Scotland we find 'doctor stones', used in healing work. There used to be many early laws, created to stop the veneration of stones.[21]

Eolh: elk rune, spirit worker, animal helper (used in many sigils for protection, warding off danger)

The Elk species (Alces alces alces, European Elk) became extinct in the Netherlands in the year 1025. The pronunciation of this letter in the Elder Futhark (Rune Algiz) was Z but this changes to R in the Younger Futhark where the rune appears upside down.[22]

After Christianization animal skins were hung in trees or donated to local priests and churches (as offerings).[23]

Sigel: The Sun

Sun is the shield of the clouds
and shining ray
and destroyer of ice *(Old Icelandic Rune Poem)*[24]

Sigel (rune) *Sowilō or *sæwelō is the reconstructed Proto-Germanic language name of the s-rune, meaning 'sun'.[25]

In the Netherlands sunset and sunrise were the time of day when sick people often prayed and asked for healing or divine assistance.[26]

Tir: Noble Warrior, restoring cosmic order

Tir, warrior, restoring cosmic balance, arrow pointing at north star. In the Elder Futhark this is Rune Tyr, named for the god Tyr, who sacrifices a hand to the Fenris wolf so he can be tied up and Ragnarok (the end of the world as we know it) kept at bay, for a time.

The Germanic tribes, as did Norse peoples, operated a Thing or Althing (*Alþingi* in Icelandic), a public assembly where major decisions were made and justice was meted out.[27]

Beorc: birch tree, (mother)

The silver birch tree is a pioneer tree, the first tree to grow back after a forest fire or logging. It is not picky about soil type and will grow anywhere, even well above the arctic circle. Some authors connect this tree to the mother goddess (such as Norse goddess Frigg) and it is said to have many healing and magical properties in Slavic and Baltic culture. In the medieval period twigs of a birch tree were said to ward of witches and 'evil' spirits. You can make a delicious detox tea from young birch leaves! Birch is often used in Scandinavian and Slavic love magic.[28]

Eh: horse rune, psychopomp, navigating other worlds, Odin's eight-legged horse Sleipnir, partnership

The pre-Christian Netherlands had an abundant population of bears and wolves while wild horses grazed in forest clearings well into the 12th century. Sleipnir is the eight-legged horse Odin rides between the worlds. This rune also carries the meaning of twinning, pairing or partnership.

Mann: rune of 'man' (all human beings), Mankind and the Ancestors

This rune represents human beings and, by extension, their ancestors. *Tuisto* or *Tuisco* is the mythical ancestor of all Germanic tribes. *Mannus* is the son of Tuisto and founder of a number of Germanic tribes.

Lagu: water

In many languages there is a connection between the words breath and air/wind and soul (see Rune OC). However, the Dutch word for soul (*ziel*) also refers to an internal or enclosed space. It is derived from the ancient word *saiwala*, meaning inland sea or belonging to the sea. This meaning shows an ancient connection to the Germanic belief that the sea represents the primordial waters from which all Life arose. This is the place where unborn souls reside and the deceased return. Germanic people visualised this as the realm of Vrouw Holle.[29]

The author of Egil's Saga described the coastal area of Frisia as flat land with fields demarcated by ditches and canals. Planks served as informal bridges to cross between fields.[30]

The earliest known inhabitants of Europe made offerings to bodies of water (rivers, creeks, swamps). Archaeologists have found evidence of this dating back to the Bronze Age. There was a time when every lake, river, pool or pond was understood to have its own indwelling deity. Large animals such as horses and cattle were offered at (or to) wells.

A Greek theologer called Clemens Alexandrinus described in the second century how Germanic women 'read water': they studied vortices and eddies in rivers to forecast the future. They also studied stagnant water collected in crevices in rocks. This is called hydromancy.[31]

In many regions in Europe people observed the custom of placing a coin in the mouth of a corpse and a coin on both eyes to pay the ferryman for delivering them safely to the underworld where the ancestors reside.

In large rivers (Maas, Waal, Rijn) we find offering sites containing swords and kettles. The swords had all been disabled, indicating the belief in a reversal: what is broken in this world becomes whole again in the other world![32] Until today people cast coins in wishing wells as payment to the water spirit for granting a wish.

Various researchers report that wells were a central feature in cults venerating the feminine sexuality. The Church referred to such holy wells as a 'cunnus diaboli' *(diabolic vagina)*.[33]

Ing: seed, fertility, reservoir of potential

Ing (Ingwaz, Yngve) is the founder of the Ingaevones Tribe. Ing is also another name for the great fertility god Freyr, (brother of Freyja). The meaning of this rune is (literally) seed and (metaphorically) life-giving spark. Can be used to stimulate the growth of slumbering abilities into full growth. Storehouse of potential energy in need of an incubation period in the dark earth.

Daeg: day, daylight, illumination, enlightenment

Daeg means day (*dag* in contemporary Dutch). This is the rune of brightness, alertness and awakening. Rune Daeg represents Midsummer (the Sun at full strength, giantess Sunna at her highest point) just as Rune Ger represents Midwinter (when the Sun is weakest).

Oethel: enclosure, homestead, ancestral home or land

"On the higher areas in the salt marshes (kwelderwallen) settlements arose. First a homestead with stables, then several cattle farms. Limited forms of agriculture were practiced, crops not averse to salty soil. The Frisians started building dykes to protect their enclosures".[34]

Farms often had a well set within its own enclosure. Fields were (and still are today) demarcated and separated by small canals or ditches.[35]

Ac: oak tree

Roman author Tacitus mentions that enormous oak trees grew on the shores of lakes in the Low Countries. As the water chewed away at the shoreline these trees would drop down and become floating islands, posing a huge danger to ships.[36]

Oak is sometimes referred to as 'iron wood'[37] because of its strength and endurance. It is often struck by lightning. Celtic Druids believed *awen* (divine inspiration or illumination) could come through lightning. This is called *courting the flash.*[38]

Aesc: rune of the ash tree, god rune

Also known as Ansuz in the Germanic world. The world tree Yggdrasil is said to be an ash tree (or a yew) and Odin hangs himself on Yggdrasil for nine days, piercing himself with his spear, to be initiated into the mystery of the runes.

Yr: tool, weapon (piece of battle gear), hand of craftsperson

In Frisia someone accused of theft had the option of challenging the instigator to a sword duel by hanging his own sword above their threshold or nailing it to their doorpost.[39]

Stone age tools, such as small axes or shards, thought to represent Donar/Thor's lightning were considered magical objects in the Low Countries of the 7th century.

Ior: 'river fish' or other aquatic animal (eel, serpent or beaver)

Some authors link this rune to the world serpent, Jormundgandr, who bites his/her own tail and holds the world together.[40] Rune Ior is perceived as a 'fish', which (in Old Norse perception) could refer to any aquatic animal, especially a beaver. Frogs and toads were associated with the element water (also water spirits) and with folk healing. Until today we associate those animals with witches! Both were said to bring rain.

Queorth/Cweorth: fire twirl, funeral pyre (cremation)

This rune is the opposite from rune Ear in that it represents a fast and all-consuming destruction by fire. It represents fire twirls used by the Vikings to ignite the funeral pyres of their warriors. Ear is slow destruction, Qweorth is an all-consuming blaze.[41]

Ear: death, grave, earth/soil, slow and gradual decay

Once upon a time criminals were executed publicly on De Dam (a famous city square in central Amsterdam) and the bodies were rowed across the water, *Het IJ*, to Northern Amsterdam, where the burial pits were. The bodies were hung up for display until the rope disintegrated and then dropped into the burial pit. In a very literal way this place was the Land of the Dead *but* there was life at the heart of this realm because the *Kinderboom* (Child Tree or Baby Tree) was situated here. Aspiring parents would row across the water at night to collect the soul of their future child. Babies were said to hang in this tree in baskets or wrapped in cloth.

In an even earlier time this area was a wild zone called Volewijck Bird District) and a breeding location for birds.[42]

Calc/Chalc: chalk, chalice

Pronounced with the guttural G (as it appears twice in the Dutch word *gracht!*) Rune of the chalice or Holy Grail. Rune of the quest and spiritual journey. Container for our spiritual learning.[43]

Stan: stone, keystone

The literal meaning of this rune is stone. In the magical or symbolic sense, it means key stone, or touch stone. It will lead you to the heart of the matter. Without this central piece structures crumble.

(Gar)

Technically speaking this rune has no place in the Frisian rune row as it is a Northumbrian rune. Said to represent Odin's spear Gungnir, interpreted by some as a kenning for world tree Yggdrasil. It points to mystery, not knowing, no answer today, in a rune reading. Only the future will reveal the answer.[43]

Appendix

Further Scholarly Discourse

Reconstructed Proto-Germanic deities

The following Proto-Germanic deities have been reconstructed by scholars (Proto-Germanic reconstructions are marked with an asterisk)[1]:

Goddesses

- *Nerþuz, described by Tacitus as Mother Earth, possibly continued in Norse Njǫrðr (Njord, Njorth).
- *Frijjō (wife, specifically here the wife of Wōdanaz), OE Frige, Norse Frigg, cf. Sanskrit *priyā* (mistress, wife).
- *Fraujō*, daughter of Njǫrðr, Norse Freyja, OHG *Frouwa*, Old English *frēo* (lady), cf. Gothic *Fráujo* (lady, mistress), German *Frau*, Dutch *Vrouw*, Swedish, Danish and Norwegian *Fru*.
- *Fullō, goddess—or *Fullaz, god—of riches, plenty. Corresponds to Norse Fulla.
- *Wurdiz (fate), Norse Urðr (Urd, Urth), Old English Wyrd.
- *Sōwilō, the Sun, Norse Sól, OE Sunne, Old High German Sunna. *Austrǭ, Dawn goddess Easter, Old English eostre, Old High German and Old Saxon *ōstara, Old French āsteron.

Gods

- *Wōdanaz (lord of poetic inspiration and frenzy), 'the Germanic Mercury', Norse Óðinn (often Anglicized Odin or, especially in older texts, Othin), Old English Wōden, Old High German *Wuotan*.
- *Þunraz (thunder), 'the Germanic Jupiter', Norse Þórr

(Thor), West Germanic Donar, Old English Þunor.

- *Teiwaz, god of war and possibly early sky god, "the Germanic Mars", Norse Týr or Tir, Old English Tiw, Old High German Ziu, continues Indo-European Dyeus.
- *Ermunaz, Saxon god (speculative, based on Nennius' Armenon). The word means strong or exalted (Old High German *ermen*, Old Norse *jǫrmaun* or *jörmun*, Old English *Eormen*).
- *Wulþuz (glorious one), possibly originally an epitheton, mentioned on the Thorsberg chape, continued as Norse god Ullr.
- *Ingwaz or *Inguz*, identified with the god addressed as *fraujaz* (lord), Old High German *frô*, Gothic *frauja*, Old English *frēa*, Old Norse *freyr*.

The 'Goddess Alphabet' of Ineke Bergman

(Het alfabet van Godinnen, Wijze vrouwen en Heiligen uit onze streken)

In 2012 Ineke Bergman created and published a list of goddesses, based on her own research. In her dedicated Facebook group[2] she later added a postscript with more detailed information about some goddesses. Members of the group have added names too.

Bergman has since made additions to her list, from an (out of print) 1836 book (titled: *In het boek Nederlandsche Volksoverleveringen en Godenleer verzameld en opgehelderd door Mr. L. PH.C. van den Bergh lid van de Maatschappij voor Nederlandsche letterkunde te Leyden en van het provinciaal Utrechtsch Genootschap*).

In her dedicated Facebook group members have added *Friagabis, Boudihillia, Fimmilena* and the Frisian goddess *Frya*. Here is my own (adapted) working list while writing this book, please note that:

- I have arranged all names in alphabetical order

- My annotations and additions to Bergman's list (including translations of Dutch words) appear in cursive script
- Deities discussed in greater detail in this book appear in bold print
- Names of saints were commonly imposed on the names of earlier (ancient) heathen gods and goddesses

The List!

- *Abnoba*, **Alfrodil**, Anbet, Anna, **Arduina**, Astrild, *Atesmerta*, Atla
- **Baduhenna**, Barbet, Berchta, Brigantia, **Brurorina,)**, Berkana *(is one of the names of the Birch Rune, sometimes called the Birch Goddess, contested by scholars)*, Boudihillia
- *Cantismerta*, Catharina, **Cunera**
- Domnu, Dorothea
- Einbeth, Eir, Ertha, Exomna
- **Fanna or Waldacha**, Feruna, Fimmilena, Flora, Freda of Ferda, Frigaholdam, Frouwa, Fostare/Fosta/Fostera/Phoseta, **Fru Freke**
- Ganna, Gerda, Gerdr
- **Haeva *or* Hafna**, Harke, Hel *(not Hela IA)*, Hertha, **Holle or Hulda** (Chapter 12), **Hludana**, Hurstrga
- Iseneucaega, Iduna *(the correct version is Idunn)*
- Jacoba, Juliana, Josefina
- Korenmoeder, Kunigunde, Kere of Ker
- Lucia, Laga
- Margaretha, Matrona *(Chapter 4)*, **Meda from Medemblik**, Mona
- **Nehalennia**, Nemetona, Nerthus
- Odilia, Ostara
- Perchta (Chapter 12)
- Quiteria?
- Rana, Roggeannegien, Roggemoer, **Rosmerta**, Rura
- **Sandraudiga**, Sif, Spin An, Spinwieven, Sunna

- **Tanfana**
- Urdr, Ursula *(Bergman calls her a Christianised version of Nehalennia)*
- Vagdavercustis, Viana from Vianen, Victoria, Vihansa, Viridecdis
- Valcallinehis (godin of the river Waal), Veleda
- Walpurgis, Wilbet, **Witte Wieven** (Chapter 7)
- Xulsigiae (Gallia Belgica) triple goddess Trier
- IJda? Yrsa (she-wolf) from Scandinavia
- Zwarte Griet

Glossary

Animism is a word derived from Latin (*anima* means breath/ spirit/life) which refers to a spiritual belief that All That Is, all beings/objects/places (think of mountains, rivers, oceans) and even phenomena (think of weather: wind, storms) possess a distinct indwelling spiritual essence. All That Is is alive and animated, full of spirit. It is a word often used to distinguish the spiritual belief systems of earth-focussed indigenous peoples from organised religions.[1]

Balkenhaas is not a hare, as the word suggests, but a cat. Dutch folklore from the Christian era reports that the Devil might appear and ask 'what is the animal in the sack?' The answer is a hare (*een haas*). The Witte Wieven (White Ladies) will ask for a balkenhaas, as payment for assistance given. In both cases the reference is to a cat, not a hare.[2]

Bezweringsformule is a magical spell or incantation.

Boeleren met de Duivel is an old Dutch term for fornication with the Devil.

Boomheiligdoom is a sacred site, sanctuary or pilgrimage destination organised around an ancient sacred tree of spiritual significance. It usually has its own body of folklore and local tales about miracles and supernatural events.

Duivelskater (also *duivekater* or *drommekater*) is a traditional festive bread that originates in Amsterdam and surroundings and is now still popular in the Zaanstreek, just north of Amsterdam. There are sources as far back as the 16th century describing this bread, and it is depicted on paintings like one from Dutch master Jan Steen from 1658 (see footnote: it is the oblong bread leaning against the wall on the left-hand side of the baker). The bread derives its name from a devil (or demon) in the shape of a black cat with glowing eyes.[3]

Oera Linda book, is a manuscript, supposedly written 4000 years earlier in fictive (fake) runes and telling the history of the Frisians, giving them a rather grandiose role on the world stage, a falsified historical account.

Flanders (Vlaanderen in Dutch) is the Dutch-speaking northern portion of Belgium and one of the communities, regions and language areas of Belgium. The demonym is Fleming and the adjective is Flemish. The official capital of Flanders is Brussels and its independent regional government handles various aspects of Flemish culture, education and community life. Flanders is the area with the largest population (but not the largest area in size). The city of Brussels (as well as many people living outside Brussels) is bilingual.

Flemish
1. An adjective relating to the region of Flanders, its people and/or their language.
2. Refers to the Dutch language as spoken in Flanders, one of the two official languages of Belgium.

(De) Geestelijke Wereld is the Dutch term for The Spirit World.

Het Dodenleger Literally Army of the Dead. See: Het Wild Heir.

Het Wild Heir (/Heer) Heir, also Heer, is an old Dutch word for *leger*: Army. It refers to a ghostly troop of hunters rushing through the sky, or over land, accompanied by terrifying sounds (the baying of hounds or howling of wolves). This happened during the Yule period, the time of winter storms. The ghostly army could have different leaders Wodan (Odin), Vrouw Holle or Perchta/Berchta and others.

Huldreslaat is sad music said to be played when Vrouw Holle and her Heimchen (troop of spirit children) ride out. In Norway it is said that this music is composed by the Huldrefolk (faerie folk), or spirits living underground, and played on a fiddle. There are tales about human musicians becoming apprenticed to the Huldrefolk and learning how to play these potent sad songs.[4]

Hunebedden *(plural, singular tense is Hunebed)* is the Dutch word for dolmens or passage graves created about 5000 years ago. Most of them are found in the province of Drenthe. They are made from smooth large rocks dating from the Ice Age (and polished by ice) weighing up to forty tons each. These boulders are so heavy that people used to believe they had been built by giants. However, today we know that around 3000 years BCE, tribes of the so called Funnel Beaker Culture built these gigantic structures to bury their dead. They may also have acted as focal points for ceremonies and initiation rituals.[5]

Ketelmuziek Implies a loud banging of pots and pans. Noise is said to have an atropopaic function: it is said to ward off bad spirits or "evil powers". It can be used to drive out demons and so increase health, vitality and fertility.

Kinderputten Literally, children's wells (or baby wells) were wells where people could pray for pregnancy and invite the soul of an unborn child to join you. According to legend there was a mysterious (mythic) tree at the bottom of such a well where newborn babies hang from the branches (like fruit). To connect with such a baby the parents needed to make a pilgrimage or quest north of their usual location. In Germanic belief North is the direction of Death, the Underworld and the Ancestors, therefore also the direction of (Re)Birth.[6]

Kinderschrik, a *child terror*, a frightening creature or phenomenon used to make children behave or keep them out of danger (e.g. away from bodies of water).

Kwelder Land created by sea water carrying mud which ultimately creates a landmass which does not flood during high water, *salt marshes* in English.

Nornen *(Schikgodinnen)* The three Norns or schikgodinnen (goddesses of fate) are often said to spin and weave the fate of all beings (not just human beings). Some academics point out that the Eddas describe them as strongly connected to water (not weaving). Other scholars connect them to the Matronae, as protective deities. The three Norns are called Urdr, Skuld and Verdandi. I sense a strong connection between Urd and Rune UR. The text Vǫluspá in the Poetic Edda describes them as living in a body of water under the world tree Yggdrasil. Dutch author Linda Wormhoudt suggests they were originally water spirits or water deities.[7]

Onttoveren is the Dutch verb for cancelling a spell or unravelling a curse cast by a witch or practitioner of magic (undoing the magic worked by another person).

Pakjesavond is a family evening spent celebrating the feast day of Sinterklaas (St. Nicholas) by exchanging gifts with a surprise element (and innovative arty wrap) accompanied by funny funky rhymes mildly teasing the recipient.

Pepernoten are ginger "nuts", small round biscuits made from gingerbread dough that are traditionally cast around rooms by Zwarte Piet when Sinterklaas visits.

Polder is a Dutch word for low-lying land reclaimed from the sea or a river and protected by dike. (My own family in the Netherlands lives in an area below sea level!)

Schikgodinnen *(zie Nornen)*

(De) Signatuurleer is the *Doctrine of Signatures*, states that herbs resembling various parts of the body can be used by herbalists to treat ailments of those same body parts.

Sinterklaas is the colloquial Dutch name of St Nicholas and the patron saint of children. He was the template for the American figure of Santa Claus. He celebrates his birthday in the Netherlands every year, on December sixth. He arrives by steamboat from Spain, accompanied by a troop of helpers called Zwarte Pieten (Black Peters) and riding a white horse called Americo across the roofs. Children set out their shoes by the chimney (or in the hall) and they receive treats and presents from him.

Spinwijf (or spinjuffer) is literally a spinner or spinning woman, she is a ghostly figure appearing as an old woman dressed in flowing white garments. Seen late at night in deserted location and observed working at her spinning wheel by moonlight. Farmers used her as a child terror, to stop children from trampling their fields.

Spook: ghost.

Strandjutter is a beach comber and *juttersgoed* is ship's cargo washed up on beaches.

Syncretism is the blending of religious beliefs from different sources and origins.

Terp (pl. terpen) A terp is an artificial dwelling mound created in areas where regular flooding from the sea and/or rivers occurs. It is intended to provide safe ground during storm surges, tidal waves and other forms of flooding. These mounds occur in the coastal regions of the Dutch provinces Friesland and Groningen but also in Germany and Denmark. This was in a period before the dikes (a type of engineering Holland is famous for) were built to hold back the sea.[8]

Tjoenster is a Frisian word for witch.

Toverkol is a woman practicing black magic and casting spells on people or animals in folklore.[9]

Varende vrouwen, wayfaring women (or varende heksen, wayfaring witches) are women/witches crossing the North Sea and travelling from Holland to England in a sieve, mussel shell or egg shell. They row or paddle across the boiling sea using a needle.[10]

Waddeneilanden – these are a string of islands following the North coast of the Netherlands. They continue further East in the form of the German East Frisian Islands. From West to East the names of these islands are: Noorderhaaks, Texel, Vlieland, Richel, Griend, Terschelling, Ameland, Rif, Engelsmanplaat, Schiermonnikoog, Simonszand, Rottumerplaat, Rottumeroog and Zuiderduintjes.[11]

The islands Noorderhaaks and Texel are part of the province of Noord Holland (where the author of this book grew up). The islands Vlieland, Richel, Griend, Terschelling, Ameland, Rif, Engelsmanplaat, and Schiermonnikoog are part of the province of Friesland. The small islands Simonszand, Rottumerplaat, Rottumeroog, and Zuiderduintjes belong to the province of Groningen. They are known for being a great holiday destination and escape from the hustle and bustle of the crowded mainland.

Zielengeleider (psychopompos or soul conductor) escort the souls of the deceased to the right destination or realm in the other world. This role is performed by gods and goddesses with a connection to death, assisted by human beings. Psychopomps can also take animal form (common are horse, dog, owl, crow, dolphin – for those who drown at sea etc.)[12]

(Het) Zomerland is the Afterlife, also called *Het Hiernamaals* in Dutch). I love this term because it connects the Netherlands today to the Neolithic period when a powerful Bird Goddess was said to welcome souls' home to her Summerland and this was connected to the migration of swans.

Zwarte Piet *(literally Black Pete or Black Peter)* – is the helper of Sinterklaas (Saint Nicholas). He carries a large sack (to stuff naughty children in), a rod (to punish those same misbehaving children) and the Big Book of Sinterklaas where he makes note of the behaviour of children. This means that children are half excited and half terrified of the Saint and his troop of helpers when they visit. Behind the scenes parents communicate with "Sint and Piet" so the children receive realistic evaluations of their behaviour, which adds to the magical and "real life" aspect of the Sinterklaas festival.

Acknowledgements

It takes a village to raise a child and a global village to write a book!

I received help from many people on my quest and would like to thank some of them by name:

Peter op 't Holt, who said: *an informative book about the pre-Christian spirituality of the Netherlands, pulling together all information available, does not yet exist – why don't you write it? (Sorry Peter for disappointing you by writing this book in English, not Dutch!)*

Sjoukje Gummels, Ytje de Meer and Annie de Meer for translation help with tricky passages in Frisian texts.

Mitchell Clute, senior producer at Sounds True, for being excited enough about this book to facilitate the first interview on the topics of this book, in his on-line community called The Shamanic Path.

Caitlin Matthews for strong words of encouragement and asking some pointed questions. Nigel Pennick for generously sharing some of his own findings and sources in the Netherlands with me.

Suzanne ter Huurne for pointing me in the direction of Ineke Bergman's Facebook community and sending me useful links and book recommendations.

Hank Wesselman for his early encouragement. (You did not see the publication of this book. May you blaze a trail in the Other World, you truly are a Spiritwalker now!)

Andrew Steed for spontaneously writing the first endorsement for this book, while it was still an infant in the cradle.

Abe de Verteller, whom I hope to meet in person one day, for his marvellous and informative website.

All my students of Old Norse and Germanic traditions who

fly between continents to work with me.

The excellent Dutch school system for perfecting my Dutch (dissolving all traces of the West Frisian dialect of my childhood) as well teaching me five additional languages by age 14! If I have made my unique contribution in this world, the Dutch education system and all my own teachers played a key role in preparing me for that! I will close with a huge thank you to my own (Dutch) teachers!

About the Author

Imelda Almqvist is an international teacher of Sacred Art and Seidr/Old Norse Traditions (the ancestral wisdom teachings of Northern Europe). Moon Books has also published her previous three books: *Natural Born Shamans: A Spiritual Toolkit for Life (Using shamanism creatively with young people of all ages)* in 2016, *Sacred Art: A Hollow Bone for Spirit (Where Art Meets Shamanism)* in 2019 and *Medicine of the Imagination – Dwelling in possibility (an impassioned plea for fearless imagination)* in 2020.

Imelda has presented her work on both The Shift Network and Sounds True. She appears in a TV program, titled Ice Age Shaman, made for the Smithsonian Museum, in the series Mystic Britain, talking about Neolithic arctic deer shamanism. She is currently working on her fifth book: about the runes of the Elder Futhark (and Uthark). Her response to the 2020 pandemic was starting an online school called Pregnant Hag Teachings, to make more of her work available on-line.

From the Author

Thank you for purchasing this book! I hope that reading it was as much of an adventure as writing it was for me! May I ask you politely to leave a review on your favourite on-line site? (Most people read reviews on amazon before they decide to buy a book!) If you would like to receive updates on courses I teach and events I participate in, please subscribe to my newsletter. I can be contacted through my website. I am always open to being contacted about public speaking and teaching in different locations. I have limited availability for on-line consultations, rune readings and mentoring sessions for shamanic practitioners and sacred art practitioners.

Wild Blessings! Imelda

Website: www.shaman-healer-painter.co.uk

Online School: Pregnant Hag Teachings
https://pregnant-hag-teachings.teachable.com/courses/

Footnotes

A brief note about spelling, translations and local customs

1. https://en.wikipedia.org/wiki/Old_Dutch
2. https://nl.quora.com/Is-West-Fries-een-dialect-binnen-de-Friese-taal
3. https://www.youtube.com/watch?v=EySS4Hq2Syc&t=315s
4. https://brilliantmaps.com/netherlands-land-reclamation/
5. https://www.youtube.com/watch?v=1Z8zbaG6xLQ
6. https://www.expatica.com/nl/lifestyle/holidays/sinterklaas-100660/
7. https://www.youtube.com/watch?v=xeeijNvZJCo
8. https://www.youtube.com/watch?v=5KfWFuHT3tQ
9. https://ourbigescape.com/10-great-traditional-dutch-recipes-holland/
10. https://www.touropia.com/tourist-attractions-in-the-netherlands
11. https://www.holland.com/global/tourism.htm
12. https://www.worldatlas.com/articles/what-are-the-provinces-of-the-netherlands.html

Introduction

1. https://en.wikipedia.org/wiki/Low_Countries
2. https://www.firstthings.com/article/2020/02/the-myth-of-medieval-paganism
3. https://www.youtube.com/watch?v=vpeJiIufd6E&t=593s

Chapter 1

1. De Friezen: De vroegste geschiedenis van het Nederlandse kustgebied, Luit van der Tuuk, Uitgeverij Omniboek, 2013/2016, p.11-12
2. https://en.wikipedia.org/wiki/Frisian_Kingdom
3. De Friezen: De vroegste geschiedenis van het Nederlandse

kustgebied, Luit van der Tuuk, Uitgeverij Omniboek, 2013/2016, p.13

4. https://willemwever.kro-ncrv.nl/vraag_antwoord/geschiedenis/waarom-wordt-nederland-ook-wel-holland-genoemd

5. https://theancientweb.com/explore/europe/netherlands/

6. https://www.youtube.com/watch?v=DECwfQQqRzo&t=1776

7. http://www.aardkundigewaarden.nl/aardkundigemonumenten/detailpagina.php?tuin_ID=616

8. https://www.thoughtco.com/polders-and-dikes-of-the-netherlands-1435535

9. From private correspondence with Nigel Pennick, quoted with permission

10. https://www.dorestadonthuld.nl/

11. From private correspondence with Nigel Pennick, quoted with permission

12. https://en.wikipedia.org/wiki/Glacial_period

13. De Friezen: De vroegste geschiedenis van het Nederlandse kustgebied, Luit van der Tuuk, Uitgeverij Omniboek, 2013/2016, p.20

14. De Friezen: De vroegste geschiedenis van het Nederlandse kustgebied, Luit van der Tuuk, Uitgeverij Omniboek, 2013/2016, p.29

15. De Friezen: De vroegste geschiedenis van het Nederlandse kustgebied, Luit van der Tuuk, Uitgeverij Omniboek, 2013/2016, p.22

16. https://en.wikipedia.org/wiki/Mythology_in_the_Low_Countries

Chapter 2

1. https://wikimili.com/en/Sacred_trees_and_groves_in_Germanic_paganism_and_mythology

2. https://thewickedgriffin.com/the-germanic-and-celtic-

tribes/

3. https://www.youtube.com/watch?v=kC2O9ri1qoM&t=8s
4. https://en.wikipedia.org/wiki/Donar%27s_Oak
5. https://catholicinsight.com/the-donar-oak-europe-and-boniface/
6. De Friezen: De vroegste geschiedenis van het Nederlandse kustgebied, Luit van der Tuuk, Uitgeverij Omniboek, 2013/2016, p.137 - 139
7. https://en.wikipedia.org/wiki/Saint_Boniface
8. https://nl.wikipedia.org/wiki/Boomheiligdom
9. In Völuspá (17-18, Hollander's translation), https://hrafnar.org/articles/dpaxson/norse/hyge-craeft/
10. https://paganmeltingpot.wordpress.com/2014/09/17/yggdrasil-yew-not-ash-tree/
11. https://treesforlife.org.uk/into-the-forest/trees-plants-animals/trees/yew/
12. https://www.abedeverteller.nl/taxus/
13. https://www.whitedragon.org.uk/articles/yew.htm
14. https://www.cancer.gov/research/progress/discovery/taxol
15. Medicine of the Imagination: An Impassioned Plea For Fearless Imagination, Imelda Almqvist, Moon Books, 2020
16. https://www.youtube.com/watch?v=k-v_-YAGpHY&t=121s
17. https://en.wikipedia.org/wiki/Irminsul
18. https://arboriculture.wordpress.com/2016/10/16/trees-and-religion-paganism/
19. https://en.wikipedia.org/wiki/Sacred_trees_and_groves_in_Germanic_paganism_and_mythology
20. https://arboriculture.wordpress.com/2016/10/16/trees-and-religion-paganism/
21. https://nl.wikipedia.org/wiki/Toponiem
22. https://mens-en-samenleving.infonu.nl/religie/49032-op-bedevaart-in-heiloo-bij-onze-lieve-vrouwe-ter-nood.html

23. Heilige Bronnen in de Lage Landen: Op zoek naar bronnen van betekenis in verleden en heden, anthology, A3 Boeken, 2013, p. 97
24. De Friezen: De vroegste geschiedenis van het Nederlandse kustgebied, Luit van der Tuuk, Uitgeverij Omniboek, 2013/2016, p.76
25. https://www.youtube.com/watch?v=4a1CSgsJV5k&t=282s
26. http://hearthmoonblog.com/the-alder-tree/
27. https://arboriculture.wordpress.com/2016/10/16/trees-and-religion-paganism/
28. http://www.thegoddesstree.com/trees/Yew.htm
29. https://en.wikipedia.org/wiki/V%C3%B6r%C3%B0r
30. https://blog.pachamama.org/people-and-trees-intimately-connected-through-the-ages
31. https://www.youtube.com/watch?v=kC2O9ri1qoM&t=25s
32. https://www.britannica.com/topic/Slavic-religion
33. https://nl.wikipedia.org/wiki/Kinderboom
34. Heilige Bronnen in de Lage Landen: Op zoek naar bronnen van betekenis in verleden en heden, anthology, A3 Boeken, 2013, p. 162
35. https://nl.wikipedia.org/wiki/Koortsboom
36. https://bertvanzantwijk.wordpress.com/2017/10/12/zak-doekje-leggen/
37. https://heavenly-holland.com/kroezeboom/
38. https://www.wensbomen.nl/
39. https://www.newsweek.com/christmas-tree-origin-story-pagan-tradition-1254178
40. https://nl.wikipedia.org/wiki/Gerlachus_van_Houthem

Chapter 3

1. https://en.wiktionary.org/wiki/kaaskop
2. Volksverhalen uit het grensgebied van Zuid-Holland, Utrecht, Gelderland en Noord-Brabant, Henk Kooijman, Amsterdam 1988. p. 206

3. http://dutchfolklore.nl/holland-cultuur/
4. https://www.bing.com/videos/search?q=heilung&view=de tail&mid=3D3005FDBF4E48F1B8423D3005FDBF4E48F1B8 42&FORM=VIRE
5. http://maxizorger.com/article/bijgeloof
6. https://en.wikipedia.org/wiki/Astrology_and_astronomy
7. https://www.academia.edu/38062735/The_Christian_Cult_ Perspectives_of_Pliny_Tacitus_and_Suetonius_behind_ the_Prosecution_of_Early_Christians
8. https://creation.com/superstition-vs-christianity
9. https://en.wikipedia.org/wiki/Christian_views_on_magic
10. https://www.christianwitches.com/
11. https://nl.wikipedia.org/wiki/Bijgeloof
12. https://axed.nl/raarste-bijgeloof-mythen-nederland-welke-geloof/
13. https://maroelamedia.co.za/goeiegoed/vermy-die-dokter-met-die-boererate/,
14. http://penguin.bookslive.co.za/blog/2015/09/04/raad-vir-elke-kwaal-van-aambeie-tot-wingerdgriep-lees-n-uittrek-sel-uit-danie-smuts-se-boererate/
15. Volksgeneeskunst in Nederland and Vlaanderen, Paul van Dijk, Ankh-Hermes, 1981
16. Volksgeneeskunst in Nederland and Vlaanderen, Paul van Dijk, Ankh-Hermes, 1981, p. 18
17. Volksgeneeskunst in Nederland and Vlaanderen, Paul van Dijk, Ankh-Hermes, 1981, p. 23
18. Volksgeneeskunst in Nederland and Vlaanderen, Paul van Dijk, Ankh-Hermes, 1981, p. 19
19. Volksgeneeskunst in Nederland and Vlaanderen, Paul van Dijk, Ankh-Hermes, 1981, p. 26
20. Volksgeneeskunst in Nederland and Vlaanderen, Paul van Dijk, Ankh-Hermes, 1981, p. 28
21. https://www.medicalnewstoday.com/articles/323538.php
22. Volksgeneeskunst in Nederland and Vlaanderen, Paul van

Dijk, Ankh-Hermes, 1981, p. 31
23. https://en.wikipedia.org/wiki/Doctrine_of_signatures
24. http://broughttolife.sciencemuseum.org.uk/broughttolife/
techniques/humours
25. https://dragonintuitive.com/way-of-sympathy/
26. https://en.wikipedia.org/wiki/William_Coles_(botanist)
27. https://www.homeopathyschool.com/why-study-with-us/
what-is-homeopathy/like-cures-like/
28. http://broughttolife.sciencemuseum.org.uk/broughttolife/
techniques/humours
29. Volksgeneeskunst in Nederland and Vlaanderen, Paul van
Dijk, Ankh-Hermes, 1981, p. 44
30. https://www.psychologytoday.com/gb/therapy-types/ani-
mal-assisted-therapy
31. http://deenametzger.net/healing-in-the-community/
32. Volksgeneeskunst in Nederland and Vlaanderen, Paul van
Dijk, Ankh-Hermes, 1981, p. 47 - 49
33. Collectie Boekenoogen (archief Meertens Instituut), SIN-
SAG 0413 - *"Zu knapp gemessen, die Seele vergessen,* 14 februari 1894
34. Volksgeneeskunst in Nederland and Vlaanderen, Paul van
Dijk, Ankh-Hermes, 1981, p. 56
35. Volksgeneeskunst in Nederland and Vlaanderen, Paul van
Dijk, Ankh-Hermes, 1981, p. 50
36. http://www.verhalenbank.nl/
37. https://nl.wikipedia.org/wiki/Broodjeaapverhaal
38. Henk Kooijman: Volksverhalen uit het grensgebied van
Zuid-Holland, Utrecht, Gelderland en Noord-Brabant.
Amsterdam 1988. p. 53
39. Verhalenbank, Collectie Jaarsma, verslag 792, verhaal 4
40. Verhalenbank, SINSAG 0404 - *Wo soll ich ihn hinsetzen?*
41. Verhalenbank, Y. Poortinga: De foet fan de reinbôge. Fryske
Folksferhalen. Baarn (etc.) 1979, p. 200
42. Verhalenbank, Willem de Blécourt, Volksverhalen uit Ned-

erlands Limburg, Utr./Antw.1981, 25 N°1.3

43. http://www.mydanishroots.com/history-culture-heritage/the-danish-language-old-norse-words-in-english.html

44. https://www.babbel.com/en/magazine/139-norse-words

45. https://taalhelden.org/bericht/fries

46. https://www.rtlnieuws.nl/magazine/artikel/4145516/5x-bijgeloof

47. http://dictionary.sensagent.com/Merkeldag/nl-nl/

48. https://answers.yahoo.com/question/index?qid=200908 18150042AAzuTDy

49. https://en.wikipedia.org/wiki/Pluto

50. https://abcnews.go.com/International/saint-saint-kind-demoted/story?id=23477573

51. https://thetemplarknight.com/2011/09/18/saints-removed-by-the-catholic-church/

52. https://forums.catholic.com/t/is-saint-christopher-no-longer-a-saint/3285

53. https://forums.catholic.com/t/is-saint-christopher-no-longer-a-saint/3285

54. https://abcnews.go.com/International/saint-saint-kind-demoted/story?id=23477573

Chapter 4

1. The Elder Gods: The Otherworld of Early England by Stephen Pollington, Anglo-Saxon Books, 2011, p.19

2. https://marjolijnmakes.com/2016/06/07/dutch-myths-arcanua/

3. Heilige Bronnen in de Lage Landen: Op zoek naar bronnen van betekenis in verleden en heden, anthology, A3 Boeken, 2013, p. 152-153

4. Godinnen van Eigen Bodem, Ineke Bergman, A3 Boeken, 2007, p.13-15

5. https://www.facebook.com/godinnenvaneigenbodem

6. http://belili.org/marija/aboutmarija

7. https://hearthfirehandworks.com/2019/06/14/the-continental-germanic-gods/
8. https://www.britannica.com/biography/Tacitus-Roman-historian
9. htmlttps://tiwisko.wordpress.com/2014/11/27/the-alcis-the-divine-twins-among-the-germanic-peoples/
10. http://www.geocities.ws/reginheim/forgottengods.html
11. https://www.timelessmyths.com/celtic/gallic.html#Abellio
12. https://mijngelderland.nl/inhoud/specials/verbeelding-van-de-waal/de-rijn-als-goD
13. https://en.wikipedia.org/wiki/Old_Saxon_Baptismal_Vow
14. https://www.britannica.com/topic/Sucellus
15. http://en.wikipedia.org/wiki/Týr
16. https://hearthfirehandworks.com/about-the-gods/gaulish-and-brythonic-celtic-gods/vosegus/
17. https://www.britannica.com/topic/Sucellus
18. https://en.wikipedia.org/wiki/Common_Germanic_deities
19. https://en.wikipedia.org/wiki/Abnoba
20. https://en.wikipedia.org/wiki/Alaisiagae
21. https://hearthfirehandworks.com/about-the-gods/gaulish-and-brythonic-celtic-gods/the-alaisiagae/
22. https://hearthfirehandworks.com/2019/06/14/the-continental-germanic-gods/
23. https://romanpagan.blogspot.com/2015/08/the-germanic-god-and-gods-of-fire.html
24. https://www.babynamespedia.com/meaning/Amma
25. https://www.abarim-publications.com/Meaning/Ammah.html#.XlQCQ25FyUk
26. https://en.wikipedia.org/wiki/Ancamna
27. https://marjolijnmakes.com/2016/06/07/dutch-myths-arcanua/
28. https://feminismandreligion.com/2016/02/24/arduinna-gaulish-goddess-of-forests-and-hunting/
29. https://en.wikipedia.org/wiki/Hyndluljóð

Footnotes

30. https://deomercurio.wordpress.com/2016/11/20/ ἐπιφανεία-of-arduinna/)
31. https://en.wikipedia.org/wiki/Astrild
32. http://www.deomercurio.be/en/rosmertae.html
33. https://www.vikingrivercruises.co.uk/ships/longships/ viking-atla.html#:~:text=Atla%20-%20Norse%20Goddess%20of%20Water.%20The%20beautiful,the%20 earth%20and%20its%20people%20fertility%20and%20harmony.
34. De Friezen: De vroegste geschiedenis van het Nederlandse kustgebied, Luit van der Tuuk, Uitgeverij Omniboek, 2013/2016, p.58
35. https://hearthfirehandworks.com/about-the-gods/continental-germanic-gods/baduhenna/
36. https://marjolijnmakes.com/2016/07/22/dutch-myths-baduhenna/
37. http://www.shaman-healer-painter.co.uk/post.cfm?p=1870
38. https://boudicca.de/2020/01/16/a-goddess-barbet/
39. https://otherworldlyoracle.com/berchta-goddess-women-children-perchten/
40. https://earthandstarryheaven.com/2016/03/23/birch-goddess/
41. https://www.facebook.com/slavicmagpie
42. https://ericwedwards.wordpress.com/2015/03/12/brigantia-goddess-of-the-brigantes/
43. https://hearthfirehandworks.com/2019/06/14/the-continental-germanic-gods/
44. https://www.behindthename.com/name/cantismerta/submitted
45. https://en.m.wikipedia.org/wiki/Catherine_of_Alexandria
46. https://omniumsanctorumhiberniae.blogspot.com/2013/06/saint-cunera-june-12.html
47. https://en.wikipedia.org/wiki/Damon
48. https://www.facebook.com/TheNephilimRising333/

posts/495397713954628:0
49. https://en.wikipedia.org/wiki/Dorothea
50. https://www.britannica.com/topic/Epona
51. https://en.wikipedia.org/wiki/Erecura
52. http://www.pitt.edu/~dash/ertha.html
53. https://www.brittanica.com/topic/Batavi
54. https://www.youtube.com/watch?v=2TaixdHbF-0&t=500s
55. http://www.ydalir.ca/norsegods/ullr/
56. https://sites.google.com/site/oeralindabook/bronnen/nederlandse-volksoverleveringen-en-godenleer
57. http://feruna.nl/
58. http://www.maryjones.us/jce/fimmilena.html
59. https://www.britannica.com/topic/Flora-Roman-mythology
60. https://www.a3boeken.nl/nl/nieuws/fostare-een-vergeten-godin-om-weer-te-beminnen-11-09-2014/
61. https://en.wikipedia.org/wiki/Frijjō
62. https://sacred-texts.com/atl/olb/index.htm
63. https://en.wikipedia.org/wiki/Frya
64. https://en.wikipedia.org/wiki/Ganna_(seeress)
65. https://earthandstarryheaven.com/2015/01/15/garmangabi-matres-and-mortality/
66. https://skjalden.com/freyr-and-the-giantess-gerd/
67. https://en.wikipedia.org/wiki/Gontia_(deity)
68. http://www.witchesandpagans.com/frau-harke-goddess-of-the-first-harvest.html
69. https://journeyingtothegoddess.wordpress.com/2012/12/25/goddess-hertha/
70. http://www.northernpaganism.org/shrines/hela/welcome/who-is-hela.html
71. https://thimsternisse.wordpress.com/hludana/
72. http://shaman-healer-painter.co.uk/post.cfm?p=1572
73. https://en.wikipedia.org/wiki/Rheda_(mythology)
74. https://www.britannica.com/topic/Idun

75. https://www.missgien.net/batavians/batavians.html
76. https://religion.wikia.org/nl/wiki/Graanpop
77. https://en.wikipedia.org/wiki/Kunigunde
78. The Krampus and the Old, Dark Christmas: Roots and Rebirth of the Folkloric Devil by Al Ridenour, Feral House, 2016, p. 183-184
79. http://www.opwegnaarhetlicht.be/HET-WIEL-VAN-DE-BELGAE.php
80. https://en.wikipedia.org/wiki/Lutgardis
81. https://thekoalamom.com/2016/07/st-margaret-of-antioch
82. https://godinnenkracht.blogspot.com/2019/11/meda-uit-medemblik
83. https://www.rmo.nl/museumkennis/archeologie-van-nederland/nederland-in-de-romeinse-tijd/de-voorwerpen/romeinse-goden-in-nederland/
84. https://www.oudwageningen.nl/wageningen/heidense-voorgeschiedenis-westberg/
85. https://www.britannica.com/topic/Nantosuelta
86. https://www.timelessmyths.com/celtic/gallic.html#Nehalennia
87. https://www.patheos.com/blogs/heathenatheart/2019/08/nehalennia-goddess-lost-to-time/
88. https://stefangourmet.com/2017/04/15/duivekater/
89. https://www.livius.org/articles/place/colijnsplaat/
90. https://orderwhitemoon.org/goddess/nemetona/index.html
91. http://www.geocities.ws/reginheim/forgottengods.html
92. https://www.druidry.org/library/gods-goddesses/bavarian-triple-goddess-study-cult-three-bethan
93. https://www.behindthename.com/name/odilia
94. https://www.goddessandgreenman.co.uk/ostara
95. http://ww1.antiochian.org/content/st-quiteria-virgin-and-martyr
96. http://www.northernpaganism.org/shrines/ninesisters/

ran/honoring-ran.html
97. http://www.holladaypaganism.com/goddesses/
cyclopedia/r/ROSMERTA.HTM
98. https://earthandstarryheaven.com/2015/02/14/rosmerta/
99. https://feminismandreligion.com/2015/07/22/rosmerta-the-great-provider-a-celtic-goddess-of-abundance-by-judith-shaw/
100. https://mainzerbeobachter.com/2017/04/26/romeinen-week-rufia-materna/
101. https://nl.m.wikipedia.org/wiki/Roermond_(naam)
102. The Krampus and the Old, Dark Christmas: Roots and Rebirth of the Folkloric Devil by Al Ridenour, Feral House, 2016, p. 145
103. https://en.wikipedia.org/wiki/Sandraudiga
104. https://nl.wikipedia.org/wiki/Sequana_(godin)
105. https://en.wikipedia.org/wiki/Sinthgunt
106. https://en.wikipedia.org/wiki/Sowilō
107. https://en.wikipedia.org/wiki/Nordic_Bronze_Age
108. https://earthandstarryheaven.com/2015/03/08/sirona-healer-goddess/
109. Heilige Bronnen in de Lage Landen: Op zoek naar bronnen van betekenis in verleden en heden, anthology, A3 Boeken, 2013, p. 13
110. http://www.geocities.ws/reginheim/forgottengods.html
111. Godinnnen Van Eigen Bodem, Ineke Bergman, self-published, 2007
112. https://www.youtube.com/watch?v=1Z8zbaG6xLQ
113. https://www.abedeverteller.nl/de-heiligenberg-een-heidense-cultusplek-bij-amersfoort/
114. https://www.secret-bases.co.uk/wiki/Vagdavercustis
115. https://www.a3boeken.nl/nl/nieuws/vergeten-godinnen-arduinna-28-07-2014/
116. https://allthatsinteresting.com/veleda
117. https://nl.qwe.wiki/wiki/List_of_Celtic_deities

118. https://en.wikipedia.org/wiki/Vesunna
119. http://ammaca.godinnen.info/
120. https://senobessusbolgon.wordpress.com/viradecdis-vira-tecthis-viroddis-uirodactis/
121. http://www.shaman-healer-painter.co.uk/post.cfm?p=2855
122. https://www.druidry.org/library/gods-goddesses/bavarian-triple-goddess-study-cult-three-bethan
123. https://en.wikipedia.org/wiki/Xulsigiae
124. https://en.wikipedia.org/wiki/Yrsa
125. https://thetroth.blogspot.com/2013/09/feast-day-of-zi-sa_28.html
126. http://www.geocities.ws/reginheim/forgottengods.html
127. http://www.godinnen.info/
128. https://goddess-pages.co.uk/the-scandinavian-cailleach-thekaellingkarring/
129. https://www.timelessmyths.com/celtic/gallic.html

Chapter 5

1. https://www.abedeverteller.nl/het-geheim-van-de-wilde-jacht-en-het-wilde-heir/
2. https://mythology.net/norse/norse-concepts/the-wild-hunt/
3. https://en.wikipedia.org/wiki/Purgatory
4. The Krampus and the Old, Dark Christmas: Roots and Rebirth of the Folkloric Devil by Al Ridenour, Feral House, 2016, p. 97
5. Nicolaas, de Duivel and de Goden, Louis Janssen, Uitgeverij Ambo, Netherlands, 1993, p. 80
6. https://en.wikipedia.org/wiki/Matronalia
7. https://www.wildgratitude.com/the-trickster-archetype/
8. The Krampus and the Old, Dark Christmas: Roots and Rebirth of the Folkloric Devil by Al Ridenour, Feral House, 2016, p. 80
9. The Krampus and the Old, Dark Christmas: Roots and Re-

birth of the Folkloric Devil by Al Ridenour, Feral House, 2016, p. 114

10. https://en.wikipedia.org/wiki/Yule_goat

11. Veneficium: Magic, Witchcraft and The Poison Path by Daniel Shulke, Three Hands Press, 2017, p. 71 - 74

12. The Krampus and the Old, Dark Christmas: Roots and Rebirth of the Folkloric Devil by Al Ridenour, Feral House, 2016, p. 202

13. The Krampus and the Old, Dark Christmas: Roots and Rebirth of the Folkloric Devil by Al Ridenour, Feral House, 2016, p. 201

14. http://www.oldcorpseroad.co.uk/folklore/the-wild-hunt

15. The Krampus and the Old, Dark Christmas: Roots and Rebirth of the Folkloric Devil by Al Ridenour, Feral House, 2016, p. 115

16. Nicolaas, de Duivel and de Goden, Louis Janssen, Uitgeverij Ambo, Netherlands, 1993, p. 83

17. https://www.learnreligions.com/the-roman-parentalia-festival-2562141

18. https://en.wikipedia.org/wiki/Dziady

19. https://www.norwegianamerican.com/dont-take-odin-out-of-yule/

20. https://en.wikipedia.org/wiki/Redbad,_King_of_the_Frisians

21. https://www.cs.cmu.edu/~pwp/tofi/medieval_english_ale.html

22. https://www.abedeverteller.nl/het-geheim-van-de-wilde-jacht-en-het-wilde-heir/

23. https://www.summerland.org.uk/?p=95

24. https://www.youtube.com/watch?v=9pB5iiXMSrY&t=68s

25. The Seed of Yggdrasil by Maria Kvilhaug, Whyte Tracks Publishing, 2017, p. 453

26. https://mythology.net/norse/norse-concepts/the-wild-hunt/

27. https://weirdcatholic.com/2018/10/08/the-wild-hunt-and-the-purgatorial-procession/
28. https://www.abedeverteller.nl/het-geheim-van-de-wilde-jacht-en-het-wilde-heir/
29. https://en.wikipedia.org/wiki/Harii
30. https://www.reddit.com/r/IndoEuropean/comments/dq483f/the_männerbund_the_indoeuropean_coming_of_age/
31. Nicolaas, de Duivel and de Goden, Louis Janssen, Uitgeverij Ambo, Netherlands, 1993, p. 105
32. https://www.eftabundance.com/morrnahsprayer.htm

Chapter 6

1. http://freya.theladyofthelabyrinth.com/?page_id=567
2. https://lifeinduesseldorf.com/history-julius-caesar-germans/
3. https://digitallibrary.tulane.edu/islandora/object/tulane%3A51740/datastream/PDF/view, p.41
4. https://www.youtube.com/watch?v=9pB5iiXMSrY&t=44s
5. https://digitallibrary.tulane.edu/islandora/object/tulane%3A51740/datastream/PDF/view, p.42
6. https://digitallibrary.tulane.edu/islandora/object/tulane%3A51740/datastream/PDF/view, p.46
7. https://digitallibrary.tulane.edu/islandora/object/tulane%3A51740/datastream/PDF/view, p.53-56
8. http://polytheist.com/the-web-of-blessings/2015/08/12/the-matronae-and-matres-breathing-new-life-into-an-old-religion/
9. https://en.wikipedia.org/wiki/Perkūnas
10. https://en.wikipedia.org/wiki/Perun
11. https://www.britannica.com/topic/Ukko
12. https://www.fairychamber.com/blog/gods-of-the-saamis-shamanism-in-action
13. http://polytheist.com/the-web-of-blessings/2015/08/12/the-

matronae-and-matres-breathing-new-life-into-an-old-religion/

14. https://bladehoner.wordpress.com/2020/01/21/ancestral-mothers-and-goddess-collectives-in-german-iron-age-votive-altars-and-inscriptions-dedicated-to-the-matrones/
15. http://www.shaman-healer-painter.co.uk/post.cfm?p=707
16. https://hearthfirehandworks.com/2017/08/08/about-the-mothers-the-matrae-and-matronae/
17. https://hearthfirehandworks.com/about-the-gods/gaulish-and-brythonic-celtic-gods/the-mothers-matrae-and-matronae/
18. https://bladehoner.wordpress.com/2020/01/21/ancestral-mothers-and-goddess-collectives-in-german-iron-age-votive-altars-and-inscriptions-dedicated-to-the-matrones/
19. https://www.facebook.com/ladyofthe.labyrinth/posts/1070422432993642
20. Oak Tree Symbolism and Meaning [A Celtic Tree of Life] (magickalspot.com)
21. https://www.bing.com/search?q=where+is+xanten&form=EDGEAR&qs=PF&cvid=b536bf0777cc45558f2c5fca4182464d&cc=GB&setlang=en-US&plvar=0&PC=DCTS
22. http://masterrussian.com/verbs/lubit_polubit.htm
23. https://www.youtube.com/watch?v=2TaixdHbF-0&t=29s
24. https://en.wikipedia.org/wiki/Fólkvangr
25. Heilige Bronnen in de Lage Landen: Op zoek naar bronnen van betekenis in verleden en heden, anthology, A3 Boeken, 2013, p. 10 -12
26. https://en.wikipedia.org/wiki/Cornucopia
27. https://lifeinduesseldorf.com/history-julius-caesar-germans/
28. https://archive.org/stream/themetamorphoses-26073gut/26073.txt
29. Dictionary of Northern Mythology by Rudolph Simek, D.S. Brewer, Cambridge, 1993

Chapter 7

1. https://dutch-folklore.fandom.com/wiki/Witte_Wieven
2. https://www.youtube.com/watch?v=HbRa35YSLu8
3. https://www.youtube.com/watch?v=YbxnLWk-YCg&t=34s
4. https://dutch-folklore.fandom.com/wiki/Spinwijf
5. https://www.youtube.com/watch?v=jp2ghXjHF7g
6. https://www.abedeverteller.nl/witte-wieven-nevelslierten-en-grafheuvels/
7. https://www.meertens.knaw.nl/cms/nl/collecties
8. https://letterpile.com/creative-writing/The-White-Women-the-Dutch-legend-of-the-Witte-Wieven
9. https://dutch-folklore.fandom.com/wiki/Witte_Wieven#
10. https://psychopomps.org/
11. https://www.ensie.nl/betekenis/bietebauw
12. https://dutch-folklore.fandom.com/wiki/Bloedkoets
13. https://dutch-folklore.fandom.com/wiki/Bloedpater
14. https://dutch-folklore.fandom.com/wiki/Boeman
15. https://dutch-folklore.fandom.com/wiki/Boezehappert
16. https://dutch-folklore.fandom.com/wiki/Elf-rib
17. https://dutch-folklore.fandom.com/wiki/Ijzeren_Veulen
18. https://dutch-folklore.fandom.com/wiki/Kladdegat
19. https://dutch-folklore.fandom.com/wiki/Loekenbeer
20. https://dutch-folklore.fandom.com/wiki/Lorrenboer
21. https://dutch-folklore.fandom.com/wiki/Man_Met_De_Haak
22. https://en.wikipedia.org/wiki/Slender_Man
23. https://dutch-folklore.fandom.com/wiki/Tongesnaier
24. https://dutch-folklore.fandom.com/wiki/Flodder
25. https://en.wikipedia.org/wiki/Flodder
26. https://dutch-folklore.fandom.com/wiki/Alruin
27. https://dutch-folklore.fandom.com/wiki/Bloedende_Wind
28. https://dutch-folklore.fandom.com/wiki/Heggemoeder
29. https://dutch-folklore.fandom.com/wiki/Olde_Marolde
30. https://dutch-folklore.fandom.com/wiki/Tante_Cor

31. https://www.beleven.org/verhaal/vaarkobke_de_tovenaar
32. https://www.beleven.org/verhaal/schele_guurte

Chapter 8

1. Een Paleis voor de Doden: Over Hunebedden, Dolmens en Menhirs, Herman Clerinx, Athenaeum – Polak en van Gennep, 2017, p.10 – 23
2. https://www.youtube.com/watch?v=2QSBLd6YQC E&t=126s
3. Een Paleis voor de Doden: Over Hunebedden, Dolmens en Menhirs, Herman Clerinx, Athenaeum – Polak en van Gennep, 2017, p.19
4. https://religion.wikia.org/nl/wiki/Johan_Picardt
5. https://www.abedeverteller.nl/witte-wieven-nevelslierten-en-grafheuvels/
6. https://www.geheugenvandrenthe.nl/stemberg
7. https://www.geheugenvandrenthe.nl/duvelskut
8. https://www.ingasteren.nl/wp-content/uploads/verhaal/Hunebed_naam.pdf
9. https://sacredtrust.org/
10. https://www.hunebednieuwscafe.nl/2016/12/een-volksverhaal-van-het-hunebed-van-havelte/
11. 'Van 's Duvels kut en Des Duvels kolse' door W.A.B. van der Sanden. Uit de Nieuwe Drentse Volksalmanak 2014: bldz. 135 – 152, quoted by Abe de Verteller, https://www.abedeverteller.nl/witte-wieven-nevelslierten-en-grafheuvels/
12. Nigel Pennick, from private correspondence, quoted with permission, YouTube channel: https://www.youtube.com/watch?v=KHtuj3qgHZg

Chapter 9

1. https://www.abedeverteller.nl/vliegen-in-zeven-en-varen-in-eierschalen-de-extase-van-heksen/

2. https://www.ancient-origins.net/myths-legends-europe/hecate-0010707

3. *The following account is related in Charles MacKay's Witch Mania: The History of Witchcraft,* http://gregladen.com/blog/2017/10/08/how-many-people-were-killed-as-witches-in-europe-from-1200-to-the-present/

4. Ecstasies: Deciphering the Witches' Sabbath by Carlo Ginzburg, The University of Chicago Press, 1989, chapter 1, p.89-110

5. Nicolaas, de Duivel and de Goden, Louis Janssen, Uitgeverij Ambo, Netherlands, 1993, p. 114

6. Maleficium: Witchcraft and Witch Hunting in the West by Gordon Napier, Amberley Publishing, 2017, p.13

7. http://www.badwitch.co.uk/2019/06/tv-mystic-britain-and-ice-age-shaman.html

8. Maleficium: Witchcraft and Witch Hunting in the West by Gordon Napier, Amberley Publishing, 2017, p.15

9. Maleficium: Witchcraft and Witch Hunting in the West by Gordon Napier, Amberley Publishing, 2017, p.16

10. Maleficium: Witchcraft and Witch Hunting in the West by Gordon Napier, Amberley Publishing, 2017, p.19 -21

11. Maleficium: Witchcraft and Witch Hunting in the West by Gordon Napier, Amberley Publishing, 2017, p.28

12. Ecstasies: Deciphering the Witches' Sabbath by Carlo Ginzburg, The University of Chicago Press, 1989, p.8 -11

13. Ecstasies: Deciphering the Witches' Sabbath by Carlo Ginzburg, The University of Chicago Press, 1989, p.24

14. Ecstasies: Deciphering the Witches' Sabbath by Carlo Ginzburg, The University of Chicago Press, 1989, p.74

15. Ecstasies: Deciphering the Witches' Sabbath by Carlo Ginzburg, The University of Chicago Press, 1989, p.106

16. Maleficium: Witchcraft and Witch Hunting in the West by Gordon Napier, Amberley Publishing, 2017, p. 28

17. https://en.wikipedia.org/wiki/Eye_for_an_eye

18. http://www.truthbeknown.com/victims.htm

19. https://en.wikipedia.org/wiki/Maleficium_ (sorcery)#:~:text=Maleficium%20%28plural%3A%20 maleficia%29%20as%20a%20Latin%20term%2C%20 %22An,cause%20harm%20or%20death%20to%20people%20or%20property.

20. Duivelskwartier 1595: Heksen, Heren en de Dood in het Vuur , Johan Otten, Uitgeverij Vantilt, 2015, p. 25

21. Medicine of the Imagination: A Passionate Plea for Fearless Imagination by Imelda Almqvist, Moon Books, 2020

22. Maleficium: Witchcraft and Witch Hunting in the West by Gordon Napier, Amberley Publishing, 2017, p.36

23. Veneficium: Magic, Witchcraft and The Poison Path by Daniel Shulke, Three Hands Press, 2017, p. 68

24. Veneficium: Magic, Witchcraft and The Poison Path by Daniel Shulke, Three Hands Press, 2017, p. 63

25. Veneficium: Magic, Witchcraft and The Poison Path by Daniel Shulke, Three Hands Press, 2017, p. 69

26. https://www.urbandictionary.com/define.php?term=necyomancy

27. Maleficium: Witchcraft and Witch Hunting in the West by Gordon Napier, Amberley Publishing, 2017, p.20`

28. Maleficium: Witchcraft and Witch Hunting in the West by Gordon Napier, Amberley Publishing, 2017, Chapter 2, Conceptions of Witchcraft p.29 - 46

29. Veneficium: Magic, Witchcraft and The Poison Path by Daniel Shulke, Three Hands Press, 2017, p.73-76

30. Trolldom: Spells and the Methods of the Norse Folk Magic Tradition by Johannes Bjorn Gardback, YIPPIE, 2015, p.33

31. http://www.albrechtdurerblog.com/the-witch-riding-the-goat-backwards/

32. Veneficium: Magic, Witchcraft and The Poison Path by Daniel Shulke, Three Hands Press, 2017, p. 71

33. https://www.youtube.com/watch?v=uQnZgKV0j9Y

&t=196s

34. http://www.shaman-healer-painter.co.uk/post.cfm?p=633
35. http://www.shaman-healer-painter.co.uk/info2.cfm?info_ id=224437
36. Ecstasies: Deciphering the Witches' Sabbath by Carlo Ginzburg, The University of Chicago Press, 1989, p.72
37. https://occult-world.com/witch-trials-witch-hunts/mora-witches/
38. https://www.abedeverteller.nl/tag/vliegzalf/

Chapter 10

1. https://en.wikipedia.org/wiki/Kobold
2. Verhalenbank, Collectie Jaarsma, verslag 468, verhaal 15 (archief Meertens Instituut)
3. https://en.wikipedia.org/wiki/Cofgod
4. https://www.abedeverteller.nl/de-oorsprong-van-de-kabouter-deel-twee/
5. https://www.differencebetween.com/difference-between-goblin-and-vs-hobgoblin/
6. http://www.shaman-healer-painter.co.uk/post.cfm?p=2114
7. https://www.abedeverteller.nl/tag/kabouters
8. http://www.verhalenbank.nl/items/show/51277
9. Witte Wieven, Weerwolven en Waternekkers, Abe J. van der Veen, self-published, 2017, full directory p. 148-182
10. Verhalen van Stad en Streek, Sagen en Legenden in Nederland, De Blecourt/Koman/Van der Kooi/Meder, Uitgeverij Bert Bakker, 2010, p. 167
11. http://www.abedeverteller.nl/de-oorsprong-van-de-kabouter-deel-twee/
12. https://www.ducksters.com/science/chemistry/nickel.php
13. https://en.wikipedia.org/wiki/Garden_gnome

Chapter 11

1. https://www.youtube.com/watch?v=9QyllfgRX_A

2. Nicolaas, de Duivel and de Goden, Louis Janssen, Uitgeverij Ambo, Netherlands, 1993, p. 29 - 39
3. https://austrianadaptation.com/perchten-austrias-wild-pagan-festival/
4. Nicolaas, de Duivel and de Goden, Louis Janssen, Uitgeverij Ambo, Netherlands, 1993, p. 13
5. Nicolaas, de Duivel and de Goden, Louis Janssen, Uitgeverij Ambo, Netherlands, 1993, p. 20 - 31
6. Nicolaas, de Duivel and de Goden, Louis Janssen, Uitgeverij Ambo, Netherlands, 1993, p. 32
7. Nicolaas, de Duivel and de Goden, Louis Janssen, Uitgeverij Ambo, Netherlands, 1993, p. 39
8. Nicolaas, de Duivel and de Goden, Louis Janssen, Uitgeverij Ambo, Netherlands, 1993, p. 47 - 50
9. https://en.wikipedia.org/wiki/Vilhelm_Grønbech
10. https://www.psychologytoday.com/us/blog/the-bejeezus-out-me/201407/oprah-carl-jung-and-remarkable-essay-about-sex-and-death
11. https://en.wikipedia.org/wiki/Saint_Nicholas_Day
12. The Krampus and the Old, Dark Christmas: Roots and Rebirth of the Folkloric Devil by Al Ridenour, Feral House, 2016
13. https://www.holland.com/global/tourism/information/events/sinterklaas.htm
14. https://www.youtube.com/watch?v=vG5Xr8uQ5l8
15. https://www.youtube.com/watch?v=2mlw5SyY0dw

Chapter 12

1. https://www.kitchenwitchhearth.net/post/frau-holda-or-frau-holle-by-gypsy-willowmoon
2. The Krampus and the Old, Dark Christmas: Roots and Rebirth of the Folkloric Devil by Al Ridenour, Feral House, 2016, p. 120
3. https://www.shamanism.com/programs/italy-shamanic-

retreat

4. The Krampus and the Old, Dark Christmas: Roots and Re-birth of the Folkloric Devil by Al Ridenour, Feral House, 2016, p. 132

5. https://www.academia.edu/3548067/From_Fairytale_To_Goddess_Frau_Holle_And_The_Scholars_That_Try_To_Reveal_Her_Origins, p.5

6. https://www.youtube.com/watch?v=9pB5iiXMSrY&t=81s

7. The Krampus and the Old, Dark Christmas: Roots and Re-birth of the Folkloric Devil by Al Ridenour, Feral House, 2016, p. 132 – 134

8. Goddess Holle: In Search of a Germanic Goddess, Garden-Stone, BoD, 2002, p.11

9. The Krampus and the Old, Dark Christmas: Roots and Re-birth of the Folkloric Devil by Al Ridenour, Feral House, 2016, p. 157

10. The Krampus and the Old, Dark Christmas: Roots and Re-birth of the Folkloric Devil by Al Ridenour, Feral House, 2016, p. 139

11. https://www.ancientpages.com/2019/12/11/gryla-cannibal-istic-evil-troll-and-her-sons-yule-lads-in-icelandic-folk-lore/

12. https://issuu.com/msmerlinsmagic/docs/witchcraft_medi-cine_healing_arts_sh

13. https://thephotographersblog.com/milky-way-myths-and-facts/

14. http://www.germanicmythology.com/original/wildhunt.html

15. Goddess Holle: In Search of a Germanic Goddess, Garden-Stone, BoD, 2002, p.114-116

16. Goddess Holle: In Search of a Germanic Goddess, Garden-Stone, BoD, 2002, p.81

17. Goddess Holle: In Search of a Germanic Goddess, Garden-Stone, BoD, 2002, p.118

18. http://www.archaeomythology.org/wp-content/uploads/2012/11/Dexter-7.pdf
19. The Goddesses and Gods of Old Europe: Myths and Cult Images by Marija Gimbutas, University of California Press, 1992, p.132
20. https://folklorethursday.com/myths/the-cailleach-irish-myth/
21. Goddess Holle: In Search of a Germanic Goddess, Garden-Stone, BoD, 2002, p.19-20
22. Goddess Holle: In Search of a Germanic Goddess, Garden-Stone, BoD, 2002, p.27-31
23. Goddess Holle: In Search of a Germanic Goddess, Garden-Stone, BoD, 2002, p.36-39
24. Goddess Holle: In Search of a Germanic Goddess, Garden-Stone, BoD, 2002, p.15
25. Goddess Holle: In Search of a Germanic Goddess, Garden-Stone, BoD, 2002, p.21
26. Goddess Holle: In Search of a Germanic Goddess, Garden-Stone, BoD, 2002, p.27
27. Goddess Holle: In Search of a Germanic Goddess, Garden-Stone, BoD, 2002, p.34-35
28. Goddess Holle: In Search of a Germanic Goddess, Garden-Stone, BoD, 2002, p.39-41
29. http://www.naturalmedicinalherbs.net/herbs/g/galium-verum=lady's-bedstraw
30. Goddess Holle: In Search of a Germanic Goddess, Garden-Stone, BoD, 2002, p.40
31. Goddess Holle: In Search of a Germanic Goddess, Garden-Stone, BoD, 2002, p.50-51
32. http://www.shaman-healer-painter.co.uk/post.cfm?p=720
33. Goddess Holle: In Search of a Germanic Goddess, Garden-Stone, BoD, 2002, p.81
34. https://www.kitchenwitchhearth.net/post/frau-holda-or-frau-holle-by-gypsy-willo /wmoon

35. https://boroughsofthedead.com/frau-perchta

36. The Krampus and the Old, Dark Christmas: Roots and Rebirth of the Folkloric Devil by Al Ridenour, Feral House, 2016, p. 157

37. The Krampus and the Old, Dark Christmas: Roots and Rebirth of the Folkloric Devil by Al Ridenour, Feral House, 2016, p. 123

38. https://fromtinypennies.com/2018/11/20/frau-perchta-terrifying-christmas-witch/

39. Goddess Holle: In Search of a Germanic Goddess, Garden-Stone, BoD, 2002, p.94

40. The Krampus and the Old, Dark Christmas: Roots and Rebirth of the Folkloric Devil by Al Ridenour, Feral House, 2016, p. 118 – 119

41. The Krampus and the Old, Dark Christmas: Roots and Rebirth of the Folkloric Devil by Al Ridenour, Feral House, 2016, p. 127

42. Goddess Holle: In Search of a Germanic Goddess, Garden-Stone, BoD, 2002, p.97-99

43. https://answersuniverse.com/if-the-female-side-of-a-family-is-called-the-distaff-side-what-is-the-male-side/

44. https://www.etymonline.com/word/distaff

45. https://en.wikipedia.org/wiki/Dís

46. https://austrianadaptation.com/perchten-austrias-wild-pagan-festival/

47. The Krampus and the Old, Dark Christmas: Roots and Rebirth of the Folkloric Devil by Al Ridenour, Feral House, 2016, p. 227

48. The Krampus and the Old, Dark Christmas: Roots and Rebirth of the Folkloric Devil by Al Ridenour, Feral House, 2016, p. 123-128

49. The Krampus and the Old, Dark Christmas: Roots and Rebirth of the Folkloric Devil by Al Ridenour, Feral House, 2016, p. 138

50. https://www.learnreligions.com/hungry-ghosts-449825
51. https://www.learnreligions.com/feast-with-the-dead-2562707
52. http://www.germanicmythology.com/original/earthmother/wildhunt.html
53. The Krampus and the Old, Dark Christmas: Roots and Rebirth of the Folkloric Devil by Al Ridenour, Feral House, 2016, p. 129
54. https://www.kitchenwitchhearth.net/post/frau-holda-or-frau-holle-by-gypsy-willowmoon
55. The Krampus and the Old, Dark Christmas: Roots and Rebirth of the Folkloric Devil by Al Ridenour, Feral House, 2016, p. 184
56. The Krampus and the Old, Dark Christmas: Roots and Rebirth of the Folkloric Devil by Al Ridenour, Feral House, 2016, p. 162 – 164
57. The Krampus and the Old, Dark Christmas: Roots and Rebirth of the Folkloric Devil by Al Ridenour, Feral House, 2016, p. 168-169
58. http://www.shaman-healer-painter.co.uk/post.cfm?p=720
59. https://www.youtube.com/watch?v=GpSLQLHN2B4&t=24s
60. The Krampus and the Old, Dark Christmas: Roots and Rebirth of the Folkloric Devil by Al Ridenour, Feral House, 2016, p. 57

Chapter 13

1. https://quotes.yourdictionary.com/author/william-shakespeare/553167
2. https://www.nytimes.com/2012/12/09/books/review/the-old-ways-by-robert-macfarlane.html
3. https://nl.wikipedia.org/wiki/Dodenweg
4. https://www.abedeverteller.nl/taxus/
5. https://en.wikipedia.org/wiki/Lychgate

6. https://en.wikipedia.org/wiki/Corpse_road
7. https://www.dbnl.org/tekst/craa001wand01_01/craa001wand01_01_0006.php
8. http://www.verhalenbank.nl/items/show/29924
9. https://aminoapps.com/c/pagans-witches/page/blog/the-historical-uses-of-labyrinths-in-scandinavia/Z6nj_D58f-Bu58lB6gwkJ7RwJj0k8V8Q1M6L
10. https://www.legendarydartmoor.co.uk/corpse_candles.htm
11. https://nl.wikipedia.org/wiki/Dwaallicht
12. https://www.youtube.com/watch?v=GpSLQLHN2B4&t=89s
13. https://soundcloud.com/fanfarejuliana/vuurgeesten-vuurbollen
14. http://www.verhalenbank.nl/items/show/51276
15. https://www.meertens.knaw.nl/cms/nl/nieuws-agenda/nieuws-overzicht/202-nieuws-2013/144360-nederlandse-verhalenbank-online
16. https://www.academia.edu/9159836/Verloren_maar_niet_vergeten._Monumenten_voor_overleden_kinderen_in_Brabant
17. Verhalen en Sprookjes op de grens van leven en dood, Bert Voorthoeve, Zeist, 1997, p.25
18. https://en.wikipedia.org/wiki/Will-o%27-the-wisp
19. https://en.wikipedia.org/wiki/Ley_line
20. https://westerngeomancy.org/the-spine-of-albion/
21. http://www.earthstars.co.uk/about/
22. http://www.leylijnen.com/sterkeleylijnen.htm
23. https://www.ridingthebeast.com/numbers/nu13.php

Chapter 14

1. https://www.huisvanhilde.nl/
2. https://nl.wikipedia.org/wiki/Klederdracht_van_Marken
3. https://onh.nl/verhaal/de-runxput-bij-onze-lieve-vrouwe-

ter-nood-nabij-heiloo
4. https://nehalennia-tempel.nl/
5. https://www.friesmuseum.nl/en/
6. Spirituele Plekken in Nederland, Henk Ganzeboom, GV-Media, 2014, p.131 – 138
7. http://www.hunebedden.nl/engels.htm
8. http://www.hunebedden.nl/ndrenthe.htm
9. https://www.hunebedcentrum.eu/
10. https://nl.wikipedia.org/wiki/Tankenberg
11. https://www.staatsbosbeheer.nl/natuurgebieden/rijk-van-nijmegen/bezienswaardigheden/koortsboom
12. https://en.wikipedia.org/wiki/Veluwe

Chapter 15
1. https://www.academia.edu
2. Ecstasies: Deciphering the Witches' Sabbath by Carlo Ginzburg, The University of Chicago Press, 1989, p.106
3. http://www.soulritual.nl/
4. Heilige Bronnen in de Lage Landen: Op zoek naar bronnen van betekenis in verleden en heden, anthology, A3 Boeken, 2013, p. 15
5. Medicine of the Imagination: A Passionate Plea for Fearless Imagination by Imelda Almqvist, Moon Books, 2020, p. 359
6. https://alforto.nl/kalender.html
7. https://www.negenwerelden.nl/2007/06/gebeden/
8. Heilige Bronnen in de Lage Landen: Op zoek naar bronnen van betekenis in verleden en heden, anthology, A3 Boeken, 2013, p. 94
9. De Friezen: De vroegste geschiedenis van het Nederlandse kustgebied, Luit van der Tuuk, Uitgeverij Omniboek, 2013/2016, p.159
10. Heilige Bronnen in de Lage Landen: Op zoek naar bronnen van betekenis in verleden en heden, anthology, A3 Boeken, 2013, p. 11

Footnotes

11. Heilige Bronnen in de Lage Landen: Op zoek naar bronnen van betekenis in verleden en heden, anthology, A3 Boeken, 2013, p. 25
12. https://nl.wikipedia.org/wiki/Hurkgraf
13. http://www.pentavisie.com/
14. Heilige Bronnen in de Lage Landen: Op zoek naar bronnen van betekenis in verleden en heden, anthology, A3 Boeken, 2013, p. 161-163
15. Heilige Bronnen in de Lage Landen: Op zoek naar bronnen van betekenis in verleden en heden, anthology, A3 Boeken, 2013, p. 212-213
16. https://db0nus869y26v.cloudfront.net/nl/Johan_Picardt
17. https://allthatsinteresting.com/veleda
18. http://www.shaman-healer-painter.co.uk/post.cfm?p=2151
19. https://shirleytwofeathers.com/The_Blog/pagancalendar/category/norse-and-viking-festivals/
20. http://www.shaman-healer-painter.co.uk/post.cfm?p=2855
21. http://www.shaman-healer-painter.co.uk/post.cfm?p=1671
22. https://nl.wikipedia.org/wiki/Nederlandse_(inter)nationale_themadagen_en_-weken#Januari
23. https://themeaningofthename.com/imelda/#:~:text=The%20graph%20below%20represents%20the%20number%20of%20people,name%20day%20of%20Imelda%20is%2013%20May%20.

Appendix – The Frisian Rune Row

1. De Friezen: De vroegste geschiedenis van het Nederlandse kustgebied, Luit van der Tuuk, Uitgeverij Omniboek, 2013/2016, p.55
2. https://www.youtube.com/watch?v=EySS4Hq2Syc&t=21s
3. De Friezen: De vroegste geschiedenis van het Nederlandse kustgebied, Luit van der Tuuk, Uitgeverij Omniboek, 2013/2016, p.58
4. Heilige Bronnen in de Lage Landen: Op zoek naar bronnen

van betekenis in verleden en heden, anthology, A3 Boeken, 2013, p. 11

5. https://www.abedeverteller.nl/witte-wieven-nevelslierten-en-grafheuvels/

6. De Friezen: De vroegste geschiedenis van het Nederlandse kustgebied, Luit van der Tuuk, Uitgeverij Omniboek, 2013/2016, p.54

7. http://www.3worlds.co.uk/Articles/Coat-of-Power.pdf

8. Heilige Bronnen in de Lage Landen: Op zoek naar bronnen van betekenis in verleden en heden, anthology, A3 Boeken, 2013, p. 10-11

9. Heilige Bronnen in de Lage Landen: Op zoek naar bronnen van betekenis in verleden en heden, anthology, A3 Boeken, 2013, p. 100

10. Heilige Bronnen in de Lage Landen: Op zoek naar bronnen van betekenis in verleden en heden, anthology, A3 Boeken, 2013, p. 26

11. Heilige Bronnen in de Lage Landen: Op zoek naar bronnen van betekenis in verleden en heden, anthology, A3 Boeken, 2013, p. 150

12. De Friezen: De vroegste geschiedenis van het Nederlandse kustgebied, Luit van der Tuuk, Uitgeverij Omniboek, 2013/2016, p.53

13. http://www.open-deur.nl/vrij-vrijen/

14. De Friezen: De vroegste geschiedenis van het Nederlandse kustgebied, Luit van der Tuuk, Uitgeverij Omniboek, 2013/2016, p.32

15. De Friezen: De vroegste geschiedenis van het Nederlandse kustgebied, Luit van der Tuuk, Uitgeverij Omniboek, 2013/2016, p.38

16. https://www.dehondsrug.nl/verhalen/ijstijden/?lang=en

17. https://en.wikipedia.org/wiki/Amber

18. https://www.ensie.nl/betekenis/dodenakker

19. Heilige Bronnen in de Lage Landen: Op zoek naar bronnen

van betekenis in verleden en heden, anthology, A3 Boeken, 2013, p. 179

20. Heilige Bronnen in de Lage Landen: Op zoek naar bronnen van betekenis in verleden en heden, anthology, A3 Boeken, 2013, p. 194

21. https://exemplore.com/wicca-witchcraft/Scottish-Witch-Remedies

22. https://en.wikipedia.org/wiki/List_of_extinct_animals_of_the_Netherlands

23. Heilige Bronnen in de Lage Landen: Op zoek naar bronnen van betekenis in verleden en heden, anthology, A3 Boeken, 2013, p. 25

24. https://www.ragweedforge.com/rpie.html

25. https://en.wikipedia.org/wiki/Sowilō

26. Heilige Bronnen in de Lage Landen: Op zoek naar bronnen van betekenis in verleden en heden, anthology, A3 Boeken, 2013, p. 24-26

27. De Friezen: De vroegste geschiedenis van het Nederlandse kustgebied, Luit van der Tuuk, Uitgeverij Omniboek, 2013/2016, p.59

28. https://pregnant-hag-teachings.teachable.com/p/classes-for-rune-magicians1/?preview=logged_out

29. Heilige Bronnen in de Lage Landen: Op zoek naar bronnen van betekenis in verleden en heden, anthology, A3 Boeken, 2013, p.9

30. De Friezen: De vroegste geschiedenis van het Nederlandse kustgebied, Luit van der Tuuk, Uitgeverij Omniboek, 2013/2016, p.26

31. Heilige Bronnen in de Lage Landen: Op zoek naar bronnen van betekenis in verleden en heden, anthology, A3 Boeken, 2013, p. 27

32. Heilige Bronnen in de Lage Landen: Op zoek naar bronnen van betekenis in verleden en heden, anthology, A3 Boeken, 2013, p. 10-11

33. Heilige Bronnen in de Lage Landen: Op zoek naar bronnen van betekenis in verleden en heden, anthology, A3 Boeken, 2013, p. 13
34. De Friezen: De vroegste geschiedenis van het Nederlandse kustgebied, Luit van der Tuuk, Uitgeverij Omniboek, 2013/2016, p.19-20
35. De Friezen: De vroegste geschiedenis van het Nederlandse kustgebied, Luit van der Tuuk, Uitgeverij Omniboek, 2013/2016, p.39
36. De Friezen: De vroegste geschiedenis van het Nederlandse kustgebied, Luit van der Tuuk, Uitgeverij Omniboek, 2013/2016, p.47
37. https://www.youtube.com/watch?v=gtWMcCd8O2 4&t=209s
38. https://www.bbc.co.uk/programmes/articles/ 43vC3LHlWykpcX4M2Ty9djJ/12-mighty-facts-about-oak-trees
39. De Friezen: De vroegste geschiedenis van het Nederlandse kustgebied, Luit van der Tuuk, Uitgeverij Omniboek, 2013/2016, p.37
40. http://www.northernpaganism.org/shrines/jormundgand/ writings/jormundgand-the-world-serpent.html
41. https://thehouseoftwigs.com/2018/10/29/hiding-in-the-shadows-helas-runes/
42. Heilige Bronnen in de Lage Landen: Op zoek naar bronnen van betekenis in verleden en heden, anthology, A3 Boeken, 2013, p. 162
43. http://www.northernshamanism.org/the-futhorc-runes. html

Appendix – Further Schlarly Discourse
1. https://en.wikipedia.org/wiki/Common_Germanic_deities
2. https://www.facebook.com/godinnenvaneigenbodem

Glossary

1. https://dutch-folklore.fandom.com/wiki/Witte_Wievenkuil
2. https://www.abedeverteller.nl/het-pact-met-de-duivel/
3. https://stefangourmet.com/2017/04/15/duivekater/
4. https://nn.wikipedia.org/wiki/Huldreslått
5. https://www.holland.com/global/tourism/destinations/provinces/drenthe/hunebedden.htm
6. Heilige Bronnen in de Lage Landen: Op zoek naar bronnen van betekenis in verleden en heden, anthology, A3 Boeken, 2013, p. 163
7. Heilige Bronnen in de Lage Landen: Op zoek naar bronnen van betekenis in verleden en heden, anthology, A3 Boeken, 2013, p. 12
8. https://en.wikipedia.org/wiki/Terp
9. http://www.woordenlijst.eu/woord_details.php?woordid=TOVERKOL
10. https://www.abedeverteller.nl/vliegen-in-zeven-en-varen-in-eierschalen-de-extase-van-heksen/
11. https://en.wikipedia.org/wiki/West_Frisian_Islands
12. https://soulsearchers.spheresoflight.com.au/the-psychopomp-or-death-walker/

MOON
BOOKS

PAGANISM & SHAMANISM

What is Paganism? A religion, a spirituality, an alternative
belief system, nature worship? You can find support for all these
definitions (and many more) in dictionaries, encyclopaedias, and
text books of religion, but subscribe to any one and the truth will
evade you. Above all Paganism is a creative pursuit, an encounter
with reality, an exploration of meaning and an expression of the
soul. Druids, Heathens, Wiccans and others, all contribute their
insights and literary riches to the Pagan tradition. Moon Books
invites you to begin or to deepen your own encounter, right here,
right now.
If you have enjoyed this book, why not tell other readers by
posting a review on your preferred book site.

Recent bestsellers from Moon Books are:

Journey to the Dark Goddess
How to Return to Your Soul
Jane Meredith
Discover the powerful secrets of the Dark Goddess and
transform your depression, grief and pain into healing
and integration.
Paperback: 978-1-84694-677-6 ebook: 978-1-78099-223-5

Shamanic Reiki
Expanded Ways of Working with Universal Life Force Energy
Llyn Roberts, Robert Levy
Shamanism and Reiki are each powerful ways of healing; together,
their power multiplies. *Shamanic Reiki* introduces techniques to
help healers and Reiki practitioners tap ancient healing wisdom.
Paperback: 978-1-84694-037-8 ebook: 978-1-84694-650-9

Pagan Portals – The Awen Alone
Walking the Path of the Solitary Druid
Joanna van der Hoeven
An introductory guide for the solitary Druid, *The Awen Alone* will
accompany you as you explore, and seek out your own place
within the natural world.
Paperback: 978-1-78279-547-6 ebook: 978-1-78279-546-9

A Kitchen Witch's World of Magical Herbs & Plants
Rachel Patterson
A journey into the magical world of herbs and plants, filled with
magical uses, folklore, history and practical magic. By popular
writer, blogger and kitchen witch, Tansy Firedragon.
Paperback: 978-1-78279-621-3 ebook: 978-1-78279-620-6

Medicine for the Soul
The Complete Book of Shamanic Healing
Ross Heaven
All you will ever need to know about shamanic healing and how to
become your own shaman...
Paperback: 978-1-78099-419-2 ebook: 978-1-78099-420-8

Shaman Pathways – The Druid Shaman
Exploring the Celtic Otherworld
Danu Forest
A practical guide to Celtic shamanism with exercises and
techniques as well as traditional lore for exploring the Celtic
Otherworld.
Paperback: 978-1-78099-615-8 ebook: 978-1-78099-616-5

Traditional Witchcraft for the Woods and Forests
A Witch's Guide to the Woodland with Guided Meditations and
Pathworking
Mélusine Draco
A Witch's guide to walking alone in the woods, with guided
meditations and pathworking.
Paperback: 978-1-84694-803-9 ebook: 978-1-84694-804-6

Wild Earth, Wild Soul
A Manual for an Ecstatic Culture
Bill Pfeiffer
Imagine a nature-based culture so alive and so connected,
spreading like wildfire. This book is the first flame...
Paperback: 978-1-78099-187-0 ebook: 978-1-78099-188-7

Naming the Goddess
Trevor Greenfield
Naming the Goddess is written by over eighty adherents and
scholars of Goddess and Goddess Spirituality.
Paperback: 978-1-78279-476-9 ebook: 978-1-78279-475-2

Shapeshifting into Higher Consciousness
Heal and Transform Yourself and Our World with Ancient
Shamanic and Modern Methods
Llyn Roberts
Ancient and modern methods that you can use every day to
transform yourself and make a positive difference in the world.
Paperback: 978-1-84694-843-5 ebook: 978-1-84694-844-2

Readers of ebooks can buy or view any of these bestsellers by
clicking on the live link in the title. Most titles are published in
paperback and as an ebook. Paperbacks are available in traditional
bookshops. Both print and ebook formats are available online.

Find more titles and sign up to our readers' newsletter at
http://www.johnhuntpublishing.com/paganism
Follow us on Facebook at https://www.facebook.com/MoonBooks
and Twitter at https://twitter.com/MoonBooksJHP